DATE DUE			

BERLIN
GHETTO

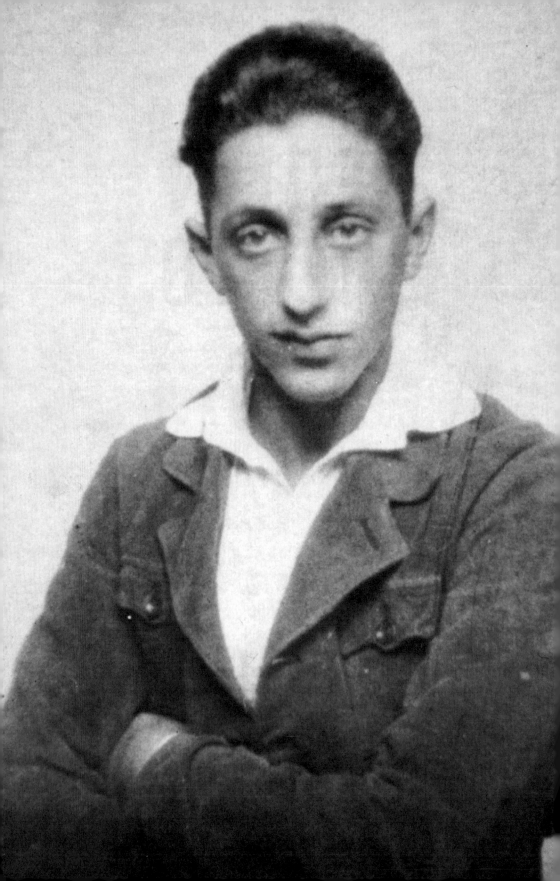

BERLIN GHETTO

HERBERT BAUM AND THE AND THE ANTI-FASCIST RESISTANCE

ERIC BROTHERS

This book is dedicated to my mentor, Dr Arnold Paucker OBE. He was always willing to help, provided me with guidance, published my first research on the Baum group and championed my work in his own writing. Without his help, this book would not exist. Dr Paucker, you have my eternal gratitude.

First published 2012

by Spellmount, an imprint of The History Press
The History Press
The Mill, Brimscombe Port
Stroud, Gloucestershire, GL5 2QG
www.thehistorypress.co.uk

© Eric Brothers, 2012

The right of Eric Brothers to be identified as the Author
of this work has been asserted in accordance with the
Copyrights, Designs and Patents Act 1988.

British Library Cataloguing in Publication Data.
A catalogue record for this book is available from the British Library.

ISBN 978 0 7524 7686 5
Typesetting and origination by The History Press
Printed in Great Britain

CONTENTS

ACKNOWLEDGEMENTS

When I began research on the Baum group, I attempted to locate as many people as possible who knew group members. I was surprised to locate two hitherto unknown members in the United States in the early 1980s: Ellen Compart – who survived the war underground in Berlin – and Alfred Eisenstädter, who emigrated to New York in 1941.

The others whom I contacted and either interviewed and/or had write depositions were either comrades, friends, relatives or associated in one way or another with Baum group members. Most, but not all, of these people took part in active anti-fascist resistance of some kind. They were Norbert Wollheim, Ellen Arndt (née Lewinsky), George Manasse, Ilse Kessler (née Prager), Margot Deutsch-Verlado (interviewed in London by Kerstin Wachholz), Günther Prager, Gerhard Zadek, Otto Wendt, Walter Sack, Kurt Siering, Manfred Lindenberger (interviewed by Herbert Lindenberger), Gerda Lüth (formerly May, née Fichtmann), Rudi Barta, Max Abraham, Herbert Ballhorn, Henry (Heinz) Sachs, Herbert Ansbach, Inge Berner (née Gerson), Fred Cassel, Ilse Heller (née Held), Inge Aptekmann (née Gongula) and Werner Rosenstock. I thank them all warmly for their assistance. I was fortunate to have been able to meet these people or contact them via telephone or in writing during the 1980s, spread as they were across the world in the US, Britain, Israel and East Berlin. I would imagine that most of them are no longer with us. I wish to add a special thank you to the late Günther Prager. He became a close friend and is sorely missed.

I wish to thank those writers and others who have assisted me on this project. Michael Kreutzer included me amongst the contributors of the exhibition *Juden im Widerstand* (Jews in the Resistance) in Berlin in 1993. He also provided me with original photographs of the Soviet Paradise exhibition from 1942, as well as the photograph of Herbert Baum used on the cover of this book. Dr Arnold Paucker OBE, the former editor of the Leo Baeck Institute Year Book in London, is a trusted mentor and advisor. The East German author and archivist Dr Margot Pikarski wrote the first complete book on the Baum group, *Jugend im Widerstand: Herbert Baum und Kampfgefährten* (*Youth in Resistance: Herbert Baum and Comrades*). She was the first writer to interview the survivors of the Baum group in East Berlin, where most of the survivors settled after the war. She gave me several photographs reproduced in this book.

Hermann Pichler, the Associate Editor of *Aufbau* in New York in the early 1980s, was very helpful in my search for survivors of the Baum group and their friends and relatives. Also during the 1980s, Diane Spielmann, librarian at the Leo Baeck Institute in New York, as well as the entire staff, did everything they could to help me. The late Yuri Suhl, author of *They Fought Back: The Story of the Jewish Resistance in Nazi Europe*, was an early mentor. My history professor at SUNY Empire State College in New York City, Tom Grunfeld, was very helpful in the very earliest stages of my planning and research. Nobel Laureate Elie Wiesel read the first version of *The Berlin Ghetto* (when it had the title *Red Flags and Yellow Stars* in the early 1990s) and was kind enough to meet with me to discuss it; at the time he offered to write the introduction to the book upon publication. Michael Berenbaum, the former director of the US Holocaust Memorial Museum, read the same version and also offered to write its introduction.

The late Erich Honecker, the former head of state of the German Democratic Republic, personally arranged a visa for myself and my wife through the GDR Anti-fascist Committee (Antifa) to visit East Berlin and meet the Baum group survivors in the summer of 1988. The late Rudolf Helmer, the international affairs secretary of Antifa, sponsored my seven-day stay. Without the assistance of Honecker and Helmer, I would not have been able to meet and interview several veterans of the Herbert Baum group. It was during that trip that I first met Dr Margot Pikarski.

I wish to thank Ruth Kysel, my English teacher from Fort Lee High School in New Jersey, who has been a trusted friend and confidant since 1971. I also wish to thank my friend Pastor Steven Vornov, also from Fort

Lee, for his enthusiasm and kind words during the final phase of this very long project.

I wish to thank my editor at The History Press, Miranda Jewess, for her help in making *Berlin Ghetto* ready for publication. Also Shaun Barrington at The History Press, who patiently helped a cranky first time author make a final deadline on a project that was 28 years in the making. Lastly, I wish to thank my wife Joan for her support over the years since I first began this project in 1983, as well as my children David, Allison and Shayne.

INTRODUCTION

I first began work on *Berlin Ghetto* as a reaction to seeing the French documentary film on the Holocaust, *Night and Fog* (*Nuit et Brouillard*), which was released in 1955. A poignant and disturbing film, its images and score haunted me for years. The absence of the theme of Jewish resistance in *Night and Fog* demanded a response. *Berlin Ghetto* is that response.

The first version of *Berlin Ghetto* was completed in 1989 when it had the title *Red Flags and Yellow Stars*. The second draft was written in 1998, having sat in a filing cabinet for about eight years. The final version was written in 2011. Even though it has always been the same book, to me it feels like three different books on the same topic. The 'first' book (1983–1989), which was typed upon a Commodore 64 computer, had a raw quality to it, employing almost exclusively my interviews and written depositions from surviving Baum group members to tell the story of anti-fascism in Berlin from 1925 to 1942. In the 'second' book (1998), I took my research and placed it within the context of German anti-fascist and communist culture, as well as the history of the German-Jewish youth movement. Some chapters of that version were unacceptable to my mentor, Dr Arnold Paucker. They were deleted when I began the 'third' book (2011). One chapter that I had planned to include that disappeared, written in 1998, was 'The Wandervogel, the "Jewish Question," and Volkish Thought'. It is nowhere to be found. All that is left of it is an interesting title.

In the 'third' book, I have taken scholarship and other material and included them in this chronicle of the Herbert Baum group. This final version of *Berlin Ghetto* places more importance upon the political life of the Baum group, while the 'first' book almost exclusively emphasised the personal, social and cultural life of these young people. When preparing the final version, I took primary source documents that originally figured in endnotes, and, by using elements of 'new journalism' made them part of the narrative.

What all the people I write about had in common was an absolute hatred of National Socialism and an almost cult-like admiration for Herbert Baum. Even though many of the people in the resistance around Baum were Jews, several were not. Therefore this is not a book about 'Jewish' resistance in Germany. To categorise it as such would belittle the significant contribution and ultimate sacrifice of the non-Jews in the Baum group, as well as their comrades in other groups. *Berlin Ghetto* is about Jews and gentiles working together in the Berlin anti-fascist resistance in what essentially was a cultural ghetto. The Jews amongst them saw themselves as German anti-fascists and thus resisted as Germans; however, they were nonetheless persecuted as Jews by the Nazi regime.

E.B., Jupiter, Florida

1

THE SEEDS OF JEWISH ANTI-FASCISM (1925–1932)

Herbert Baum enjoyed reading and learning about the world around him. At one time he wanted to pursue a career in science, perhaps in engineering. But he also knew that as a Jew he would have to work harder than others to get what he wanted out of life. Herbert, his sister and parents had immigrated to Berlin from Mosina, Posen, after the First World War, when the province of Germany in which they lived was handed over to Poland as part of war reparations. The Baum family lived on Köpenicker Strasse, which stretched between the two downtown Berlin districts: Mitte and Kreuzberg. Both districts had large working class populations with significant concentrations of communists and socialists.

Around the corner, on Brückenstrasse, lived Rudi Barta. The two boys met in 1925, when Herbert was thirteen and Rudi was eleven. They were members of a Jewish youth group loosely connected to the *Roten Falken* (Red Falcons), the children's organisation of the majority Social Democratic Party (SPD). Their group was led by Walter Link, who held meetings in his apartment on Alte Jakobstrasse in Mitte. The boys later joined a *Roten Falken* troop.

They wanted to join an agit-prop group and become politically active. With the help of a social democrat mentor named 'Li,' they were introduced to Maria Hodann, the wife of the sexologist Dr Max Hodann. Herbert and Rudi were the only Jews in the circle around Mrs Hodann. With her they attended performances of plays produced and directed by Erwin Piscator at the Volksbühne Theatre. They saw *Battleship Potemkin* by

Soviet director Sergei Eisenstein, and went to the then recently acquired Egyptian exhibition at the Pergamon Museum on Berlin's Museum Isle on the Spree river.

Rudi felt that his and Herbert's involvement with the socialists was not very successful. The group was composed of the children of non-Jewish Berlin proletarians, and Rudi stated that 'Everything remained superficial – we were too far apart in both descent and upbringing.' This was, however, an important point in Herbert and Rudi's political development as socialists. Rudi writes, 'In his [Herbert's] quiet way he always pleaded for justice … He always spoke against poverty. It was in such a logical and simple way that everyone not only understood him, but also agreed with him. He had all the ingredients of a born leader.'[1] Together they attended a course in historical materialism taught by a member of the *Sozialistische Arbeiter Jugend* (Socialist Workers' Youth, or SAJ), the major youth movement of the SPD. Herbert and Rudi later took a class in Marxist theory sponsored by the SAJ.

The two boys even tried to get their parents to become politically active. This was a difficult task, however, since their parents had come from the East to the bustling metropolis of Berlin in search of a better life; they were not interested in politics, wanting to keep a low profile. Herbert's family life was quiet and close-knit with only relatives or Jewish friends around. Even though there were Jewish schools in Berlin, Rudi and Herbert both attended a German *Realschule* (A six-year school that led to an apprenticeship). This school had about two or three Jewish students for every 30 gentiles. Assimilation into all aspects of German life and culture was stressed. Rudi's parents even warned him to stay away from the 'dark' children – the Jewish ones![2]

In 1927, the Jewish socialist group led by Walter Link declared itself to be affiliated with the Zionist *Kadimah*. Since Herbert and Rudi had no interest in Zionism, they joined the *Deutsch-Jüdische Jugendgemeinschaft* (DJJG), a non-Zionist German-Jewish youth Bund that year.[3]

The DJJG was founded, according to Werner Rosenstock, 'to counterbalance *Kameraden*. As a genuine youth movement, the *Kameraden* had become selective in their membership … They could not, and did not want to, serve as a mass organisation for … young German Jews.'[4] The DJJG was a relatively small youth movement, with a sizable majority of the members in Berlin and additional sections in Leipzig and Dresden. Rosenstock writes that the DJJG 'had an impact which was greater than warranted by its numerical limitations. This was mainly due to the personality under whose spell the group leaders of the DJJG worked, Ludwig Tietz,' who was well known for 'his unreserved personal care and understanding for those who worked with and under him.'⁵

Rosenstock, the national leader of the DJJG, discusses its development:

[T]he Bund became an educational community, laying stress on the fertile tension between the youth leader and his younger followers who had to be brought up in the image of the movement. Discipline, authority of the leader and unreserved loyalty to the Bund were the most visible manifestations. As far as the Jewish aspect was concerned, it has to be realised that the decision to join a Jewish youth movement was not necessarily motivated by the desire for Jewish commitment. More often than not it was, in the first place, based on the longing for a community life as offered by the [German] youth movement ... The German Jews, especially in Berlin and the other large cities, were a self-contained community. While they were professionally and, to some extent politically integrated into their environment and although the rate of intermarriage was rising, most of them did not mix socially with non-Jews. It was against such a background that young Jews felt impelled to build up their youth movements amongst contemporaries of their own background.⁶

The members of this bund took part in various activities, including rambles in the forest, campfire cookouts, sing-alongs and serious discussions led by a group leader, who determined the philosophy of his group. Rudi Barta writes, 'We did not live at home ... we only ate and slept there. Our lives developed – mostly out of protest – in other directions.'⁷ Herbert and Rudi grew up and were shaped by the different youth movements.

Their new group had its home base on Wehlauer Strasse, where the leaders were generally conservative and belonged ideologically to the part of German Jewry that was for full assimilation into the German *Heimat*. The youngest group leader amongst them was Norbert Wollheim, who was Herbert and Rudi's first group leader in the DJJG.

The highlight of belonging to the DJJG was not the weekly *Heimabende* (meetings). Rudi Barta writes,

[T]he real life for us boys started Sunday mornings and sometimes already Saturday afternoons, when we met under the bridge at the Alexanderplatz [train] station. The environs of Berlin were beautiful. Between long marches, plays and jointly preparing simple meals, we developed a deep relationship with the nature around us ... like the romantic *Wandervogel* scout troops we met along the way.[8]

Max Abraham, a young DJJG scout at the time, remembers his friend and leader Herbert Baum:

> We all went for rambles where 'Hebbi' [Baum] took part ... and showed a paternal leading capacity ... [L]ater on he started to be less Jewish and more oriented towards socialism, but all members were Jewish so eventually he started to form his own group with a very strong socialist leaning.[9]

Another friend of Herbert and Rudi was Rita Resnik, a beautiful, petite girl who spoke with a thick Russian accent, having emigrated from Kishinev in the Soviet Union with her mother in 1918. Rita's father, whom she never knew, was a Russian Jew. Rita joined the DJJG when she was eleven; she considered the bund to be 'a youth organisation of bourgeois Jewish children from law-abiding lower middle-class families.'[10] It was 1928 when she met Rudi and Herbert. Together they made music, sang songs, read books and went on rambles. Herbert always teased Rudi about Rita even though there was only ever a platonic friendship between them. Herbert ribbed his friend about her anyway.[11]

Martin Kochmann, Herbert's oldest school friend, also belonged to the DJJG. Herbert and Martin had known each other since 1922, when they were both ten years old. They attended the Carl-Michaelis-Realschule in Kreuzberg and were in the same class until 1928, when they both graduated and began apprenticeships to learn a trade. Both boys' families could not afford to keep them in academic education. Herbert began training to be an electrician, while Martin began classes in business administration.[12]

It was in 1928 that the 'core' of the future Baum group was formed, composed of Herbert and Martin – who had been friends for years – and Sala Rosenbaum and Marianne Cohn, who became the girlfriends of Martin and Herbert respectively. Sala had immigrated with her mother to Berlin from Poland. Marianne Cohn was ten years old when she joined. She was bubbly, vivacious, and could be a bit domineering at times. The Cohn family, which included five children, lived at Richardstrasse 48 in Neukölln. Marianne's parents were assimilated German Jews who only observed the high holy days. She was not as serious as Herbert, and relished the novels of Stefan Zweig, Franz Werfel and Thomas Mann. Marianne loved to joke around with her friends, while Herbert had his nose buried in the revolutionary pages of Marx and Lenin.[13]

Margot Deutsch, a close friend of Marianne's sister Beate, was also in the group. Margot went on many hikes and outings with Marianne, Herbert and Beate. She recalls that Herbert was very pleasant and easy going, and remembers the many intense discussions they had. 'We all had to try to get to the bottom of every problem that ever existed in the whole world … [it was a] time for the youth to analyse nearly everything they could think of.' They read books together, went to concerts, the theatre and even the opera when they could afford it. It did not matter if they disagreed with each other's philosophy because they were good friends. The sense of belonging was more important than sharing the same ideology.[14] Some of the people they met around this time were Aribert (Ari) Steinbach, a boy with a healthy sense of humour who was a talented musician, Harry Oshinski, a brilliant student who was always open to adventure and Walter Fuchs, Barta's friend and neighbour, who suffered greatly due to his strong Jewish appearance.

Herbert Baum was itching to become more politically active. He felt that socialism was the answer but which direction should he follow? His background was in the socialist and Jewish youth movements, but he was also fascinated by communist thought. He consumed many texts, including Marx's *Communist Manifesto* and *Capital*, Lenin's *State and Revolution* and Trotsky's *My Life*. Baum saw these writings as providing the answer to Germany's socio-economic ills and believed that radical politics would help bring about the end of anti-Semitism.

Rudi Barta writes, 'Slowly we developed our own leadership qualities and were made responsible for groups of smaller children, or *Pimpfe*, with whom we grew.' This was in 1929, when Herbert was made a group leader of his own DJJG group on Wehlauer Strasse in Prenzlauer Berg. Walter Sack was also a member of the group; a few years younger than Baum, they had originally met at synagogue when they attended religious school together preparing for bar mitzvah. Walter and his friend Ari Steinbach (see above) believed in an evolutionary form of socialism. Walter and Ismar Zöllner (Herbert's cousin) worked side by side as apprentices in Walter's father's blacksmith shop, which was attached to their apartment on Skallitzer Strasse in Kreuzberg.[15]

Gerhard Zadek was also in the Jewish youth movement with Herbert Baum. His father, a Jew from Magdeberg, came to Berlin in 1914 in search of work as a tailor, but was conscripted into the German Army to serve in the First World War. After the war ended, he opened a small tailoring business down the street from the Alexanderplatz. Gerhard was born in 1919, and he and his family lived in a dank apartment near the Alex. During the late 1920s, Gerhard and his friends played in the Alexanderplatz; they wanted to visit the wooded outskirts of the city, but could not afford the train fare. The big square – and the neighbourhood around it – was grey and ugly. There was no place for children to play safely. Old buildings, large department stores, noisy taverns, pornographic peep shows and the gigantic police headquarters that stretched from the centre of the Alex to the massive Alexanderplatz train station set the mood of this part of the Mitte district of Berlin. The Alex was populated by seedy characters – petty thieves, pimps and prostitutes – and peddlers selling matches, pencils, apples and other cheap items.

The Zadek family were amongst the thousands of extremely poor Jews in Berlin during the Weimar period. All the family members worked long hours in the tailoring shop in order to survive, but they were always short of money and food. Gerhard shared his parents' worries and sometimes went to a welfare kitchen in the neighbourhood to get hot meals. He and his friends collected rubbish, old clothing and sometimes even bones to make money, with which they could travel to other parts of Berlin; sometimes they would walk as many as eight kilometres if they had no money for the U-Bahn or S-Bahn.

One day in 1929, Gerhard and his friends were standing in front of the synagogue on Kaiserstrasse when an older boy told them that they should get out of the neighbourhood and see the countryside. One boy asked him his name. 'My name is Herbert Baum.' He suggested that the boys join the DJJG and go for organised rambles and attend lecture and discussion groups in the evening. Upon Baum's prompting Gerhard joined the DJJG, which he considered the beginning of his political life. Shortly thereafter he met Baum's friend, Walter Sack. Zadek recalls that at group meetings led by Baum and his girlfriend Marianne Cohn, he and the other boys were jealous of Marianne's close relationship with Herbert and treated her poorly. However, they eventually came to care for her almost as much as they did for Herbert.

The rambles in the countryside were stimulating for Gerhard and the other boys, as were the discussions on the writings of authors such as Upton Sinclair and Emile Zola. They also studied Marxist works and texts on life in the Soviet Union, books that gave Gerhard an insight into socialism and communism. He came to consider himself a communist. His casual meeting with Herbert Baum on Kaiserstrasse had truly changed his life.

Gerhard and other boys in the DJJG had numerous run-ins with members of the *Hitler Jugend* (Hitler Youth). The DJJG scouts wore a handkerchief with a red border to identify that they were members of a Jewish group, which made them the targets of older toughs. These boys, who were about five years older than Gerhard and the others, waited in the darkness until the young Jews approached, then would pounce and beat them up. Gerhard lost a tooth during one of these fights, an experience that made him more defiant.

Gerhard Zadek joined the sports group *Fichte* and the communist scouting group *Rote Pfadfinder*, which held meetings on Munzstrasse. During this time he participated in 'war games'. He and other boys went on weekend outings in the town of Grunke, where a farmer let them sleep in the hay loft, and they took long walks in the countryside. Gerhard credits his healthy lifestyle to his meeting Baum and his membership of the DJJG.[16]

Franz Krahl also joined Baum's DJJG group in 1929, shortly before Germany was shaken by the Great Depression:

> Up until that time our discussions on *Weltanschauung* [world view] centred on God, the ideal human society, and its potential values. As the political situation worsened, we then focused on the topics of anti-Semitism, Zionism, growing up, and sexuality, all of which grew in importance to us. We also developed questions and possible answers to the socio-political problems of the day.

Herbert Baum guided his group in the study and discussion of basic Marxist texts, including *Wages, Price, and Profit*. Heated discussions ensued, with Walter and Ari favouring less radical policies, while Franz believed that there was not enough time to let socialism evolve naturally, and that revolutionary steps had to be taken.[17]

By this time Herbert Baum was sure that communism was the only path to follow, a conviction bolstered by the growth of the National Socialist movement. He became an extremely persuasive communist and sought converts throughout Berlin. Marxism-Leninism became Herbert's 'religion'. As the Nazis gained momentum, his stance became more militant. He eventually came to the conclusion that only a revolution could give Germany a fair and equitable socialist society. Herbert Baum was forceful – one could say possessed – about his ideals and convinced many people to share his radical political line. In 1931 he made his ideological if not cultural break from Judaism and joined the *Kommunistischer Jugendverband Deutschlands* (Communist Youth League of Germany or KJVD), the youth wing of the *Kommunistische Partei Deutschlands* (Communist Party of Germany or KPD). Following Baum's lead in making a total commitment to communism were Marianne, Martin, Sala and Franz, amongst others.[18] Other people joined the SAJ at that time. Rita Resnik considered this a 'friendly parting of ways.'[19]

Baum led DJJG meetings at different buildings owned by the Jewish community, as well as in his family's apartment on Köpenicker Strasse, with Marianne as co-leader. Amongst the group of about 20 boys was Herbert 'Rabauke' Ballhorn. He writes: 'My memory of Herbert Baum is that of a wonderfully warm and fair-minded teacher-leader who encouraged and nurtured young kids to become adults … he was a born leader.'[20] After the group was freed from the somewhat limiting institutional restraints of the DJJG, Herbert accelerated the Marxist-Leninist education of his young scouts. Ballhorn continues: 'Judaism and Zionism played no role … Slowly, seemingly by chance and without intent we edged towards social issues … [and] had entered the mainstream of communist thought. Herbert … was very subtle and clever about it.'[21]

On Sunday afternoons Herbert had his group meet with members of the *Roten Falken*, the socialist children's group. The first get-togethers were a bit strained; many of the Jewish boys were middle class while the young socialists were strictly working class. Ballhorn remembers that the Jews dressed better and had a somewhat more selective use of the German language, which only helped magnify the differences between them. On the other hand, the rampant anti-Semitism of the day made the Jews wary of this or any other gentile group.

There were many barriers that Baum needed to break down in order to make the two groups cohesive. He achieved it by putting the Jewish boys on an equal ideological footing with the socialists through political indoctrination. The Falcons were shocked by the Jews' knowledge of Marxist-Leninist concepts and theories. Ballhorn recalls that 'It seemed to me that our handful of Jewish boys were better equipped and versed in socialist theory than the Red Falcons themselves. Herbert had done a good job on us.'[22]

Initial problems faded after a few meetings as friendships between youngsters in the two groups developed. They found a common language: their talks stressed the concepts of solidarity, brotherhood and class struggle. On a very small scale Herbert Baum had reached his goal of ending anti-Semitism and brought about equality by applying socialism. He also used 'war games' to speed up the interaction between the two groups. One game took place in the Grunewald forest of Berlin in 1932. After a picnic and political talk, the boys were divided into 'Red' (socialist) and 'Brown' (fascist) groups. Ballhorn states, 'Darkness was falling and I was crawling towards the "enemy" alone, undetected and from an unexpected angle. By doing this, I earned some extra points and at the end of the game Herbert praised me for it. I felt very proud.'[23]

2

THE SEARCH FOR A GERMAN-JEWISH
IDENTITY IN THE YOUTH MOVEMENT

The attitude of the *Wandervogel* and the Volkish movement towards Jews made it clear to many German Jews that they would never be considered 'pure' Germans, and that attempts at assimilating into German society were foolhardy at best. However, as there was no Jewish nation, many considered assimilation the only pragmatic solution.

Zionism had become an important driving force for a segment of German Jewry at the end of the nineteenth century. The Jewish youth movement, which originated in Germany, began in 1912 with the founding of the *Jüdischer Wanderbund Blau-Weiss* (*Blau-Weiss* or 'Blue-White'), a Zionist organisation. *Blau-Weiss* had its roots in the Zionist students' movement of the 1890s. The *Kartell-Convent der Verbindungen deutscher Studenten judischen Glaubens* (KC) was a group of Jewish university fraternities that fought anti-Semitism as exponents of German liberalism. One of their acts of self-assertion was to aggressively provoke duels with anti-Semitic students who had offended Jews with vicious comments or deeds. These Jewish students, however, were not the type to seek an answer to Jewish problems outside the borders of Germany.[1]

The first attempt at a true Zionist organisation was the *Bund Jüdischer Corporationen* (BJC), which was an umbrella organisation of many Jewish Student Unions (VJSt) from German universities. At their *Kartelltag* (Annual Assembly) in Breslau in 1902, they adopted the following programme: 'The BJC is the rallying point of all Jewish students who feel themselves consciously as Jews and desire to participate in developing a living Judaism.'

The basic concept was to shape a Jewish consciousness into an activist form of Zionism. The VJSt sections of the BJC

> were academic fraternities conforming to patterns established at German universities. They held weekly drinking parties (*Kneipen*) and trained their members in the art of fencing in order to be able to fight duels ... At festive occasions ... the BJC corporations ... sported ... banners [that] featured the colours blue, white, and yellow – the yellow signifying the colour of the yellow spot of medieval days.[2]

The BJC's basic purpose was to educate – but not indoctrinate – the membership about Zionism, thereby making Zionist activity a personal duty and focus of every student.

A second Zionist organisation that complemented the BJC was founded in 1902. Begun at Berlin University, the *Freie Verbindung Hasmonaea* was founded and led by Egon Rosenberg. The *Hasmonaea* began as a fraternity that pledged to 'further the Zionist idea'. During special events, its members wore a wide band across the chest with the gold-black-gold fraternity colours and a Star of David embroidered on the band.[3]

Enzo Traverso, in his critical book on the Judeo-German symbiosis, presents a view of German Zionism before the First World War:

> [T]he Zionists seemed unwilling to renounce their Germanity. Franz Oppenheimer ... was as 'proud' of being German as he was of his Jewish origins... 'My Germanity,' he [said], 'is as dear to me as my Jewish ancestry ... I embrace both the Jewish national sentiment and the German.' At first, the Zionists were proud to acknowledge their roots in Western civilisation and German culture; the establishment of a Jewish State in Palestine seemed to them a valid objective for the oppressed, persecuted *Ostjuden* of the Czarist Empire, not for the German Jews. Before it became an assertion of ethno-cultural, even national, identity, belonging to the Zionist movement often took the form of philanthropic activity within Judaism ... [Oppenheimer] made a clear distinction between ethnic fellowship ... and national and cultural belonging ... As against the Eastern Jews, endowed with a national tradition and culture, the Jews of Central Europe identified with German tradition and culture. It should not be forgotten that for Theodor Herzl, founder of political Zionism, Germany remained in a way the source of any national regeneration

of Judaism, as is shown by his wish to make German the language of the future Jewish state of Palestine.[4]

In 1905, Kurt Blumenfeld, a Zionist, joined a BJC-affiliated fraternity in Konigsberg. He felt that the BJC had to eliminate its cautious approach and openly promote the Zionist cause in order to attract more Jewish students. He presented a theory of 'post-assimilationist' Zionism. Walter Gross explains Blumenfeld's ideas:

> 'German Jews ... had completed the assimilationist process; to them Zionism was a necessity in order to ... become harmonious personalities who were not ... thrown off balance by some hidden desire to get rid of their Jewishness. Blumenfeld's appeal was ... to those who were de-judaised. He spoke to the highly sensitive assimilated Jew who believed that Jewish heritage was no longer of any import ...'[5]

The traditional Jewish reproach against Zionism at that time was that it displayed disloyalty to the German fatherland. Blumenfeld's response was that a Zionist Jew was not an ethnic German, and he demanded that Zionists see themselves solely as children of the Jewish people. He felt that it was untenable for Jews to identify with the German Volk; once they accepted that they belonged to Jewry, they would be authentic Zionists.[6]

In 1912 members of the KZV (*Kartell Zionistischer Verbindungen*) and the BJC joined together to found the Zionist *Jüdischer Wanderbund Blau-Weiss*. Two years later, on 19 July 1914, the KZV and the BJC officially merged to form the *Kartell Jüdischer Verbindungen* (KJV). Its aim was 'to educate its members as men who will be conscious of the national unity of the Jewish people and are resolved to stand up for a renewal in Eretz-Israel which will be worthy of its history.'[7]

The end result of Zionism was to be the formation of a Jewish state populated with Jews from around the world on *aliyah* – emigration to Palestine – in the holy land of biblical Judaism. German Zionists, however, had problems with *aliyah*, one being their belief in the superiority of German culture. During the 1920s, Fritz Lowenstein, the former editor of *Jüdische Rundschau*, wrote from Haifa that the arrogance of Germans in Palestine towards the *Ostjuden* was uncalled for, especially since the Germans were having difficulties adapting to their new environment. They were struggling with the somewhat primitive rustic conditions and had trouble learning Hebrew.[8]

Felix Rosenbluth, the president of the ZvfD (*Zionistische Vereinigung für Deutschland*) from 1920 to 1923, wrote that there was

> a certain inflexibility in the German Zionist type, whose disadvantages show up especially at times of economic or vocational crisis – a certain inability to adjust and adapt to new situations ... In the case of many German Zionists a certain stiffness, which manifests itself to advantage in business affairs as stability, and a certain attachment to orderly circumstances, make for a greater despondency in the face of reversals and hardship.[9]

There was a belief in the Zionist movement that German Zionists would never be successful in Palestine due to their aversion to becoming farmers. One Zionist asked, 'Do we want our wives to become peasants? Do we want to marry peasants?' The attitude prevailed that while agricultural work was fine for Jews who had no other choice, it was hardly appropriate employment for cultured, educated Zionists from Germany. In other words, for the *Ostjuden*, *aliyah* was necessary, while it remained a luxury for the German Zionist.[10]

In a speech at the 1920 Delegate Congress, Otto Warburg, the president of the World Zionist Organisation, said that

> there should be no great expectations of the German Zionists as agricultural workers. For this purpose we have countless masses in the East ... The German Zionists [can] find other vocations ... in industry and as middle level bureaucrats ... For this the better preparation can be found not in the East, but right here in Germany.'[11]

Blau-Weiss, the Zionist Jewish youth movement, was, according to Stephen M. Poppel, 'indistinguishable in most regards from the German *Wandervogel*.'[12] Gerhard Scholem was very critical of *Blau-Weiss* accusing the organisation of taking many of the elements of the German *Wandervogel* and giving them priority over Zionism. Scholem, who was seventeen years old at the time, co-edited and published three issues of *Blau-Weiss Brille* between summer 1915 and the beginning of 1916. Chanoch Rinott explains that Scholem's views were heeded and had a lasting effect because he wrote with the voice of experience. Rinott presents Scholem's views on *Blau-Weiss* and Zionism from articles published in 1917:

1. The demand for ideology and for its realisation in action. A young Jew has to be a 'whole Jew,' not only an 'athletic Jew' (*Muskeljude*) or a 'Wanderer,' and not only a 'philosopher.' And action means 'to go to Eretz Israel.'

2. Zionism has become 'much more inner-directed, much more personal'; and that makes the problem of emigration much more acute. Law and medicine are not very useful professions to achieve this goal. Many Zionists found a 'very comfortable way of life in the *Galut*' and left emigration to the Russian Jews. The commitment to go to Palestine is the response to Herzl's demand, who spoke at the Sixth Zionist Congress (1903) of the 'signal for the exodus of the masses.' [...]

4. Hebrew, Jewish learning and Judaism have so far been 'an alien plant in the *Blau-Weiss Bund*'; but nowadays 'a youth movement that is not based on Hebrew-isation' is no longer conceivable. Unless these demands are realised, no 'wholeness of Judaism, full of content, can be created.'[13]

When *Blau-Weiss* members began university, they often joined the KJV, which was often a difficult transition. The outlook of *Blau-Weiss* was shaped by the *Wandervogel*, the German youth movement that spread the ethos of returning to nature and shaking off society through outdoor pursuits, while maintaining a nationalistic philosophy. They had believed in the value and life-reforming mission of Youth, but 'were taught to respect the *Alten Herren* [older KJV alumni]. They had grown up in the atmosphere of *Wandern* and *Gross Fahrt*, of romanticism ... [Thus] the teaching of Zionism as a systematic philosophy of Jewish life ... struck them as arid intellectualism.'[14]

The leadership of *Blau-Weiss* felt that all paths must lead to Palestine and began to develop plans for a settlement of its own there. It attracted many children of anti-Zionist parents, including young people from the upper echelons of Jewish society. Secondary school students, as well as commercial apprentices and first-year university students joined *Blau-Weiss* in significant numbers. These were the perfect recruits to become Zionist pioneers: they had few economic worries and did not have the responsibility of family life to tie them down. Older members went on *Hashshara* (vocational training) with German peasants. Individuals went to Palestine, hoping that thousands of German Zionists would follow them there.

An official *Blau-Weiss* document states that this Jewish hiking movement was founded

... solely out the necessity of working for the physical, spiritual, and moral training and toughening of Jewish youth. A relatively great part of our youth suffers under the harmful influences of big city life. We regard it as our task to take them away from the influence of the movie theatre ... away from the company of materialistic ... adults ... The *Blau-Weiss Wanderbünde* [hiking leagues] seek to lead the young man to nature, [and] within nature to achieve his spiritual and moral rehabilitation and the awakening of an idealistic view of life.[15]

Blau-Weiss blossomed into a movement of significant importance and numerical strength. However, it stayed away from any kind of political party affiliations, as did the *Wandervogel* and the *Bünde*. The *Bundesleitung* (leadership council) ran the *Bund* in a somewhat authoritarian manner; the *Bundestag* (Congress) of *Blau-Weiss* proclaimed the 'Law of Prunn' in August 1922, which placed every member under the unconditional authority of the *Bundesleitung*.[16] At the meeting, under the leadership of Walter Moses, a new constitution was promulgated. It declared

[T]he grand tasks [of the *Blau-Weiss*] require a leader and armies – a leader to command and an army to serve, together a tightly ordered organisation. The first epoch of carefree existence is past ... The hope for the fulfilment of life through the triumph of freedom will be replaced by the stern faith in the triumph of might ... Membership in the *Blau-Weiss* imposes ... obligations that encompass the whole realm of life ... The orders of the leadership or its deputies demand unconditional obedience ... Personal interests are secondary to the demands of the *Bund*.[17]

Gerhard Scholem resumed his criticism of *Blau-Weiss* after the Prunn meeting. He, along with fourteen others, signed a declaration condemning 'the growing absolutism of *Blau-Weiss*' and spoke of 'the bankruptcy of everything Jewish [in the *Bund*].' Those who signed the document felt that *Blau-Weiss* should be integrated into 'working Palestine'.[18]

The *Bund* achieved its greatest success between 1924 and 1926, when hundreds of *Blau-Weiss* pioneers settled in Palestine. The number of German émigrés to Palestine was 180 in 1924, 630 in 1925 and 242 in 1926.[19] The leadership wanted them to remain together as long as possible and establish *Blau-Weiss* craft and agricultural endeavours. The *Blau-Weiss Werkstatten* (artisans) and an agricultural settlement were the first two economic concerns founded by these German Zionists.

Despite the *Blau-Weiss*'s popularity and numerical strength, it never achieved a position of central importance in mainstream Zionist affairs. This was because of its stubborn insistence – based upon its overall philosophy, inspired by the German youth movement – that it should be separate from the world of adult politics. The attitude of *Blau-Weiss* is summed up in this contemporary deposition:

> We are not ... Zionist, as our ill-wishers say of us. We are Jewish. For us that says more. We are also a youth movement. As such we stand above parties. Nothing Jewish is foreign to us. We even venture to use words like 'freedom,' 'Palestine,' 'Shalom,' and sing Jewish freedom songs. But nothing would be so foolish as to deliver up the Jewish youth to a [political] party.[20]

There were problems in Palestine: the *Blau-Weiss* settlers spoke little Hebrew; they were not socialists and did not wish to be merged into the labour movement; and were perceived to be separatists by the official Zionist authorities in Palestine. Walter Moses instilled a separatist attitude amongst the young people because he thought that German Jews would not succeed in Palestine through social fragmentation.

Moses realised that it would come down to a fight for public money in order for *Blau-Weiss* to thrive in Eretz-Israel. He saw his *Bund* as the vanguard of German Zionism, but without significant financial aid their time in Palestine would be short-lived. In the end no aid was provided for the pioneers. Walter Gross writes: 'The Zionist Central Committee in Germany declined to earmark the proceeds of its fund raising activities for the acquisition of ... land on which the *Blau-Weiss* pioneer group might be settled. The proposal to give preference to their own fellow countrymen was considered inadmissible on ideological grounds.'[21]

The abandonment of *Blau-Weiss* by the Zionist Central Committee in Germany helped bring about its collapse in Palestine. The fact that members were generally not well prepared for life there did not bode well for its continuation either. *Blau-Weiss* was dissolved in Germany in 1926.[22]

While the *Blau-Weiss* Zionists partially reached their goal of sending people to settle Palestine, the *Kameraden, Deutsch-Jüdischer Wanderbund* (*Kameraden*) was never able to unify the three distinct opinions that centred upon what it meant to be a Jew in Germany. *Blau-Weiss* and *Kameraden* were inspired by romanticism and the German youth movement, and the former had answers while the latter came up with many questions. The *Kameraden*, founded in 1916, was confronted with the dynamics of the issue of being Jewish in Germany. To these young people, the question became a personal challenge. What did Judaism mean to them? What should they believe in order to be Jews? If they were non-believers, were they still Jews and should they remain Jews? It essentially boiled down to this: were they 'German Jews' or 'Jewish Germans'?[23]

The largest section of *Kameraden* – *Der Kreis*, led by Hermann Gerson – made a strong commitment to reconnect with Jewish religion and traditions. They considered the Judaism as practised by their families to be empty and confusing. They endeavoured to learn Hebrew and celebrate a more or less traditional form of Friday night services. The Buber-Rosenzweig translation of the Bible was studied and analysed in an attempt to grasp the meaning and evolution of Jewish religious and cultural traditions. These small steps towards Judaism did not automatically make them Zionists or Jewish nationalists.

The second section of *Kameraden* felt that they were 'blood Jews' but intrinsically Germans by virtue of language, culture and homeland. This smaller group was markedly different from *Der Kreis*, and the promulgation of their views was a thorn in the side of the larger section.

The third section did not have a positive attitude about being Jews. They were non-believers who made no attempt whatsoever to learn about Jewish culture, and saw Jews as just a 'sociological group'. Anti-Semitism – they believed – could be eliminated through a very close integration with the German people. Some felt their future lay in the bourgeoisie, while an ever-growing segment joined the workers' and proletarian parties of the left.[24]

The conflicts within *Kameraden* reached their height in 1931, when Hermann Gerson, the leader of *Der Kreis*, said, 'The consequences of our actions can only lead to the development of a political *Bund*. For me, this can only mean [a] socialist [organisation].'[25] Gerson wanted to change *Kameraden* into a non-Zionist youth movement based upon Marxist and Jewish ideals. The other factions in the *Bund* bitterly opposed this position. Dr Ernst Wolff, the leading ideological rival of Gerson, challenged the members to reaffirm their connection to the German nation. The nationalists felt that German values were equal to Jewish ones, and that it was important for assimilated Jewish youth to take their rightful place in the German youth movement.[26]

Kameraden could not exist forever with the conflict between the majority Jewish-national *Der Kreis*, the ultra-nationalist section and the left-socialist section. The organisation decided to split up on Whitsunday (15 May) 1932 at a major meeting in Kassel. Three movements emerged from the break-up: the *Der Kreis* majority took the name *Werkleute* (Craftsmen or Artisans), the rightist minority became the *Schwarzes Fahnlein, Jungenschaft* (Black Squad) (SF), and the socialist minority was called the *Freie deutsch-jüdische Jugend* (Free German-Jewish Youth) (Fd-jJ).

How did *Kameraden* remain together for so long (1916–1932) considering the constant ideological infighting? Eliyahu Maoz explains that 'If *Kameraden* did not disintegrate much earlier, this was due to two reasons: first the common zeal for hiking, camping, culture – all these typical activities of a youth movement, and secondly the indecision of quite a large number of the members.'[27]

The 400 ultra-nationalist members who founded the *Schwarzes Fahnlein, Jungenschaft* after the Kassel meeting, openly sought to belong to a German *Volksgemeinschaft* by assimilating themselves into the German youth movement. While camping and hiking, members learned about medieval architecture, the songs of the German bunds and gained a familiarity with the German countryside. They placed a special emphasis on the glorification of German military virtues – even after Hitler took power. The members were middle- and upper-class youngsters, who, like most Jews in the youth movement, felt that the bourgeois values of their parents were empty and rejected them completely. The SF did not partake in the 'middle class' vices of smoking, drinking or premarital sex; they wanted to create an alternative lifestyle for themselves based upon the ideals of the *bundisch* youth movement.

This anti-bourgeois attitude had first developed in the parent movement of the SF, the *Kameraden*. An emphasis on group solidarity and group action characterised the focus of *Kameraden*: to create a true sense of belonging through community-building activities. This attitude was demonstrated at their annual winter camp when food and money were shared equally.[28] The *Schwarzes Fahnlein* felt a strong connection with German and European culture, as did all Jewish youth movements. The difference was that in the SF, German culture assumed supreme importance. This led to total cultural and intellectual assimilation.

The SF members refused to renounce their identity as Germans. From April 1933 until its end in December 1934, the SF joined with other 'right of centre' Jewish organisations in an attempt to convince the Nazis that the van-guard of assimilated Jewish youth was ready and willing to participate in the 'new' Germany. The SF wanted to find an accommodation with the National Socialist regime in order for its members to take part in the *Arbeitdienst* (work service) and, hopefully, later join the Nazi-led German Army.

The SF's campaign to play a part in Hitler's Germany included sending petitions to the Reich Chancellery, glorifying the First World War veter-ans from the *Wandervogel* who died in combat, and marching in German Memorial Day Services. According to Carl J. Rheins,

> This pronounced identification with nationalist German values after Hitler had come to power had the effect of isolating the SF within the Jewish community in Germany. By 1934 the SF … [was one of] only two German-Jewish youth organisations which continued to adhere to a total German *Weltanschauung* despite the fact that many Jews had already been expelled from the Civil Service, the free professions and the secondary-school system.[29]

The SF made their wishes public in statements that were tentative but hopeful. The following, written by *Bundesführer* Gunther Ballin in May 1933, presents a carefully worded plea to not be forgotten in the creation of a 'new' Germany:

> We want to be the *bundisch* movement of those willing to share, without compromises or reservations, in the responsibility for Germany; not only because Germany is where we live, but because she is the object of our hearts and our love … [we have] tried to secure ourselves a place within the German *bundisch* youth and to maintain it through our work, our attitude and our willingness.[30]

The next *Bundesführer*, Paul 'Yogi' Mayer, felt that only the SF amongst all other Jewish bunds would be able to create an elite corps deserving of a role in the new German state. 'We do not want to be a mass youth organisation. We want to be only a *Fahnlein* (military squad)! The best are enough.' Membership in this model unit was based upon strict adherence to a community of heroic virtues, as well as the 'physical and moral bearing of the individual.'[31]

Despite the anti-Semitism and legislative restrictions upon Jews, the lead-ers of SF rejected a rational and pragmatic approach. Instead, they favoured an idealistic attempt towards participation in the nationalist revolution. Paul 'Yogi' Mayer writes:

> We stand and wait, 1000 young Jewish Germans. We are waiting mute, silent, but with faith. And because we wait like this, we have a great opportunity, namely that of some time being able to find the way to our German *Volk* in honour.

It is highly probable that the twelve- to fifteen-year-old rank and file members of SF had no idea of their leaders' attempt to integrate them into a German *Volksgemeinschaft* and partake in the 'Brown Revolution'. The youngsters enjoyed the day-to-day activities of the *Bund*, identified with romantic *bundisch* values and felt a strong connection with the German fatherland.

The *Heimabend* – the weekly group meeting common to all Jewish youth bunds – typically began with singing songs that glorified Germany's medieval past. Songs about the *Bauernkrieg* (the Peasants' Revolts) were very popular. The values these songs lauded included: 'bravery in the face of the enemy, an admiration for the professional soldier class and a romantic fascination with the medieval peasantry. [Most songs] ... did express a certain nihilism that was typical of Germany in the early 1930s.'[32]

The songs the SF members sang stressed the militaristic element of German society. Part of one such song, written by 'Oka' and published in the SF organ, *Der Fahnentrager*, is reproduced below:

> A regiment moves into enemy land
> hot is the sun, and white the sand.
> Songs ring out,
> Sounds vibrate,
> Proud flags fly toward the east ...
>
> Drum, you speak of love and death,
> Drum, you signal our agony.
> Over the entire host
> strays just one more
> last ray of a reddish sun...
>
> Weapons clang in the dark night
> Soldiers march in silent watch.

Stars announce
as they are fading
a new day which brings us battle ...

Carl J. Rheins explains that the SF emphasised German values rather than Jewish ones. For the most part, Jewish or Hebrew language songs were not sung. Literature with a Jewish theme, such as the work of Sholem Aleichem, was not read at the *Heimabende*. 'The SF's excursions ... had a marked military air which, although present in other Jewish youth groups in Germany, was particularly pronounced in the SF to a point where other Jews found it irritating.'[33]

Werner Angress, historian and former *Schwarze Fahnlein* member, writes:

> The image of the ... [SF] was really that of the non-Jewish *Bund*. The same literature which was popular in the German youth movement was read around our campfire in the German forest. Our songs ... were in some way concerned with war or expressed that rather romantic and unstructured longing that was part and parcel of all the *Bünde*.[34]

The rural excursions of the SF included activities modelled upon German military tradition. Roll call took place at 6.00am. Members presented themselves for inspection, hair neatly combed, uniforms in order, belt buckles polished, bodies rigidly at attention. Guard duty was the responsibility of all troopers; the SF had to constantly be on guard against attacks by the *Hitler Jugend*. The boys completed long hikes, sometimes a distance of 27km – while carrying full army packs. Members were to engage in 'tests of courage' such as jumping through fire. These feats and exercises helped to instil pride and boost self-esteem. The SF troopers would return to school without the feelings of inferiority engendered by the rampant anti-Semitism of the time and the membership of many of their gentile classmates in the Hitler Youth.[35]

The SF's *Bundesführer*, Gunther Ballin, saw membership in his organisation as a buffer against Zionism. In May 1933, four months after the Nazis took power, Rheins writes, 'Citing the *Bund's* pronounced German outlook, Ballin argued that only by enrolling their children in an appropriate *bundisch* youth organisation could National-German Jews be assured that their offspring would not be exposed to Zionist ideology.'[36]

The only other organisation to have a similar outlook to the SF was the *Deutscher Vortrupp* (DV). The close ties between the two German-National Jewish bunds were permanently broken by a bitter controversy surrounding a manifesto signed by SF members and their friends. The document, signed in July 1934, in Breitenhees, proclaimed:

A communal solution to the Jewish Question does not exist. Every attempt of emancipation as a group is inevitably bound to fail ... There remains merely a completely individualistic way which only individual people can take on their own account, and which will have to be taken by means of a total separation from Jewry in every form ... Thus for all to whom Germanism is the factual basis of their lives there is no other way which could lead to a satisfactory solution.[37]

The editorial in the August 1934 issue of *Der Deutscher Vortrupp* attacked those who signed the manifesto, charging that they had betrayed the Jewish community by promoting a worthless individualistic solution to the Jewish Question in Germany. The *Israelistisches Familienblatt* took the SF to task for 'destroying the internal unity of the Jewish youth movement in Germany by abandoning the historic Jewish tradition of communal resistance to external political pressure.'[38]

It was the 'ultra-German nationalist' emphasis which the National Socialist regime perceived as a threat to Aryan racial superiority. The Nazis could not accept the idea that young Jews would ever consider becoming part of the German *Volksgemeinschaft*. This ran counter to the orthodox Nazi doctrine of the racial differences between Aryan and Jew. Those Zionist organisations which advocated immediate emigration were favoured by the Nazi regime. Simultaneously the authorities cracked down on Jewish assimilationist groups which still sought a role for Jews in Nazi Germany. Therefore it is not surprising that less than six months after the signing of the Breitenhees Manifesto, the Nazis ordered the liquidation of the SF.

Werner Angress recalls the last gasps of the *Schwarze Fahnlein*:

I remember a ceremony, indelibly impressed upon my mind, which took place on 2nd December 1934 in Berlin, at which Leo Baeck officially dedicated the book of the *Kriegsbriefe gefallener deutscher Juden* [war letters of fallen German-Jewish soldiers]. The *Bund deutsch-Jüdischer Jugend* and *Schwarze Fahnlein* stood to attention while Leo Baeck spoke of his experiences as a rabbi during the First World War. After the sermon we marched out in formation, flags flying. Yet four days later the order came ... for the *Schwarze Fahnlein*, to be dissolved. We moved out at night and to my great distress my flag ... was burned.[39]

3

THE 'RED ASSIMILATION'

Herbert Baum and his friends' commitment to communism as well as their decision to join the KJVD (Communist Youth League of Germany) in 1931 was not the act of a few solitary Jews leaving the fold, but rather a widespread movement amongst young Jews: the 'Red Assimilation' of 1927–1932. Werner Rosenstock, who was a leading member of the DJJG during that time, writes that

> especially in Berlin, many young Jews … regarded communism as the answer to the political crisis in Germany. [They were] … antagonistic towards the continuation of a collective Jewish existence. They dissociated themselves with their community of origin, because they considered it to be a bourgeois society and, as soon as they were no longer minors, gave up their membership in the Jewish communities to become 'dissidents' like their Gentile comrades.[1]

Why did young Jews turn to communism? An eloquent answer is provided by Berliner Herbert Ansbach of the KJVD and a comrade of Herbert Baum:

> My father, who earned the family income as a small merchant, was quite religious. He regularly went to synagogue, and so did I. When I started seeing the misery of life of poor people, I felt hatred against those who were responsible for it. I lost confidence in a God who tolerated such injustice. So I started to find out why that should be so. When I was

fourteen, I began to ask questions and to read all I could get hold of, and was most impressed by the explanations given by Marx, Engels and Lenin. Love for human beings, hatred against those who prepare for war and make profit out of the blood of innocent people, and knowing how that can be changed, made me a communist.[2]

Another young communist Jew from Berlin, the theatrical set designer Wolfgang Roth, writes:

Rudi Pieroth, a quarrelsome and quick-witted communist, became my best friend and advisor ... in painting and ... in politics ... I became more occupied with politics, wanted to fight for a better world. We lived in a strange blend of absolute desperation and enormous zest for life ... We were so young, so enthusiastic, and had answers for everything ... we wanted to help the masses.[3]

Why did communism appeal to young German Jews? They felt strong bonds with both German and European culture; familiarity with Jewish traditions ran a distant second.[4] This dualism in German-Jewish youth culture set the stage for an intense search for a philosophy or ideology that one could grasp as both a German and a Jew.

The lines were drawn: Nazis and communists were fighting in the streets of Berlin and other cities. If one wanted to stop the Nazis from taking power, the best choice for a young activist was to join the communist youth in the KJVD. They were militant and anti-fascist. Arnold Paucker writes that 'where Jewish youth – against the advice of the official Jewish leadership – engaged in resistance activities, they for the most part joined the communists.'[5]

One of the goals of the National Socialist Party – which in 1931–1932 was pushing itself closer to legitimate political power – was the total elimination of foreign influences, which included the 'foreign' Jew in their midst, from German culture altogether. The KPD had positioned itself in its propaganda as *the* anti-fascist party and it was presumed in some quarters that it would come down to a civil war between these two militant revolutionary parties. A radicalised young Jew had no choice but to join the communists.

Many young German Jews rejected the values and aspirations of their parents' generation, especially their 'materialistic ambitions'. When children asked their parents for a 'Jewish' answer to a problem or issue, none was forthcoming. Rinott writes: 'Kafka's complaint about his father, that parents had no answer to give their children about being Jews, remained valid. The older generation was obviously ready to pay the price for growing assimilation … The distinguishing marks of Jewish life were receding even more into the background.'[6] This alienation from Judaism pushed some Jews towards communism, which provided an intense sense of purpose as well as a community with numerous cultural institutions. There was a common language and dogma that, in some ways, resembled a religion. Also one did not have to be born a communist in order to become one.

Rinott writes, 'The sources of Jewish knowledge were unknown … [and] a youth rarely found in his family traditions that had any meaning for him.'[7] This alienation from Judaism led some to search beyond the religion for an identity that fitted their outlook and personality. Zionism did not become a major issue amongst young German Jews until after 1933 for obvious reasons. There were numerous examples, however, of Jewish socialists and communists of German heritage. Karl Marx, the father of scientific socialism, although a convert to Lutheranism as a young boy, was born a Jew. There were a significant proportion of Jews in the KPD, as well as leading party functionaries such as Ruth Fischer. The two martyrs and founders of German communism, Rosa Luxemburg and Karl Liebknecht, were born Jewish.

Another aspect to consider is the Jewish element of the proletariat and the working class, especially in Berlin. A portion of these poor young Jews who were amongst the proletariat – even if their families were apolitical – felt an affinity with the German workers' movement and not the Jewish community. There were also Jewish families in the working class districts of Berlin who were already active in the trade union, social democratic or communist movements. These youngsters were predisposed to radical militancy either through life experience or their family's political orientation. Wolfgang Roth presents a bleak view of proletarian life as a young Jewish boy in Berlin:

[W]hat did children from tenement houses like me experience in the neighbourhood of the Schlesischer train station? Maybe seeing how the cheap prostitutes in their high laced boots dragged customers to their dark dwellings on our Muncheberger Strasse…? Or perhaps watching how different gangs … often [had] brawls, when they returned from the funeral of one of their members who had been shot dead?[8]

What influenced Herbert Baum to become a communist and join the KJVD in 1931? He lived in a working class district that included a large number of communists, an environment that must have had an impact on the young man. Furthermore, an event in autumn 1932 probably solidified his loyalty to the cause. At this time communists in the nearby district of Neukölln, where Herbert's girlfriend Marianne Cohn lived, organised a rent strike when Nazi Brownshirts (members of the SA) 'occupied' a bar in their building. The bar had been a leftist meeting place, but business was poor due to the poverty of the local communist patrons. The Nazis promised the owner that they would drink at least one barrel's worth of beer each day if they were given run of the place. This caused anger amongst the local communists; they saw the Nazi action as an attempt to move into 'their' territory. The situation was made more volatile by Nazi attacks on communists and the Brownshirts' drunken rowdiness.

A significantly high number of tenants participated in the strike, but it was not effective, as many residents were welfare recipients and had their rent paid directly to the landlord. Others were threatened with eviction, which put them back in line. On 15 October 1932, activist communists began a demonstration about one kilometre away from the bar. These marchers were primarily members of the paramilitary *Roter Frontkämpferbund* (Red Front Fighters League or RFB). A few dozen demonstrators began to march towards the bar while shouting 'Down with fascism' and singing the *Internationale*. Upon reaching the tavern, some communists took out pistols and fired inside. Four patrons were wounded, including the owner of the tavern, who later died from his wounds.[9]

What was it like to be a German communist during the early 1930s? The party was legal and protected by law; their deputies sat in the Reichstag with National Socialists, Catholic Centrists, Social Democrats and representatives of the other political parties. The party newspapers' headlines screamed openly to readers for revolution and strikes. Communist meetings were given police protection. The RFB was one of four legal private armies in Weimar Germany.[10]

The communists promised a good fight against the fascists; they had a proven track record to their credit. Herbert Baum became a communist because he felt that it was the only way to fight fascism effectively; the 'Red Assimilation' was not just a fashionable trend for Baum and his friends. Communist-inspired anti-fascism became a way of life for them and many other young Jews in Berlin. They saw no other path.[11]

4

STALINISM IN THE COMMUNIST PARTY OF GERMANY

O great Stalin, O leader of the peoples,
Thou who broughtest man to birth.
Thou who fructifies the earth,
Thou who restorest the centuries,
Thou who makest bloom the spring,
Thou who makest vibrate the musical chords …
Thou, splendour of my spring, O thou,
Sun reflected by millions of hearts.

A. O. Avidenko[1]

During the years of the Weimar Republic, the Communist Party of Germany (KPD) found itself increasingly submitting to Soviet authority. Its overall strategy was determined solely in Moscow, where the Soviets also created and destroyed the leadership cadres. Weitz writes that 'KPD factions rose and fell depending on the Comintern's assessment of the tactics appropriate for a particular period and, more often and more fatefully, on personal and political alignments between German communists and their Russian mentors.'[2]

The Comintern determined that Soviet control would be the norm; Lenin's 'Twenty-one Conditions' of 1920 stated that all communist parties were to model themselves upon the Russian party. Leaders of the KPD often travelled to Moscow to meet with the Executive Committee of the

Communist International (ECCI) to discuss important matters concerning German communism. Agents who were given special powers were assigned to the KPD Politiburo by the ECCI. Thousands of German communists journeyed to the Soviet Union during the 1920s, since the experience resulted in enhanced status upon returning to Germany. By the end of the 1920s, it was common knowledge that in order to advance in the ranks of the KPD one had to have trained at an academy or institute affiliated with the Comintern, the Communist Party of the Soviet Union (CPSU) or the Red Army.[3]

When necessary the KPD co-opted topics and language from rival political parties, a concept that had originated in Stalinist Russia. This trend continued virtually until the German invasion of the Soviet Union on 22 June 1941 (Operation *Barbarossa*). This included the opportunistic and cynical use of anti-Semitism by the party when attempting to exploit nationalist sentiment for tactical reasons. One striking example is found in a speech given by the Jewish KPD leader, Ruth Fischer, at a students' meeting on 25 July 1923:

> The German Reich will be saved only when you, together with the German nationalists, understand that you must fight hand in hand with the organised masses of the KPD; those who combat Jewish capital are already fighting in the class struggle, even if they are unaware of it. Stamp out Jewish capitalists! String them from the lamp posts.[4]

The push for the Stalinisation of the Communist Party of Germany began in 1925. Included in Stalin's twelve conditions for the bolshevisation of the KPD (February 1925) were:

> 10. It is essential that the party systematically improve the social composition of its organisation and purge itself of disruptive opportunistic elements. Its aim must always be maximum unity.
> 12. It is essential for the party to develop a rigorous proletarian discipline based upon ideological unity, clarity about the goals of the movement, unity in practical activities, and determined dedication to the party's tasks by the party masses.[5]

Stalin also outlined steps to restructure the German party organisation at the tenth KPD conference (12–17 July 1925):

a.   Establishment of order in the central party apparatus.
b.   Creation of politically more reliable and organisationally strong dis-
     trict leadership and strengthening of its authority.
c.   Continuing close contact with the district branches.
d.   Creation of a bolshevist corps of party functionaries.
e.   Organisational preparation for and supervision of the carrying out of
     party campaigns.
f.   Reorganisation on the cell principle.[6]

The Stalinisation process of the KPD included fusing the KJVD (the youth
section) with the main party and the Stalinist line. When the Comintern
issued an open letter censuring the Fischer-Maslow group – the left-wing
party leadership deposed by Stalin in late 1925 – the KJVD unconditionally
endorsed the letter at its ninth congress in Halle (October 1925).

It was at a party workers' convention of the KPD (1 November 1925)
that a resolution was passed in order to give the KJVD more 'support' and
tie it more closely with the party. The youth organisation was essentially
made part and parcel of the KPD itself. It was required that every party cell
have a parallel KJVD cell, and that each local branch of the party must have
a local youth group attached to it. Regional chairmen of the party were
responsible for the administrative work needed to achieve this; the steps
included recruiting drives for the KJVD and assigning party cadres to focus
on youth work.[7]

The KJVD now began a new developmental phase – closely aligned with
German and international communism – which led to its bureaucratisation
and militarisation. One section of the League Discipline Statute that the
KJVD adopted in Halle read: 'It is the duty of all League members and units
to maintain the most rigorous discipline. The resolutions of the Communist
Youth International, the KJVD Congress, the Central Committee [of the
KPD] and all other authorities are to be meticulously executed.'[8]

Considering the above, it makes perfect sense that Ernst ('Teddy')
Thälmann, the popular KPD leader from 1924 until his arrest in 1933,
gained his position by following Stalin. A former longshoreman and
transport worker, Thälmann sided with Stalin in the Kremlin's political
infighting and steered the KPD towards heavy dependence on the Soviets.
The authoritarian style of Soviet politics under the ever-growing power
of Stalin became the working model for the KPD. Following the Soviet
model, true power in the KPD was firmly in the hands of the Politburo,

which was dominated by Thälmann and the Comintern agents who were responsible for the KPD. Determination of a communist party member's loyalty in Germany became contingent upon enthusiastic support for the Soviet Union. Any party member who disagreed with political decisions made by the KPD Politburo, the Comintern, or even Stalin himself, could be deemed 'disloyal' to the party as well as to international communism. The KPD 'now became entwined with the authoritarianism that marked the Stalinist revolution from above in the Soviet Union.'[9]

Leon Trotsky wrote a critical evaluation of the KPD's reliance upon Stalinism.

> After gathering into its hands the apparatus of the Comintern, the Stalinist faction naturally transfers also its methods over to foreign sections, i.e., to the communist parties in the capitalist nations. The policy of the German leaders has for its counterpart the policy of the Moscow leadership. Thälmann observes how Stalin's bureaucracy rules the roost, by condemning as counter-revolutionary all those who do not recognise its infallibility. Wherein is Thälmann worse than Stalin? If the working class does not willingly place itself under his leadership that is only because the working class is counter-revolutionary ... Within the Soviet Union ... the victorious revolution has created material grounds for repression. Whereas in ... Germany, ultimatism ... hinders the advance of the Communist Party to power ... the ultimatism of Thälmann ... is ridiculous. And whatever is ridiculous is fatal, particularly in matters concerning a revolutionary party.[10]

Even before the KPD's 'Stalinisation', the mass of radical working people looked to the Soviet Union as the revolutionary model that would have to be followed in order to bring about 'Soviet Germany'. German communists were unable to destroy capitalism, while the Soviet Union, according to available information, was on its way to building socialism and was a land of peace and prosperity; the Soviets had also apparently abolished exploitation. It was therefore agreed that the Soviet Union deserved the enthusiastic support of all German communists, and, by the early 1930s, communist functionaries had learned that opposition to the Soviet Union's policies led to expulsion from the party.[11]

KPD press accounts presented the Soviet Union in glowing terms: men and women heroically giving of themselves to build 'the socialist fatherland of workers of all countries,' where Soviet workers and peasants have 'chased their exploiters to the devil ... Russian workers have food to eat, while in Germany workers go hungry. In Russia peasants have land, while in Germany hundreds of thousands of settlers and small peasants wait for an acre to feed themselves.'[12]

Arthur Koestler, a KPD member in Berlin, told a party functionary of his desire to give up his job as a journalist in order to work as a 'party propagandist or, preferably, as a tractor driver in the Soviet Union.' This was during the forced collectivisation period, when the Soviet press was pleading for tractor drivers. Koestler was told by the functionary that, 'the first duty of every communist was to work for the revolution in his own country; to be admitted to the Soviet Union, where the Revolution had already triumphed, was a rare privilege, reserved for veterans of the movement.'[13]

Eric D. Weitz writes:

German communists did not only read about the Soviet Union. Solidarity with the Soviet Union became inscribed in the cultural and political practices of the party ... Communists every year celebrated the anniversary of the Bolshevik Revolution and commemorated Lenin's death along with Luxemburg's and Liebknecht's in the LLL festivals ... Already in the 1920s workers and children's delegations visited the Soviet Union, and raising the necessary funds served as another form of public mobilisation. Visits to revolutionary Russia [were] ... inspirational to many KPD members who wrote suitable reports for the party press upon their return ... Party cells in German and Russian factories established relations in which they corresponded and sent aid to one another...

Solidarity with the Soviet Union was made more urgent by the constant threats it endured, from English imperialists and American finance capital to the German bourgeoisie and every other reactionary force around the world. '[Soviet Russia] is flesh of the flesh and blood of the blood of working people ... [where] the working class is proving that it ... has the power to govern and ... can secure to all workers a free, humane, and happy existence.' Solidarity with the Soviet Union therefore required 'the greatest vigilance, energy, and resolution!'[14]

Stalinism was very evident even in the individual party cadres. In 1932, the typical German communist cell had about 20 members and held meetings once or twice a week. All party cells were led by a 'triangle': *Pol.-Leiter* (political leader); *Org.-Leiter* (administrative organiser); and *Agit-Prop* (responsible for agitation and propaganda). All meetings were begun with a political lecture that was given by either the *Pol.-Leiter* after a briefing at the KPD district headquarters, or by an instructor from headquarters itself. The purpose of each lecture was to present the correct party line on specific issues of the day.[15] This same leadership and organisational style was used by the KJVD during its underground phase (1933–1936).

The lecture was followed by a 'discussion' unique to the communist party. A basic rule of communist discipline was that when the party adopted a certain line concerning a given problem, all criticism stopped; further criticism was considered 'deviationist sabotage'. It was natural, therefore, that these 'discussions' took the form of one member after another standing up to recite approving variations in Stalinese of the themes discussed by the lecturer. Koestler writes, 'We groped painfully in our mind, not only to find justifications for the line laid down, but also to find traces of former thoughts which would prove to ourselves that we had always held the required opinion.'[16]

There were two KPD slogans that vividly illustrate the party's attitude towards open discussion of the official party line. The first, 'The front-line is no place for discussion,' demands total submission to party policy, especially during times of struggle and persecution. The second slogan was 'Wherever a communist happens to be, he is always on the front-line.'[17] Thus, since a communist is always in the midst of ideological or physical struggle, any open discussion would thereby weaken the strength and resolve of the party.

As previously stated, the Stalinisation of the KJVD led to bureaucratisation and militarisation; this meant that it became a rather 'un-youthful' youth movement. It got to a point that completely confounded Ernst Thälmann, who gave a temperamental speech to the Central Committee of the KJVD in autumn 1932. His address was very critical and inadvertently spelled out the problems within Stalinism in the party and youth league:

> We need a more revolutionary team spirit in the work of the League. Let's get rid of the authoritarian tone. The KJVD is not the army! Every trace of bureaucracy must be ruthlessly stamped out ... The all too prevalent flat, monotonous language, the impersonal, cold, academic tone in discussions must go.
>
> Why don't we assume the romantic revolutionary voice of the broad masses of young workers? Why do we go about our work in such a dry, sober spirit? We need more liveliness, more enthusiasm, more verve, more

dynamism, more passion! We must create magnets to attract young proletarians to the KJVD.

In essence, the Communist Party of Germany shot itself in the foot by
slavishly following the Stalinist line. The KPD was obviously under Soviet –
read *foreign* – control, while its rival extremist party, the National Socialists,
was solely a German creation. The communists were saying, 'Use the
Soviet-Communist culture as a model to improve your wretched capitalist
German society,' while the Nazis said, 'Germans, take your inner greatness
and superiority and show the world what you can do!'

During the 1920s, the self-respect of Germans was extremely low. This
was due in part to the hyper-inflation of 1923 and the enormous cost of
war reparations to the Allied powers. The root, however, of all of Germany's
economic ills, and thus its political and social problems, was 'war guilt' and
the notorious Treaty of Versailles. Germany was told over and over again by
foreign powers that it was solely responsible for starting the First World War.
Under Versailles, foreigners dictated to Germany exactly what it could and
could not do. Thus Germany was truly under foreign control, which stoked
the embers of a strong nationalist sentiment.

Hitler inflamed the masses with his fiery speeches that demanded throwing off the yoke of Versailles and setting Germany on the path to greatness
by making its own destiny. As the protocols of Versailles were being silently
disregarded, or *de facto* eliminated, the Nazis gained strength and electoral
power. This was also due to the unstable political and economic situation
that stigmatised the Weimar Republic, factors that also enabled the KPD to
gather mass support as well as greater success in the voting booth.

In the long run, however, what ultimately doomed the communists in
their bid for complete power in Germany was their kowtowing to Moscow
on virtually every party issue and policy. Stalinism caused the militant KPD,
considered the second strongest communist party after that of the Soviet
Union, to collapse in the early stages of the Hitler dictatorship. It was obvious that the majority of the German people wanted no part of a movement
that was under the strict control of a foreign power. The Treaty of Versailles
and its effects were imprinted on the collective memory of Germany. They
would never again allow a foreign power to tell them what to do. This set
the stage for the ascent of Hitler. The German people were much more
receptive to the philosophy of their inherent superiority than to subservi-
ence to foreigners.

The KPD – even before being forced to go underground – became a fragmented organisation riddled with distrust, as a result of the paranoia which permeated the Soviet party in the wake of the Stalinist purges of 'Trotskyite traitors'. In the Soviet Union, informers were everywhere and the innocent as well as the guilty were swallowed up. Arthur Koestler explains the conflict in German communist culture in 1932:

> The party was preparing to go underground ... The new recruit to the party found himself plunged into a strange world, as if he were entering a deep-sea aquarium with its phosphorescent light and fleeting, elusive shapes. It was a world populated by people with Christian names only – Edgars and Paulas and Ivans – without surname or address ... It was a paradoxical atmosphere – a blend of fraternal comradeship and mutual distrust. Its motto might have been: Love your comrade, but don't trust him an inch – both in your own interest, for he may betray you; and in his, because the less he is tempted to betray, the better for him.[18]

5

DESCENT INTO DARKNESS (1933)

The communists called for a general strike to begin on 30 January 1933, but no one – including the communists themselves – took this order seriously;[1] the party's influence over the working class had slipped away. On the same day, shortly before noon, the following oath of office was recited stiffly by a man with a Charlie Chaplin moustache:

> I will employ my strength for the welfare of the German people, protect the constitution and laws of the German people, conscientiously discharge the duties imposed on me and conduct my affairs of office impartially and with justice to everyone.[2]

Adolf Hitler had legally attained the Chancellorship of Germany, after President Paul von Hindenburg had decided the day before to invoke Article 48 of the Weimar constitution. This article provided Hitler with dictatorial powers to 'protect the state from overthrow'. He drew upon this law to convince the elderly President and his cabinet to dissolve the Reichstag and order new elections for 5 March.[3]

The following day, 31 January, the future propaganda minister Josef Goebbels wrote a diary entry after meeting with Hitler:

> In a conference with the Führer we establish the directives for the struggle against the Red terror. For the present we shall dispense with direct counter-measures. The Bolshevist attempt at revolution must first flare up. At the proper moment we shall then strike.[4]

On 4 February, Hitler persuaded Hindenburg to legalise the suppression of meetings that would 'endanger public security',[5] legislation introduced to weaken the opposition Social Democratic and Communist parties in their election bids. Even though the National Socialists were the largest party after the 6 November 1932 election, 33 per cent of the vote was not nearly enough for a majority in the Reichstag. Since there was a need to expand their power base, the Nazis used their newly found legal authority to target the socialists and communists. SA troopers broke up legal social democratic rallies and leading socialist newspapers were suspended.[6] The Brownshirts also invaded the taverns where communists and social democrats held open meetings.[7] However, even with seemingly endless provocation and repression, the predicted 'Bolshevik revolution' that Hitler, Goebbels and Göring needed to unleash a wave of terror never materialised.

Hermann Göring, in his role of Prussian Minister of the Interior, stated that demands made on the police force continuously strained its resources. In a decree of 22 February, Göring declared that 'the voluntary support of suitable helpers to be used as auxiliary police officers in case of emergency can no longer be dispensed with.'[8] To that end, 50,000 men were mobilised. 10,000 came from the German National People's Party's private army, the *Stahlhelm*. The black-shirted SS, originally Hitler's elite bodyguard unit, numbered 15,000. The SA, at 25,000, had the highest representation in this supplemental police force. These men wore their own brown uniforms with white arm bands labelled 'auxiliary police'.

Göring's 'volunteers' strutted around, rubber truncheons and pistols stuffed in their belts, travelling on trams, buses and trains for free. They entered cafes and restaurants, carrying souvenir photographs of Hitler, Göring and Goebbels, which they then sold to frightened patrons at exorbitant prices while wielding their weapons menacingly. Terror-stricken waiters served them at side tables. To reward their 'service to the state', each 'volunteer' was paid three marks a day from the police treasury.[9]

The communists seemed blind to the seriousness of the political situation. On 23 February, Max Brauer, a leading social democratic politician, met in Berlin with Ernst Torgler, the chairman of the communist delegation in the Reichstag. He asked Torgler whether the communists would consider making peace with the Social Democratic Party (SPD) in order to create a united front alliance. Torgler said, 'It does not enter our heads. The Nazis must take power. Then in four weeks the whole working class will be united under the leadership of the communist party.' Reflecting upon Torgler's answer, Bauer felt that he must have been suffering from stress.[10]

A few days later, Bauer met with the Soviet Ambassador, Chinchook, in Hamburg. He asked him the same question he asked Torgler and then had a feeling of deja vu: 'No, they [National Socialists] must come to power now, and then at last the old fight will come to an end. In four weeks the communists will have the leadership of the whole working class.'[11]

Later that month, a leading KPD member named Heskert fled to Moscow. Upon his arrival, he publicly declared before the Executive Committee of the Comintern that what had occurred in Germany had confirmed Comrade Stalin's predictions. He also said that social democracy and fascism were twin brothers. A Comintern resolution dated 1 April 1933 stated that the Nazi dictatorship in Germany has freed the masses from the influence of social democracy and thus 'accelerated the tempo of the evolution of Germany towards proletariat revolution.'[12]

'The Reichstag building is on fire!' Word spread around Berlin on the evening of 27 February as Hermann Göring arrived at the scene. With flames crackling behind him, he proclaimed:

> This is the beginning of the communist revolution! We must not wait a minute. We will show no mercy. Every communist official must be shot, where he is found. Every communist deputy must this very night be strung up.[13]

The first consequence of the fire was the arrest of 4000 known communist activists, including every KPD candidate for the 5 March Reichstag elections.[14]

A presumably insane Dutch communist, Marinus van der Lubbe, was found after he had set a few small fires in the Reichstag's basement. It was unlikely, however, that he could have set the entire building on fire by himself. The appearance of this young Dutchman gave Hitler the opportunity to exploit the Reichstag fire to the limit. In order to halt 'communist acts of violence endangering the state', the next day Hitler convinced Hindenburg to sign a decree 'for the protection of the people and the state'. It included

> Restrictions on personal liberty, on the right of free expression of opinion, including freedom of the press; on the right of assembly and association; and violations of the privacy of postal, telegraphic, and telephonic

communications; and warrants for house searches, order for confiscations as well as restrictions on property, are also permissible beyond the legal limits otherwise prescribed.[15]

In separate decrees issued shortly thereafter, the death penalty replaced life imprisonment for many offences, including treason, arson and railroad sabotage. 'High treason' was poorly defined in order to include all forms of dissidence, including published materials.

In National Socialist parlance, 'election campaign' meant bloody street battles with communists and social democrats. During the period 30 January–5 March, which encompassed the election campaign, the German press reported the murders of 51 anti-fascists, while the Nazis claimed eighteen dead during the same time period. The Brownshirts had swarmed all over Germany to defeat the 'Marxist' enemy.[16]

The new Chancellor's decrees crippled the parties of the left and helped boost the Nazi vote to 44 per cent in the 5 March election. The communist party was virtually crushed by this time. In addition to those communists already arrested, KPD leader and presidential candidate Ernst Thälmann was arrested and shipped off to a concentration camp. Thousands of communists fled Germany, and SA storm troopers and their police collaborators wrecked, burned and looted Social Democrat and Communist party offices. Brownshirts also assaulted and arrested these parties' municipal officials and deputies.[17]

The KPD was completely unprepared for its virtual destruction within a year of Hitler taking power on 30 January 1933. For some strange reason, however, the Nazi takeover had no impact whatsoever on the KPD's politics or propaganda. In the official view of German communism, Hitler's regime was just another form of vicious, fascistic capitalism.[18]

The failure of the KPD to jointly nominate a candidate with the SPD has been seen by Arthur Koestler as a primary reason for Hitler's attaining power in 1933. But the party instructor for Koestler's cell lectured that backing the candidacy of Hindenburg along with the social democrats as a 'lesser evil' was a complete fallacy, 'a Trotskyite, diversionist, liquiditorial and counter-revolutionary conception'.[19]

The main enemy of the communists had always been and remained the social democrats. This rival workers' party, the SPD, was dubbed the 'twin brother' of the Nazis and the 'major prop' of capitalism. Despite being Nazism's 'twin brother', the KPD made what could at most be called feeble attempts to include the SPD in a united front against Nazism in 1931.[20] Even though the 'Fascist beasts' were just that, the communists' 'main pre-occupation was with the Trotskyite heretics and Socialist schismatics.'

It must be remembered that the Nazis and communists did find common ground upon occasion. In 1931 communists and Nazis collaborated in the referendum against the social democratic government. The autumn of the following year saw 'brown' and 'red' join hands in the Berlin transport workers' strike.[21]

Despite the legality of the party and most communist activity, the summer of 1932 saw the KPD in the midst of preparation to go underground. The party cadres, which had numbered around 20 members up until this time, were now cells composed of 'Groups of Five'. Only the leader of each 'Group' knew pertinent information about the other four members.[22] Looking back, Arthur Koestler writes: 'To prepare for a long underground existence in small decentralised groups meant that our leaders accepted the victory of Nazism as inevitable … [and] that the party would offer no open, armed resistance to the ascent of Hitler to power …'[23]

Considering the KPD's nonchalant attitude about and devious partnership with the Nazis and their hatred of 'social fascists' and 'Trotskyite heretics,' it can confound a researcher to try and pin down a consistent German communist policy. The meaning of the word 'fascist' had been watered down by the party because it had used the 'fascist' label to describe every German government from 1929 up to Hitler in 1933. The communists were unable to grasp the fact that they had 'authentic' fascists on their hands until it was too late.[24]

Leon Trotsky, writing in exile in Turkey on 25 August 1931, rhetorically asks:

If the Social Democracy is a variety of fascism, then how can one officially make a demand of social fascists for a joint defence of democracy? … the [communist] party did not put any conditions to the National Socialists. Why? If the Social Democrats and the National Socialists are only shades of fascism, then why can conditions be put to the Social Democrats and not to the National Socialists?[25]

The former commander of the Red Army continues:

The circular letter of the Central Committee of the German Communist Party to all units on 27 July [1931] most mercilessly lays bare the inconsistency of the leadership ... the essence of the letter ... [is that] ... there is no difference between the Social Democrats and the fascists, that is, that there is no difference between the enemy who deceives and betrays the workers, taking advantage of their patience, and the enemy who simply wants to kill them off.[26]

The Chancellor started spinning his web to enlist the support of the German Nationalists and Catholic Centrists in the Reichstag in order to pass the Enabling Act; Hitler needed a two-thirds majority to pass this bill. It was officially called the 'Law for Removing the Distress of People and Reich' and took all power away from parliament and gave it to the Reich cabinet for a four-year period. Laws enacted by the cabinet were to be drafted by the Chancellor and 'might deviate from the constitution'.[27]

Shortly before the Enabling Act was to be voted on, a story appeared in the Nazi Party newspaper *Völkischer Beobachter*. It described a concentration camp that was being set up on the grounds of a former gunpowder factory outside Munich near Dachau. It would concentrate 'all communists and, where necessary, *Reichbanner* and social democratic officials ... [who] cannot be allowed to remain free as they continue to agitate and to cause unrest.'[28]

The first working session of the Reichstag began on 21 March; all the communist deputies and 26 of the social democratic deputies were missing. The final vote on the Enabling Act was 441 for, and all 94 social democrats in attendance against. The National Socialist deputies stood as one and with their arms held high in the party salute, sang the 'Horst Wessel' song: 'Raise high the flags! Stand rank on rank together. Storm troopers march with steady, quiet tread ...'[29]

During May 1933 – when thousands of communists were imprisoned in concentration camps – the KPD Central Committee stated that it had pursued an 'absolutely correct political line ... before and during Hitler's coup', while the 'brutal social fascists ... have openly gone over to the fascists' auxiliary service, where they promote cooperation with the fascist bourgeoisie and applaud the fascist state's control of workers' organisations.'[30]

Seven months after Hitler took control of Germany – in the summer of 1933 – a clandestine document written by an unidentified leading KPD member was sent to the Comintern in Moscow. The communiqué read, in part, that the KPD had succeeded not only in beating back all the voices of panic, but had also put an end to the retreat. The party has been able to strengthen the cadres and rally the masses for the counter attack ... In the last weeks it has become clear that the entire party is on the march and that our authority in the working class is on the rise.[31]

Even after the virtual eradication of the KPD through the destruction of its institutions, publications and cadres, as well as the incarceration of its leadership and thousands of rank and file party members, functionaries of the party continued to adhere to the Stalinist line regarding fascism in Germany. This was probably through fear of what might happen to them if they dared to express their real thoughts or opinions in conversation or in an official correspondence to their 'bosses' in Moscow.

6

PERSECUTION, SETBACKS AND THE BEGINNING OF RESISTANCE (1933)

Considering the situation in Germany in 1933, it is clear that anti-fascists did not have an easy time operating at any level. This was especially true in Berlin. People who became active resistance fighters had to learn techniques to protect themselves and others from discovery by the authorities. Any slip-up could mean a prison term, confinement in a concentration camp or even death. When seeking sympathisers one always had to be on the lookout for Gestapo infiltrators or agent provocateurs.

The KPD advised through the underground that no more than five people should meet at one time; no lists of people or records of any kind should be kept; and that messages were to be oral only. The Communist Party of Germany also recommended that codenames be used as a means of protection, and that any person could act the role of courier provided that only a bare amount of information was given. But however difficult the situation or dangerous the work, there were always people willing to work for the cause. Persecuted communists, social democrats, trade unionists and Jews made up the bulk of the German resistance – they had the most to lose under Nazism. Any efforts to create a national movement were severely cramped, however, by the possibility of a death sentence for 'high treason' and other loosely defined crimes.

1933 was a very bad year for German communism. Top people fled to form parties-in-exile in Paris (KPD) and Prague (KJVD), while thousands of others escaped to wherever they could. A great number were sent to concentration camps. Known party members who remained in Germany were kept under surveillance, which rendered them useless for resistance.[1] By the end of 1933, between 60,000 and 100,000 communists had been interned by the Nazis.[2] Weitz writes that despite this, however, 'Within Germany communists numbering in the tens of thousands pursued active resistance in the 1930s despite the continual rounds of arrests by the Gestapo.'[3]

Times were also getting tougher for the Jews of Germany, as after the Enabling Act was passed, Hitler turned his attention to them. A boycott on 1 April 1933 saw the Brownshirts position themselves in front of Jewish-owned or managed shops throughout Germany. They prevented people from entering stores and held large placards that read, 'Don't Buy from Jews.' They marked the store windows with a large Star of David and the word '*Jude*' in order to 'inform' the public that these were Jewish stores.

It was on this day that Georg Manasse, a nineteen-year-old from Pomerania, arrived in Berlin. He was shocked by what he saw and remembers vividly that people who attempted to enter Jewish stores were either photographed or taken away by force. Georg had engaged in quite a few street fights with Nazis in his hometown, and the boycott reminded him of those times. He took the U-Bahn train to a station in the Charlottenburg district of Berlin, where he was to live with his mother and other relatives.

One day Georg took a walk around his new neighbourhood and met three thirteen-year-old boys: Heinz Birnbaum, Sigi Spivak and Jack Rosenbach. They told Georg about the youth group that they belonged to which had a firm foundation in Judaism. It was neither Zionist or assimilationist, and concentrated on scouting, hiking and discussions about Jewish history and culture. Georg expressed an interest in joining and his new friends brought him to a meeting where he was almost immediately made the leader of a group of 20 young boys. This was probably *Werkleute*, which was one of the three Jewish youth movements formed after the dissolution of *Kameraden* in 1932. Since Georg was new to Berlin, the three young scouts became his official tour guides. Georg felt the closest to Heinz and they became good friends. Heinz Birnbaum, a Jew of Polish heritage, lived in a large apartment in the middle-class district of Charlottenburg with his parents, sister and two other relatives. The Birnbaums were relatively well-to-do; Heinz's father ran a business distributing eggs to small grocery stores throughout the city.

Georg got along well with young boys and Heinz looked up to him as a big brother figure. It was a perfect match. Heinz was very receptive to Georg's views and made them his own. They were both interested in

Zionism and tried to find a synthesis between it and socialism. They spent time at each other's homes and Georg joined Heinz in his favourite prank: making crank calls to people on the telephone. Heinz helped Georg with family chores; one time they moved some furniture across Berlin in a big two-wheeled wagon.

Because their Zionism ran counter to the *Werkleute* movement's philosophy, Georg and the three boys were forced out of their scouting group. Georg joined *Hechalutz* (a Zionist Jewish association which aimed to settle members in Israel) and the boys became members of *Habonim*, the children's Zionist bund. Shortly after Heinz joined *Habonim*, he told Georg, 'I met this very interesting man whom I would like you to meet. His name is Herbert Baum.' Heinz was taken with Baum's forceful personality and dedicated anti-fascist stance. He was invited to Baum's flat and brought Georg along. Herbert was there with his girlfriend, Marianne Cohn. The four young people discussed Hitler and the situation in Germany. Baum declared that he was a strong believer in communism and felt that it was the solution to Jewish problems; he did not see Zionism as the answer. 'Jews have to stay in Germany and fight together with all other German anti-fascists to topple Hitler.' Even though Georg did not believe in communism, he did agree that all anti-fascists should work as one. Party affiliation was not important – working against the regime was.

From the pamphlets Herbert created, Georg suspected that he was involved in the KJVD. He never knew for sure because such questions were generally not asked. Heinz slowly came under Herbert's influence and drifted away from Georg. Heinz was, according to Georg, 'like putty in Baum's hands'.[4]

The KJVD had 55,000 members in 1932. This made it a numerically small organisation compared to other KPD mass organisations. The Communist Youth League of Germany, however, played a significant role in the early stages of anti-fascist resistance, especially when it was expected that a crisis within the regime would throw Germany into a situation that was ripe for a successful communist revolution. Opposition from young people was inspired by the Nazis' totalitarian attempt to give absolute control to the *Hitler Jugend* over all youth activities outside of school and the home. Young communists were, in the face of a fascist dictatorship, willing to become overtly political and to make daring sacrifices.[5]

Heinz Birnbaum remained a member of *Habonim* even though he submitted himself totally to Baum's *Weltanschauung* (world view). Many times

Heinz tried to bring Georg Manasse into the Marxist-Leninist fold. This was one of the methods Baum used to gain converts and bring new people into the resistance. Georg remained a non-communist anti-fascist, however, and limited himself to socialising with Heinz, Herbert and Marianne. One afternoon the four of them met with a group of non-Jews wearing swastikas in the Grunewald forest in outer Berlin. These friends of Baum's were former social democrats, communists and trade unionists who now belonged to the *Deutsche Arbeiter Front* (DAF), the Nazi union that all workers joined. Everyone used nicknames – Herbert was 'Hebbi,' Heinz was 'Bobby' and Georg was 'Ariel'. An object was hidden somewhere in the woods and Herbert had a map marked with a cross. After a long search, the group located the object. The young people had a cookout followed by a political talk.

A while after the outing, Heinz and Georg met on the streets of Charlottenburg. Heinz put off his friend somewhat by making fun of his involvement in Zionism and bragged that the communist movement was stronger than before Hitler. Heinz also told him that he had landed an apprenticeship as a tool and die maker at Butzke and Company, a large pipe manufacturing concern. Since he was unable to complete his education, Heinz had decided to learn a craft in the metal trade. By this time he had made his final ideological break from Zionism and was completely won over to the communist cause. Birnbaum came to the conclusion under the influence of Herbert Baum that 'our place and fight is in Germany.'[6]

Since it was difficult to come across much unbiased information about Germany and other countries within Germany itself, people in the resistance took trips out of the country to secure printed material. Herbert Ansbach, a young communist Jew active in the KJVD, went to Paris from Berlin to attend the 'World Congress of Youth Against War and Fascism'. Before leaving Paris, Ansbach asked for money to purchase a revolver in Berlin. His friend laughed and said, 'I cannot do that, but we can give you a bomb to carry back.' On the train bound for Berlin, Ansbach was handed a tightly wrapped package. He later discovered that his 'bomb' was in actuality 20 brown-covered pamphlets about the Reichstag fire of 27 February 1933, and the trial that followed.[7]

Herbert Baum was extremely active in the creation and distribution of such illegal communist literature. It was only a few days after Hitler became Chancellor that Baum directed a number of his young DJJG scouts, including Herbert 'Rabauke' Ballhorn, to either sell or distribute the *Rote Fahne*, the KPD publication, printed in secret. During this time Baum attempted to both solidify and expand his sphere of influence in Berlin. He did this by maintaining his contacts and developing new ones in Jewish youth movements. He was able to give these youngsters hope and widen the effectiveness of the underground.[8]

It was during the spring of 1933 that Baum placed Walter Sack in a KJVD cell of five members. Walter was a few years younger than Herbert; they had attended religious school together and were in the DJJG at the same time. The year Baum joined the KJVD, 1931, was the year Sack joined the ranks of the SAJ youth movement of the Social Democrats. Walter became a communist, however, which led to his joining the illegal KJVD.

Walter also joined the *Ring, Bund deutsch-jüdische Jugend* (Bund of German-Jewish Youth, or more commonly *Ring*) in order to become the leader of a large group of children. The *Ring* was founded in 1933 when the DJJG was disbanded. This movement, similar to the DJJG, was made up of assimilated Jews who took pride in their German heritage and wished to remain in Germany. According to Walter, 'these connections were all about Herbert Baum.' His group became known as the *Dritte Zug* (third troop). Sack employed the diverse activities of the *Ring* – the rambles, meetings, music, discussions and readings – to introduce basic ideas of communism and socialism to Jewish youngsters. Walter's comrades in the *Ring* who had a similar political outlook, Judith Kozminski and Ari Steinbach (a Social Democrat who was not involved with the KJVD), steered their troop members towards socialism in a similar manner. Walter and Ari often led troop meetings together. In addition to reading books by Jack London and Upton Sinclair, the youngsters read popular Soviet youth books that had been translated into German. These books included *Schkid: The Republic of Thugs* and Nikolai Bogdanov's *The First Girl*, in which a Komsomol member shoots his beloved comrade during the Russian Civil War to protect her from the shame of being publicly declared a 'loose' woman by counter-revolutionaries. The older children under the tutelage of Sack, Steinbach and Kozminski began to read excerpts of Marx's *Communist Manifesto* and *Capital*.[9]

It was around this time that Rudi Barta and Herbert Baum both tried to influence their youngsters to choose one of them to follow. Rudi felt that Herbert was looking for stronger commitments from his troop. He was pleading for people to go into active, serious political work (without mentioning any names of parties or institutions), while Rudi took a more moderate stand as an assimilated German Jew working against the Nazis.

Barta felt it was a friendly competition between the two friends. Rudi had followed Herbert's path for a few years, but he developed his own philosophy before the Nazis came to power.

Herbert and Rudi led their troops under the banner of the *Ring*; Walter and Ari's group and Judith Kozminski's made it a quartet of *Ring* troops with an anti-fascist bent. Herbert Budzislawski became the first youngster to declare his loyalty to Herbert. This was despite the fact that Rudi was close to his sister Ruth and the rest of the family. Following him was Siegbert Rotholz and others.

The youngsters would do anything their troop leader asked of them; such was the strong appeal of the youth movement and the charisma of the leaders. Nobody questioned their leader's political or social decisions. If someone felt uncomfortable about their group, that person would join another more to their liking. Quite a few youngsters tried out different troops until finding one that gave them a sense of purpose. Barta states that Judaism was not an important element of their lives: 'We did not know much and did not try to transfer it to our groups.' On Friday evenings Rudi tried to create a religious 'atmosphere' but with no success. 'We did not know enough to carry it off.'[10]

It was in the *Ring* that Ellen Compart found a place to be herself in 1933. Born and raised in the working-class Prenzlauer Berg district of Berlin, Ellen felt that some form of socialism would enable people to get the most out of life. Ellen's first *Ring* troop leader was Rudi Barta, who led *Heimabende* in buildings owned by the Jewish community on Choriner Strasse, Oranienburger Strasse and Rykestrasse. A typical discussion led by Rudi went along these lines:

> If we want a better world we must never cease to search, never cease to learn, never be afraid to revise or moderate – and must be prepared to do so over and over again. We must learn to understand ourselves and others to reach the common goal: the end of Hitler's Reich.

Ellen and the others were made aware that there were many small cells of anti-fascists in Berlin. It was suggested that people visit with any group if invited, but they were told never to reveal any names or details about other groups. Anyone who said 'no' to the regime was a potential friend. It did not matter much if the philosophy differed, for only in unity could there be strength. Contact between groups was through a few individuals who used code names; this was for everyone's protection and to lessen the risk of revealing information when under duress. The shared outrage made any such groups and their members allies and friends. The need and desire to protect each other was strong.[11]

Ellen and her friends were deeply disturbed by the Jewish boycott, but it was the numerous anti-Jewish laws that really hurt them and their families. Only a few days after the boycott ended, on 7 April, the first anti-Semitic law was put into effect. The 'Law for the Restoration of the Professional Civil Services' legalised the removal of Jews and political opponents of the Reich from the civil service. A companion law cancelled admission to the bar of 'non-Aryan' lawyers. Jews were also excluded from serving as lay assessors, jurors, commercial judges and patent lawyers. They were prevented from working as panel physicians, dentists and dental technicians in state social insurance institutions. Jewish journalists lost their jobs on newspapers; Jewish conductors and musicians could no longer work in orchestras; and Jewish professors were kicked out of their universities.

On 25 April, the 'Law Against the Overcrowding of German Schools and Institutions' was enacted. This law limited the attendance of 'non-Aryan' Germans to a proportion to be 'determined uniformly for the entire Reich territory'. The ratio of new pupils was set at 1.5 per cent until the number of 'non-Aryan' students would be reduced to approximately 5 per cent. On 29 September of the same year, the Reich Chamber of Culture was established, banning Jews from working in the cultural and entertainment fields: art, literature, theatre and film.[12]

In less than a year, Hitler had removed the Jews from public life, the government, culture and the professions. In effect he had impoverished those Jews and their families. The children of these unemployed Jews saw that their future held nothing for them and that the only way to change the course of their lives was either to emigrate or actively work against the National Socialist regime. By the end of 1933, a total of 37,000 Jews had left Germany.[13]

Ellen Compart and her friends did not have the option of leaving Germany. They remained and with the help of their *Ring* troop leaders adapted as best they could to the 'new' Germany. Ellen attended the *Heimabende* led by Walter Sack and Ari Steinbach; she remembers that Walter was the practical organiser and that Ari was the creative, inspirational force. Sack and Steinbach once took the youngsters to the Katakombe, a famous Berlin cabaret know for biting anti-fascist satire even after Hitler took power.[14] The compere, Werner Finck, was a controversial figure whose intricate web of half-sentences came across as a suggestive, indirect opposition to Hitler. Shortly after the Nazis came to power, Finck appeared on stage at the Katakombe holding a flower-crowned photo of the Führer, walking slowly from one side of the stage to the other, saying: 'shall we hang him here … or should we hang him here? … He'd better be put against the wall …' Upon noticing Gestapo men in the audience, Finck would ask them after a complicated joke, 'Do you follow? … Or have I got to follow you?' When a storm trooper heckled him, yelling, 'Jew-boy,' the unflappable MC would snap back: 'You're wrong – I only *look* that intelligent!' Finck would occasionally stiffen his arm in the Nazi salute and shout, 'That's how deep we're in the shit!'[15]

Ellen and the others went to the popular cabaret, which was tucked away in an elegant part of town, where they saw a show entitled, 'The Courage to Laugh'. The walls were covered with caricatures of famous Berlin entertainers and actors. One of the skits they saw that night featured a 'Survival Coach' who displayed his goods on a table in a market place, which he sold while singing a patter song. He held up a body ointment to protect against the electric cattle prods of the police, inflatable wigs that were really helmets, a smokescreen in a spray can and a stink-bomb in a gelatin capsule that was activated by being stepped upon. Near the end of his song, the police arrived in a helicopter and the 'Coach' was carried away while tossing leaflets into the audience. Another skit featured dreams that could be purchased for as little as 25 pfennig, including one where people find themselves confused by having more than one political party to vote for at election time.[16]

It was the books of Germany's great writers and philosophers that took these young people out of their tight, cramped world and set them free to think and dream, but even these were targeted by the swastika. On the evening of 10 May 1933, a torchlight parade of thousands of students marched to a square on Unter den Linden opposite Berlin University. The torches were put to an enormous mountain of books. As the fire grew in intensity, many more books were thrown in until 20,000 were consumed by the flames. Dr Josef Goebbels addressed the enthusiastic crowd of students. He said, in part, that 'The soul of the German people can again express itself. These flames not only illuminate the final end of an old era; they also light up the new.'[17]

During this time, Herbert Baum was working as an electrician for a small private contractor in Berlin. After finishing school in 1928, he had attended classes at a technical school while completing an apprenticeship which lasted from 1928 to 1931. Even though he was the only Jew in the shop, he was well liked by his co-workers and it has been reported that he attempted to persuade them to become anti-fascists. Herbert was still following his dream of becoming an engineer. He had begun taking night classes at the Beuth-Schule to become an electrical engineer, which was very difficult considering the strict quotas imposed on Jews in all German schools. Herbert's girlfriend Marianne had trained to become a Kindergarten teacher and held down a job in a Jewish school. The two young people were deeply in love and decided to live together. They found an affordable flat at Stralauer Strasse 3/6 in Friedrichshain where they began a happy life.[18]

7

ACTS OF REBELLION (1934)

Herbert Baum, Marianne Cohn and their close friends Martin Kochmann and Sala Rosenbaum worked in resistance to a limited degree during most of the first year of Hitler's regime. Their work consisted mainly of distributing illegal anti-fascist newspapers and pamphlets, and maintaining contact with underground KJVD members and others who were sympathetic to the cause.

Due to the relentless persecution of both communists and Jews, it was not until the late autumn of 1933 that a workable resistance was formed in Berlin by the KPD-in-exile in collaboration with existing KJVD cells; this was coordinated in Berlin by Alfred Lischeski and Kurt Siering. This development gave the circle growing around Herbert Baum a strong framework within which to conceive and implement acts of resistance.[1]

Kurt Siering, a German gentile, originally met Herbert Baum during 1932 in the KJVD. In collaboration with a few comrades, Kurt created and distributed an underground newspaper called *Rote Sturmparole* (Red Storm Parole). He was instructed by the leadership of the KJVD to work directly with Baum and concentrate on activities with the young Jews in the group.[2]

In 1934, Baum was made leader of the then underground KJVD sub-district southeast, which was based in Neukölln. This group included Sala Rosenbaum and Martin Kochmann, Marianne Cohn, Herbert Ansbach, Rita Resnik, Heinz Birnbaum and Werner Steinbrink.[3] Werner Steinbrink was a non-Jewish communist from the same neighbourhood where Herbert Baum and Martin Kochmann grew up. He was quite educated, having passed his Abitur after taking evening classes. Afterwards he took classes to train to become a laboratory technician.[4]

Herbert Baum kept his communist work separate from his activities in the *Ring*. The same was true for Walter Sack, who also belonged to an underground KJVD cell and led his children's group in the *Ring*. The communist cells were illegal and dangerous, while the *Ring* was a 'legal' organisation affiliated with the Jewish community. It therefore provided an excellent cover for anti-fascist work. Herbert initiated interaction and contact between *Ring* and Zionist *Haschomer Hazair* members. In this way the communist resistance was widening its base of support within government-sanctioned Jewish youth movements.

It was becoming increasingly dangerous to distribute leaflets by hand on a regular basis, so Herbert Baum devised a new strategy. He took a large vegetable can used in restaurants, which he emptied and cleaned out. In the bottom half he placed explosives, which he covered with a round metal plate. The next step was to apply chemicals over the plate to prevent the top half of the can from burning. He fastened a timer with a clock on the side of the can and then carefully stuffed flyers into the top half.

Baum's KJVD comrade, Herbert Ansbach, initiated contact between the Red Students League, to which he belonged, and Baum, who persuaded a law student at Berlin University to help him with the first 'leaflet bomb' action. The can was placed in a crowded room at the *Staatsbibliothek* (State Library) on Unter den Linden. The timer was set and it went off with a boom, spitting leaflets all over the room. Fifteen minutes later a number of black cars screeched to a halt in front of the building and Gestapo men poured out. They took everyone into custody, but soon let them go. The success of the leaflet bomb gave Baum the courage to repeat the action.

With the help of a member of the Nazi Radio Workers Bund, one of Baum's comrades gained access to an important radio show at the Funkturm building. He placed the leaflet bomb in a flower box behind the podium and sat in the audience. The show began and out stepped the Nazi propaganda minister, Dr Josef Goebbels, who opened it with a brief speech. Suddenly, a shot went off behind him, and small, round Soviet star emblems and leaflets flew over his head and into the audience. Goebbels ducked under a desk and then scrambled out of the room. A few minutes later, SS men, police and firemen arrived and attempted to collect the 500 small slips of paper, but they only managed to gather up 30. The rest of them disappeared as souvenirs. On the small slips of paper it was printed: 'Hear the voice of the truth – tune in to Radio Moscow!'

The third – and most dramatic – leaflet bomb action occurred on 11 July 1934. Eight people were involved – five from Baum's KJVD cell – including Baum himself. He and Werner Steinbrink planned and implemented both the procuring of the necessary ingredients and the action itself. It was a busy summer's day when eight cans were placed atop 5 Bahnhof Alexanderplatz, near the Tietz and Karstadt buildings. The timers were set and an hour later all eight cans exploded, filling the air with leaflets that read: 'Today the millions march to celebrate the October Revolution, and in Germany the workers and peasants shall overcome fascism and rejoice!'[5]

Georg Manasse was worried about Herbert's anti-fascist flyers. Herbert told Georg that they must be given out and thrust a package into his hand. 'Go on, give them to friends,' Baum told Georg. Georg recalls that he 'was very scared … [Baum] had such a strong influence on people.' Manasse says that Baum was extremely persuasive: 'You could not say no to him … He had this charisma.' Georg handed out a few copies and destroyed the rest. He never let Herbert give him any more.[6]

Baum's KJVD cell performed yet another daring resistance act on 1 August 1934. This was called 'Anti-War Day' by Berlin anti-fascists because it was the 20th anniversary of the beginning of the First World War. The KJVD activists took children's lettering stamp sets and created short anti-fascist slogans. They set the type, applied coloured ink with a roller, and stamped the slogans on small pieces of paper.

Baum and his comrades met at a bustling avenue in Kreuzberg. Half of them were riding bicycles, while the others were on foot, carrying the cans. They placed the cans on the ground and lit them; a different coloured smoke spewed from each. When startled pedestrians stopped in their tracks, the anti-fascists on bicycles threw hundreds of small slips of paper into the air and on the ground, and then sped off. Two of the slogans read: 'Freedom for Thälmann' and 'Against Fascist War Preparation'. One anti-fascist who acted the role of 'pedestrian' reported back to the group that many people had picked up the leaflets to read them.[7]

One week later, on 8 August, seven KJVD southeast members, including Baum's oldest friend Martin Kochmann, were arrested. The charge was 'preparation to commit high treason' and the Gestapo alleged that they had organised a group in order to overthrow 'the constitution of the Reich'. A few days later, on 11 August, Kochmann was sent to Alt Moabit prison, where he remained during the investigation. Herbert Pasler – who had joned the KJVD in 1934 – was also arrested. He paid membership dues to either Kurt

Siering or Otto Wendt; one of them then gave Pasler illegal literature to read. This material included *Rote Sturmparole* and *Junge Garde Süd-Ost*.

The Gestapo discovered that Martin Kochmann was a trip organiser of a Jewish hiking group that was led by someone known only as 'Bubi' (one of Baum's cover names), and believed that Herbert Pasler's KJVD group had joined the 'unpolitical' hiking group in autumn 1933. Kochmann had met Bubi on the street in late July or early August 1934. He was informed that Pasler, whom Kochmann had visited at his home upon occasion, would wait for him on Manteuffelstrasse in order to give him something. The two young men met where planned, and Pasler gave Martin a package containing 100 anti-fascist flyers. Kochmann threw out the package after seeing what it contained.

Kochmann strongly denied any connection to the KJVD, and insisted that the German-Jewish youth group he led was cultural and not political. He claimed that he was unaware of any communist infiltration by Bubi, and that he met with Pasler only to discuss art history. The Gestapo did not believe him, but since they did not have any strong evidence supporting their theory of his group's communist infiltration, he was released.[8]

The arrest of Martin Kochmann and the six others was indeed a blow to Baum and the KJVD. It had become clear to Baum that Kochmann's arrest was due, in part, to the leaflet bombs. It was now far too dangerous to continue the 'bombings,' so new, less dramatic distribution methods had to be developed. To that end, Baum and his comrades concentrated on forming new ties and strengthening existing ones between organised and unorganised communists and social democrats, liberal and radical Jewish youth groups, and sports clubs throughout Berlin. Even though Baum's operation was based in Neukölln, his network of contacts spread throughout the city.

Baum's KJVD cell met every Saturday either in Baum or Sala Rosenbaum's apartment to plan resistance actions for the coming week. In the wake of the arrests, a new three-person committee was formed: Herbert Baum, Herbert Ansbach and Werner Steinbrink. Ansbach took over Martin Kochmann's role in the cell, while Steinbrink and Siering performed other functions. Each of the three leaders had numerous small cells to supervise and indoctrinate. This was exactly the same structure the party had decided upon in 1932 for the KPD cadres, with the three-person 'triangle'.

Every other week there were mass meetings in the forested suburbs of Berlin. These sessions were held in order to develop a better understanding of Marxist political ideology, and to maintain social contact.

Each gathering was held in a different location using a wide variety of inconspicuous covers. Outings were camouflaged as boat trips, garden parties, sports meets, picnics, birthday parties and other 'legal' activities. The people attending these gatherings were both Jews and gentiles. There were always anti-fascists standing guard to warn the leaders of the approach of Nazi officials, police or *Hitler Jugend*; the meeting could then be turned into a harmless social function in a few seconds.

Herbert Baum and Werner Steinbrink were responsible for choosing the time and place of these events. They also chose the cover and briefed everyone on what to bring and wear. Books used at the meetings – often smuggled in from abroad – were torn apart and stored in small quantities in several apartments around town. The Central Committee of the KPD-in-exile often determined the themes and ideas for discussions. Amongst them were: 'The Danger of War through Imperialistic Fascist Regimes', 'The Situation in Germany' and 'Class Struggle under Fascism'.

The three-man KJVD committee of Baum, Ansbach, and Steinbrink created and published a bi-weekly newspaper, *Junge Garde Süd-Ost*, as well as numerous flyers. These anti-fascist publications were distributed by members of the various cells in Baum's KJVD underground group. Steinbrink was the editor-in-chief, while Baum and Ansbach wrote articles and flyers. Baum was also responsible for the distribution of the illegal materials.[9] Gerhard Prauge, a gentile member of Baum's KJVD group, had a duplicating machine on which he printed communist literature, including the KPD's *Rote Fahne* and the KJVD's *Junge Garde Süd-Ost*. He was also given the task of infiltrating the *Hitler Jugend*, enabling him to provide Herbert with valuable information.

Otto Wendt was one of the young gentile KJVD members who made the switch from social democracy to communism; he was a member of the SAJ – the youth organisation of the SPD – until 1931. During that year, the SPD was fighting for the construction of two expensive battleships. Since millions of people were out of work, many left-wing party members protested this move openly, leading to thousands of people being thrown out of the SPD and its youth movement, including Wendt himself. He then joined a youth group connected to the *Sozialistische Arbeiterpartei Deutschlands* (SAPD), which was politically between the SPD and the KPD. In October 1931, he joined the *Sozialistische Schule Bund* (SSB), which was a branch of the KPD.

Shortly after the Nazis banned socialist and communist youth groups, Wendt joined Baum's underground KJVD group. Two other members of the KJVD group, Ansbach and Steinbrink, were also members of the SSB before its dissolution. Wendt was responsible for maintaining contacts between the KJVD and former SAJ and SSB members. He was also in charge of circulating anti-fascist pamphlets and literature amongst his numerous contacts in the underground.

Wendt's job in a bank was an asset to Baum's group, as it meant he could supply it with large amounts of mimeograph paper, the type used for duplicating flyers. Supply had become difficult because the Gestapo had given an order to all stores that sold paper that anyone purchasing ten or more sheets of mimeograph paper had to show his or her identification card, their name being added to a list for possible interviewing by the Gestapo. New members of communist cells were told to bring ten sheets of such paper as membership dues.

Wendt recalls that 30–40 young communist Jews joined the KJVD subdistrict southeast from 1933 to 1934. According to Otto, they joined not as Jews combating anti-Semitism, but as anti-fascist Germans of Jewish heritage. All KJVD members treated each other as equals, no matter their religious, ethnic or socio-economic status.

After the Nazis' rise to power, Wendt, amongst others, was dispatched to warn comrades in Scandinavian countries to stay put. Otto was in contact with the Berlin families of many KJVD émigrés and spoke with them often. He was told of many instances when the Gestapo visited their homes asking the whereabouts of these known communists. Returning to Berlin would put them at risk of being arrested.

Otto was friends with a boat captain who regularly sailed from a Baltic port in Prussia to Copenhagen for day trips. Thus Wendt was able to spend about six hours in the Danish capital without using a passport. While there he met up with friends from Berlin, as well as Danish communists and social democrats who invited him to return. This was considered an important contact for the KJVD group in Berlin, and he made several trips during the 1930s.

He arranged for food parcels to be sent to his home through his contacts in Denmark. Since Wendt's father was unemployed, he did not have to pay custom fees for one package per month. He distributed the food to KJVD members and Jewish families in need. This was his unofficial contribution to *Rote Hilfe* (Red Help), the international workers' charitable organisation. Since it was illegal in Nazi Germany, each underground group or individual contributed to it in their own way. It was not organised by a central organisation, but people kept the name and spirit of *Rote Hilfe* alive as a sign of solidarity with those who could not survive without material assistance.[10]

Besides engaging in acts of rebellion, the young people of the KJVD and the *Ring* maintained an energetic intellectual life. Ellen Compart writes: 'If there would have been a statement of purpose [for the *Ring*] it would be to give Jewish youngsters a self-image and an ideology to live with and to live for in the face of Nazi propaganda that claimed they were lowly creatures – inferior, evil parasites and worthless.' The various *Ring* troop leaders tried to make it possible for Ellen and the others to grow and become useful citizens. The *Ring* groups led by Ari Steinbach, Walter Sack and Rudi Barta focused upon an evolutionary form of socialism. At *Heimabende*, Ellen and the others were trying to find the way to a better world. To do this, they had to know the basic concepts of differing political systems. German fascism was being experienced first hand and parents spoke of hardships under the Kaiser. The Weimar Republic had promised so much and failed completely. The group knew little of America, and only heard stories about inequality, racism and the glorification of wealth; it seemed that American democracy left a lot to be desired.

They tried to learn whatever they could about socialism in its various shapes and forms. They read, discussed, analysed, dissected, agreed with, rejected and repeated the process over and over again. They immersed themselves in Hegelian philosophy and analysed the influence Hegel had on Marx and Engels. The young people saw Marx's peaceful and humane society, in which each individual would make the most of his or her potential, as a goal worth fighting for. Ellen Compart writes:

Marxist thought was heady stuff for a downtrodden, persecuted, and impoverished young person whose right to exist was denied. It sounds very utopian today, as it did then, but we were treading water and reached for the stars since there was nothing else to reach for ... Man's understanding of the forces that enslave him will make a historic difference; he can then engage in social planning for the betterment of all. The seizure of the means of production puts an end to the domination of one class in society over another. The struggle for individual existence comes to an end and man can finally cast himself off from the realm of necessity into the realm of freedom, and alienation will cease.

After hearing these concepts and ideas time and time again, Ellen would lie in bed unable to sleep, and think, 'If only it could all happen tomorrow morning at nine o'clock!'[11]

8

ARRESTS AND PERSECUTION (1935)

At the beginning of 1935 Nazi newspapers announced planned blackouts and air raid exercises in Berlin. Upon discovering the date of the first blackout of the city, Baum's KJVD committee went to work. Herbert Baum, Herbert Ansbach and Werner Steinbrink created a poster specifically for the occasion, and distribution plans were worked out by the committee, as were escape routes and assigned areas for each person. The blackout provided a perfect cover for hanging the posters. The next day walls across the city were covered with hundreds of posters that read: 'Today rehearsal, tomorrow dreadful reality!'[1]

Herbert Baum and the others prepared leaflets to distribute by hand in factories – a dangerous task. Escape routes were prepared well in advance and briefings were held regularly to ensure the participants' safety. When shifts changed at factories, the young anti-fascists were there to hand out flyers to the workers. The leaflets warned against the exploitation of workers in preparation of a fascist-initiated world war, and the powerful monopoly of large capitalist concerns. Marxist-Leninist concepts were used to attempt to connect the anti-fascist resistance with the working class of Berlin.[2]

While in *Hechalutz*, the Zionist organisation, Georg Manasse came to know a fellow Zionist named Harry Salinger, a half-Jewish former KJVD member. He had spent six months in a Berlin prison after being caught distributing communist propaganda in 1933. Salinger had become friends with his cell mate, a former social democrat named Bruno who had been arrested for falsifying election results. Bruno, a short and stocky Catholic of Polish descent, had a job in construction on the new autobahn project. After their release from prison, they remained friends.

Harry told Georg that he had extra tickets for a choral concert and gave him a few. Georg then gave them to Heinz Birnbaum, Herbert Baum, Marianne Cohn and one to either Sigi or Jack, while Harry gave one to Bruno. The young people met at their seats at the Berlin Philharmonic. The performers were former leftists who were now underground. They gave their proceeds to imprisoned anti-fascists and their families. They sang songs by German and Austrian composers, including Schubert and Schumann.

During the interval, Georg and the others walked to a small room to stretch their legs. They discussed the upcoming plebiscite in the Saar and how important a 'no' vote could be against the regime. Georg felt comfortable with Bruno because he was an anti-fascist like his friends; it was also important that Bruno was not Jewish. Manasse was the most vocal about his hatred of National Socialism while Heinz and the others did not say much, probably because they did not know if Bruno could be trusted. After the concert, Heinz, Herbert and Marianne went out together, while Georg, Harry and Bruno took the U-Bahn home.

A few days later Georg called Harry from a pay telephone; he had lent Harry a book and wanted to get it back. Harry told him later in the conversation: 'You know, Bruno is really good at distributing anti-fascist literature. I gave him 30 of those illegal newspapers and he sold all of them. He called me the other day and asked if I could get him about 50 more copies of them.'

'He said all of that over the telephone?' Georg nervously asked.

Georg cut the conversation short because he had a strong feeling that something was very wrong. At this point in the regime, phones were being tapped and Harry had been in jail. There was a strong possibility that Salinger was being followed. Georg rushed home and destroyed anything in the apartment that smacked of 'subversion'.

His suspicions were confirmed a week later when four Gestapo men came to his apartment. His mother answered the door.

'Is there an 'Erich' Manasse here?' one of them asked.

'No, there is no one by that name here,' his mother replied. 'My son's name is Georg.'

'Yes, that is it, that is him,' he replied.

The men then entered the apartment. They may have confused the name 'Erich' with 'Ariel,' Georg's nickname. The Gestapo men were polite to his relatives as they searched the apartment. They found a gun and were delighted until they discovered that it was a legal starter pistol. They also found a Soviet coin and a book entitled, *The Descent of Judaism*. The men laughed, assuming that it was a Nazi book, when in actuality it was an illegal communist book about the Jewish Autonomous Region of Birobidzhan in the Soviet Union. They did not bother to read any of it.

Georg was taken to a car in front of his apartment building and driven to Gestapo headquarters at the Alexanderplatz. During the ride he told his escorts,

'I would like to know what is going on. I did not do anything illegal. I am not interested in Germany and do not want to change anything here. I am a Zionist and am trying to get out as soon as possible.'[3]

Georg Manasse was taken to an office where a clerk instructed him to sit down. He saw a document lying on a table that read: 'In the issue of high treason against Harry Salinger and his comrades'.

Amongst the names listed was that of 'Erich' Manasse. He now knew where he stood. An extremely polite and smooth Gestapo man entered the office to begin the interrogation. He knew all about the evening of the concert.

'Have you been to the Philharmonic during the past two weeks?'

'Yes.'

'With whom were you there?'

'I was there with Harry Salinger.'

'Yes, we know about Harry. But who were the others?'

'Others? There were so many people there, it was so crowded – I do not know.'

The questioning continued along these lines for a while. The officer then suddenly left the room. Since Manasse would not budge from his professed ignorance, different tactics were employed. Three SS men entered the room carrying revolvers and heavy strips of wood. Georg was beaten and called obscenities by the three men. A fourth man stood quietly in the background.

This man was an acquaintance from Georg's home town in Pomerania. They had known each other for many years and had engaged in street fights – on opposite sides – between Nazis and anti-fascists before 1933. He escorted Georg to the bathroom where they discussed a mutual friend, and he must have had some respect for Georg as he did not denounce him to the interrogator.

The officer returned and was 'shocked' by Georg's split lip and other wounds. 'Oh, Mr Manasse, what happened to you? Oh my God, this must be a mistake!' The interrogator sat down and continued:

'Would you like a cigarette?'

'No, I do not smoke.'

'How about some coffee?'

'No, thank you.'

'Perhaps *now* you can tell me the names of those people with whom you were with – ?'

'I really would like to tell you, Sir, but I do not know any other names. I went with Harry Salinger. He gave me a ticket.'

'Well then, what about 'Bobby'? What about 'Hebbi'?'

Of course, Georg knew 'Bobby' was Heinz and 'Hebbi' was Herbert Baum. He kept repeating the same questions in many different ways. After a while, the beatings would start up again. Georg heard screaming and crying all night, although during the day it was frighteningly silent. Torture and beatings only occurred after sundown. He was kept in solitary confinement in a windowless, insect-infested cell and no doctor cared for his wounds. He was comforted by the fact that he did not implicate his friends. He recalled what anti-fascists often repeated, 'If you give the Gestapo no information they will eventually stop, but give them a little and they will torture you for everything you have got.'[4] After three or four days the beatings ended but he remained incarcerated.

Georg Manasse's mother had hired a Jewish lawyer, a Dr Braun, to handle the upcoming trial. Georg told him everything that happened at the concert, and was told that the charge against him was 'preparation of high treason', which consisted of buying an illegal newspaper from Harry Salinger and sitting in on open trials to study the National Socialist judicial system. This activity was a common anti-fascist practice during the 1930s.

Manasse had never purchased anything from Salinger and decided to see what he could do to have him change his testimony. He made a point of finding the leader of Harry's group and spoke with him privately when the prisoners were taken to the showers. Manasse whispered to him, 'Why did Harry say that I bought an illegal newspaper from him for five pfennig? It is simply not true.' The man assured him that he would speak to Harry about it. It later came out that Salinger told the district attorney that he was tortured and gave false information about Manasse in order to stop the beatings.

Georg was transferred to Alt Moabit prison, where he remained until his trial. His cell mate was a personable Pomeranian Nazi with whom he got along well. When the trial began, it was discovered that Harry Salinger

had been institutionalised when he was younger. Combining this with his saying that he lied about Georg did not make his testimony very credible. Nonetheless Harry was sentenced to five years and later ended up at Dachau concentration camp, where he perished in 1940.

Georg was freed due to lack of evidence, having been imprisoned from 8 March–21 June. Bruno was mentioned during the trial but was not arrested. It can be assumed that he was an agent provocateur for the Gestapo. Upon Manasse's release from Alt Moabit, he had to sign documents stating that he had been treated 'fairly'; if he refused then he would remain incarcerated. Georg had to report to his local police station daily and was placed under a 10.00pm curfew.

Having no desire to remain in Germany, Georg used his Zionist contacts to arrange his emigration to Palestine. He had made a point of not seeing friends because he felt his movements were being watched, but shortly before leaving on *Hachshara* at a kibbutz in Slovakia he saw Heinz Birnbaum at the Liberal Synagogue on Kaiserstrasse. They spoke briefly during the service and Georg told Heinz of his experiences in prison and court. They never saw each other again.[5]

During Georg's ordeal, the strain of working under the threat of arrest took its toll on other group members. On one occasion Rudi Barta took several of his young *Ring* troopers out in the woods for a ramble, and after dark they sat round a campfire to sing. One young man started to play a soft, sweet melody on a harmonica. He then played a song; some people began singing while others listened and held their hands close to the fire. It was an inspirational song about the goodness in people.

One member, Emma Goldemann, responded negatively to the lyrics: 'Who are we kidding? We see cruelty and hate propaganda all around us. The Nazis want to wipe us out. We know about persecution first hand; we know about concentration camps – our future is more than uncertain. Why do we still sing this song?'

Rudi looked around and felt the youngsters' anger and frustration. He asked a few simple questions in order to channel their energy into positive contemplative thought: 'Do we like ourselves? Do we approve of what we do in our lives? Are we doing the best we can?' He had each youngster answer one at a time. After hearing their responses he asked another question: 'How many people have our love, approval and esteem – how many can you think of whom you look up to?' Everyone could name more than four people. Rudi pointed out that even in the dangerous situation they all found themselves in there were people worthy of respect and admiration. He then asked, 'Would more people be good role models for us if circumstances were different?'

The group discussed how environment affects people, and that the solution was not changing people but the situation they were in. It was decided that people are basically good. The youngsters now felt more positive about their own lives despite what was going on around them.[6]

Günther Prager was one of Rudi Barta's young scouts. He was born in 1921 in a small apartment on Mulackstrasse in the poor and crowded Scheunenviertel neighbourhood near the Alexanderplatz in Mitte. His parents and older brother Ernst had emigrated to Berlin from Silesia near East Prussia before he was born. Even though Berlin never had an official Jewish ghetto, this area took on the appearance of one. Many of the *Ostjuden* who came to Germany first settled in the Scheunenviertel. Grosse Hamburger Strasse, Gipsstrasse and Rosenthaler Strasse were some of the many amongst narrow streets lined with tenement buildings full of poor Jewish families.

In fact, Prager had no idea that he was born on the 'Mulackei' until he was a teenager. When walking down the street together with his mother, a prostitute approached to speak with them. She had lived in the same building as the Pragers, and told Günther stories about bouncing him on her knee as a baby. Prager recalls that his mother was very embarrassed about meeting this woman, and they never walked down the 'Mulackei' together again.

When Hitler took power Günther was eleven years old and his brother was fifteen. Günther spent most of his free time playing in the streets of the neighbourhood where they lived. This upset Ernst, who was in the KJVD and was a dedicated communist; he wanted his little brother to be politically active. To this end he arranged for him to join a children's group affiliated with Herbert Baum. Prager read and discussed many books at group meetings led by Rudi Barta, his first troop leader. The major thrust was learning about socialism. He discovered 'how to fight against fascism' and proudly stated that he and the others 'grew up as anti-fascists'. His brother Ernst was also a great influence upon him. He worried about Günther, and wanted him prepared for what the future might bring under Nazism.

Prager was in occasional contact with Herbert Baum, and was in groups led first by Rudi Barta and later Judith Kosminski. Prager recalls that Barta was like a big kid with the other boys. All of the girls were after Rudi, and vied for his attention. Prager looked up to Baum and Barta as role models; they gave him something to hold onto for the future.

Günther's group had contacts with many different youth groups, such as the Marxist-based Zionist *Haschomer Hazair*, with whom they discussed communism and Zionism and whether Jews should remain in Germany or emigrate to Palestine.

According to Günther, 'Baum was very conspiratorial.' He always told the youngsters not to tell people about their talks and the books they read. Baum warned them of what could happen if it became common knowledge. They heeded his word, for the discussions they held could easily have fallen under the Nazi crime of 'high treason'.

Ernst Prager was deeply involved in anti-fascist resistance work, but his brother did not know about it at the time. Ernst worked in a printing shop where he printed illegal flyers and brochures on his own time. Upon occasion, Ernst asked Günther to deliver a large package to Walter Sack. Prager never asked what was in the parcels; he just tied them to his bicycle. One such delivery on 1 May 1935 was a close call. He turned a corner and found himself riding towards hundreds of Nazi storm troopers gearing up for a big rally. Prager nervously peddled through the throngs of SA men – then the package fell off his bike! A storm trooper picked up the package and yelled at Günther for not tying it up properly. He showed Prager how to secure so it would not fall off again and they tied it together. A minute later Prager was off, on his way to Walter Sack.[7]

It was around this time that Rudi Barta came to a very difficult decision. When the Nazis took power, Barta felt very strongly that 'we have to stay in Germany as Jews – fighting against this passing adventure Hitler – but knowing our heritage and continuing it!' To the young people in his group he declared that he now had his doubts about his work and purpose in Germany. He was invited to join the *Blau-Weiss* Zionists and spend a year with them in Czechoslovakia. (Even though *Blau-Weiss* was disbanded in Germany in 1926, it remained intact in Czechoslovakia during the 1930s, see Chapter 2.) Barta had decided to see if Zionism was the answer for him. It was, and a year later he returned to Berlin and became a group leader in *Habonim*, the children's Zionist movement.[8]

Another member of *Habonim* was Siegbert 'Sigi' Rotholz, who had been in the DJJG before 1933, and later switched from Rudi Barta's *Ring* troop to that of Herbert Baum. In 1935 Sigi became friends with a boy named Willy Holzer when they met at Prenzlauer Allee 6, which was commonly called 'PA 6'. Located in the working class Prenzlauer Berg district of Berlin, the street level of the building was the central headquarters and meeting place of *Habonim*. Social democrat and communist youth groups also met and recruited there; 'conversions' were common amongst Jews in the different youth movements. Left-leaning Zionists read and studied Marx and there was much common ground between them and the communists and socialists. Herbert Baum could be found at PA 6 from time to time.

Willy Holzer met the then 15-year-old Sigi Rotholz in the *Bet Chaluz* at PA 6. Sigi was serving an apprenticeship to become a furniture upholsterer at the time. Holzer reports that Sigi was either apolitical or politically cautious; he never took part in the discussions. The two boys were close friends for over a year, but then lost contact with each other in 1936 when Willy left *Bet Chaluz* and Sigi left for a few years on *Hachshara*.[9]

Ellen Compart met Sigi Rotholz at a meeting of the *Ring* in 1935. Ellen also attended meetings in his parents' apartment at Rombergstrasse 11. 'Siegbert never had a comfortable or easy life,' Compart states. 'His parents struggled daily just to survive. Sigi and a large number of relatives all lived together in a dark and gloomy basement apartment on Rombergstrasse. The family was very poor, but it was not their fault. The children were intelligent and studious.'[10]

The military draft was put into effect in Germany on 20 March 1935. Herbert Baum tried to influence as many young men as he could to work against the regime from within the armed services. He used his contacts in German gentile sports clubs to set up meetings where he lectured on anti-fascist ideology in order to help develop anti-fascist cells in the German Army.[11] Baum willingly involved himself in extremely dangerous actions against the state. That was his nature – he could not sit by and watch National Socialism destroy his country. After all, he and all of his friends were Germans. It was the Nazis who branded German Jews the enemy of the fatherland. This was further brought home to him when he was thrown out of the night classes he was taking to become an electrical engineer at the Beuth-Schule. The Jewish quotas had been exceeded.[12]

One night Ari Steinbach opened up a *Ring* meeting as follows:

How does one establish the right of a Jew to be? – a fact that the Nazis would like to deny. Being born. We have no say in the matter – no chance to say, 'Thanks, but no thanks.' The only choice we have is to look at it as a curse – or a blessing. Being here is a reality, which in itself gives one the right to be – and do not forget that. Now where do we go from here – and how?

The group agreed that being a Jew in Hitler's Germany greatly accelerated the growing up process, but aside from that they were not unique. The soul searching questions they had were the same as any group of youngsters their age. They discussed teenage suicide and parents who did not know any other way to punish except with violence. One youngster suggested that group members tell their parents how they felt about physical punishment while stressing their love. One young man tried this and reported he got my face slapped for the attempt. 'My father said, 'You ought to love me without a "but!"'

The importance of having dreams and ideals without forgetting the reality of Nazi Germany was discussed, as was the developing and preserving one's self-respect and building trust by accepting people as they were. It was asked if knowledge about the outside world was of value. 'Yes,' one person said. 'It gives us our place in the whole enchanted loom, and having goals for ourselves and the world gives us a connection.' They talked of global and cosmic cohesion, and one youngster said, 'Global I can reach, but cosmic is too far out!'[13]

On evening in October, Herbert Ansbach rode his bicycle from his apartment in Kreuzberg to a flat at Alte Jakobstrasse 6 in Mitte for a KJVD meeting. The apartment was sparsely furnished. Ansbach arrived and sat on a wooden chair next to Marianne Cohn, Martin Kochmann and Sala Rosenbaum. They faced Herbert Baum. Ansbach reports:

'Erich' (as we called the 23-year-old Herbert Baum) is sitting on a folding bed. We others are sitting on wooden chairs in a circle. He speaks in a low voice. The latest flyer action was a success. All around Alexanderplatz we pasted up our flyers for the anniversary of the October Revolution. Even police headquarters managed to get one. Very risky, but very effective. Some flyers were posted on the S-Bahn – 'Erich' gives me a slightly reproachful look. 'That is too risky,' he says. 'It endangers us as well as our cause. We cannot afford that.'

The group of five also discussed the KJVD publication *Junge Garde Süd-Ost*. Herbert had arranged a hiding place for the new mimeograph machine. The last one had been confiscated by the Gestapo when a comrade in Pankow was arrested.[14]

Also active in the anti-fascist scene at this time was Alfred Eisenstädter, who had moved to Berlin from Nuremberg in 1930 when he was fourteen years old. Up until the time Hitler took power, Alfred was active in social democratic youth groups, including the *Rote Falken* and the *Sozialistische Schule Gemeinschaft*. The Eisenstädter family lived in a new apartment building in Neukölln until Alfred's father's salary was cut in 1933; they then moved to the more affordable Hansa Viertel part of town.

The only youth groups that Alfred could belong to were the legal Jewish organisations under the umbrella of the Jewish community of Berlin. In 1934 Eisenstädter joined the *Ring*, which he considered a very loose organisation. This was due to the fact that his group leader was *not* Jewish; he was given his group because his Jewish girlfriend led one of the other troops. His *Ring* troop was not at all active like Ellen Compart's, and Alfred saw his time there as mere socialising.

This was not how Alfred Eisenstädter wanted to spend his time. He had utter contempt for the National Socialist regime and wanted to do what he could to help bring about its dissolution. Alfred asked around and heard about a group of Jews who were involved in resistance work. He decided that he would make contact with the group and join them.

Alfred met 'Kurt Schiller,' the leader of this group; in actuality 'Schiller' was Herbert Baum, but it was a while before Eisenstädter learned his true name. He was taken into the confidence of Herbert, Marianne, Sala and Martin. Alfred left the *Ring* because he wanted to stop socialising and put all of his effort into anti-fascist work.

He greatly respected Herbert Baum: 'He had an absolute conviction – he was not a complicated man, he was a straightforward, honest, and convinced man ... he was totally committed to the communist party and was the one with connections to it.' Even though Alfred was a socialist, he had no problem with Herbert's communism. Young anti-fascists saw the overthrow of the regime as their common goal and did not let their differing affiliations to communism, social democracy or Zionism get in their way.

Shortly after joining with Baum, Alfred met Walter Sack and his friend (Baum's cousin) Ismar Zöllner, who both worked for Walter's father as apprentice blacksmiths. Walter led meetings in his parents' apartment, which was attached to the shop on Skallitzer Strasse in Kreuzberg. Alfred became good friends with Ismar, but had only limited contact with Walter, whom Alfred considered as important to the movement as Baum himself. Eisenstädter reports that when he first joined the resistance the Baum circle was a two-tier organisation. Baum, Sack and the other older people formed a makeshift 'politburo' and the young *Ring* members were the 'masses'. Most of the youngsters knew nothing about any connections to the KJVD or other communists.[15]

The KJVD leadership in Berlin put together a report on Herbert Baum's KJVD sub-district southeast. It detailed the inroads the group were beginning to make. Dated November 1935, the document reads, in part:

> Sub-district southeast has about 30 members. Its leadership is three-man strong. The main work of this sub district lies in the sports clubs. Fourteen comrades are in total in seven sports clubs and there have red sport groups clustered around them. In collaboration with them the comrades are performing anti-fascist work. Our comrades in many different kinds of sports clubs occupy functions such as a demonstrator, team leader, etc. The sub-district has nabbed four men active in sports, and a larger number of red women athletes, in the interests of influencing the work in the fascist sports organisations.
>
> There is a cell of twelve Jewish comrades that has gathered together a circle of about 30 youths that they are influencing. In the firm Butzke are four comrades, who regularly sell 30 newspapers. In the steelworks (airplane assembly) where 600 men are employed are five comrades. A contact to the constabulary is being made, through sports to the Marines and Infantry.... The position of the SAJ was very strong in the time of legality in the sports club; that is well known. The same is true of the sports clubs now. The sub-district is very active, regularly distributes a newspaper and pamphlet. We know about arrests of about eight comrades in this sub-district in August 1934.[16]

Alfred Eisenstädter became an apprentice in a Jewish-owned machine shop called Steinrück. It was there that he met Felix Heymann, who lived in an apartment in the front of the shop building. They became close in a short time and considered themselves best friends. Alfred later recruited Felix into the resistance.

A small group met regularly to read and discuss illegal literature. Eisenstädter states that the main job of the group at that time was the indoctrination and recruitment of new members. Each person brought in one person, and it was an ongoing process. The young people went on weekend trips to a farm in Storkow, 30km east of Berlin. They gave the farmer some money and he let them sleep in a barn or in the hay loft. Other times they camped out in the woods with their sleeping bags and bicycles. They enjoyed these rambles, sitting around a campfire cooking meals, and singing working class songs. Alfred had a 9mm handgun that had been given him by an anti-fascist who left Berlin. He kept it hidden in the basement of his apartment building and carried it occasionally. Felix tried to convince him that they should go into the woods and try it out but they never did.[17]

9

THE BRUSSELS CONFERENCE AND THE 'TROJAN HORSE' POLICY (1935–1936)

The Seventh World Congress of the Communist Internationale (Comintern) took place in Moscow from 25 July–20 August 1935. The major theme was the need to fight fascism and the dangers of a possible world war. The Congress called for cooperation and a coalition of all anti-fascist forces in the struggle against National Socialism. It was at this Congress that delegates called for the building of a new relationship between communists and social democrats. This 'popular front' would help defend the rights and liberties of all, and help destroy fascism wherever it reared its head. Of course, this campaign was to be guided by the Soviet Union through the Comintern.[1] Weitz writes, 'With great fanfare the popular front became the official strategy of international communism, enabling most European communist parties to ride a wave of popular anti-fascist sentiment.'[2]

Arthur Koestler, a KPD member and journalist at the time, vividly recalls the introduction of the popular front:

All revolutionary slogans, references to the class struggle and to the Dictatorship of the Proletariat were in one sweep relegated to the lumber room. They were replaced by a brand new façade, with geranium boxes in the windows, called 'Popular Front for Peace and against Fascism'. Its doors were wide open to all men of good will – Socialists, Catholics, Conservatives, Nationalists. The notion that we ever advocated revolution and violence was to be ridiculed as a bogey refuted as slander spread by reactionary war-mongers. We no longer referred to ourselves as …

communists…we were just simple, honest, peace-loving anti-fascists and defenders of democracy.[3]

Anton Ackermann, the KPD leader of Berlin, went to Moscow as a delegate – along with four other Berlin communists – where he spoke about the underground communist resistance in his city. Ackermann called attention to the fact that the Berliners were working with their hands tied: they had no direction from Moscow or even Prague, where the KJVD had fled in 1933. They felt incapable of working without political guidance.

Shortly after the Seventh Internationale, a KPD-in-exile sponsored conference was held outside Moscow. Called the Brussels Conference in order to hide the whereabouts of KPD officials, it focused on the strategy and tactics discussed at the Seventh Internationale. The goal of the conference was to apply Leninist theories to create a socialist 'democracy' in Germany. It was decided that KPD and KJVD instructors would be sent to Berlin and throughout Germany in order to inform underground communists about the 'popular front' policy and the Brussels Conference, as well as to provide help in developing anti-fascist cells in industry.[4] The Brussels Conference also affirmed the popular front policy, as well as the leadership of the KPD-in-exile, Wilhelm Pieck and Walter Ulbricht.

The conference demonstrated the need for dramatic structural change within the Communist Party of Germany. KPD functionaries active in the underground made it very clear to the delegates that keeping the party centralised had enabled the Gestapo to penetrate it. In response to these complaints, the KPD restructured itself through decentralisation. Border secretaries in Prague, Brussels, Amsterdam, Zurich and Forbach (the Saar) would now be responsible for maintaining contact with small groups of active anti-fascists throughout Germany.

The KPD approached the 'popular front' policy negatively and at times worked actively to undermine it. Therefore the German communists were the only party in Europe who did not create a popular front. When considering the possibility of a united KPD-SPD anti-fascist party, the KPD included conditions that read like those of the Weimar Republic. A united labour party could only be formed, according to the KPD, if its adherents agreed to the 'necessity of the overthrow of the bourgeoisie and the creation of a dictatorship of the proletariat in the form of soviets'.

Nonetheless the final resolution of the Brussels Conference called for a struggle for 'all democratic rights and freedoms' and peace. Weitz writes that the pamphlets 'distributed within Germany no longer expressed the exclusive language of class, but called for anti-fascist unity, freedom of conscience, and a democratic Germany.' The SPD, however, was yet again blamed for events in Germany by the communists. Wilhelm Florin, a Politiburo member of the KPD, declared that the SPD 'bore the historic guilt for the victory of fascism'.[5]

It was also at the Brussels Conference that the 'Trojan Horse' tactic was officially adopted by the KPD; this was a position raised at the Comintern's Congress earlier in the summer. The 'Trojan Horse' was a policy whereby communists would join Nazi organisations to enlist support and weaken the regime from within. The major target of the 'Trojan Horse' was the *Deutsche Arbeiter Front* (DAF), but overly optimistic party leaders also foresaw underground communists ferreting themselves successfully into the SA and SS.

It was around the time of the conference that Alfred Eisenstatdter was planning to take his summer vacation in Prague. Herbert Baum had not received any party directives for a while and felt at a loss. Of course, he had no idea of the resolutions made at the Seventh Internationale or the Brussels Conference – or even that the conferences had taken place. Upon hearing about Alfred's plans, Baum said, 'Look, I'd like you to get in touch with someone in Prague; I need to know what direction to take.' Alfred met Baum's contact man – a member of the Centre of the KJVD – in an open area of Prague and had a discussion with him about the situation in Germany. The man then told Eisenstädter:

> Baum must not do anything that will cause tension with the Gestapo. Too many losses have been suffered. Many anti-fascists have been killed or put in concentration camps during the last three years. It has been decided that communists will work through legal German organisations. All the Jews in Baum's circle must get into legitimate Jewish groups. There are to be no overt acts of resistance and absolutely nothing should be published.

Eisenstädter asked why there was a policy change concerning overt resistance. The KJVD contact told him that it was due to events during the plebiscite in the Saar,

> Members of the Communist Youth League – in old fashioned style – went around and painted slogans on chimneys and houses. The Nazis had expected that and went around from place to place and arrested them all.

Alfred did not like the man and was not shy about voicing his objections to this KJVD directive. He had joined forces with Herbert Baum so he could fight German fascism, but now he was being told to sit on his hands until further notice.

Whilst in Prague, Alfred stayed in a youth hostel and spent his vacation with Czech *Blau-Weiss* Zionists. Upon his return to Berlin, Eisenstädter gave Baum a detailed report of what he had been told. Herbert listened carefully and followed every point of the communist directive. Thereafter the 'Trojan Horse' tactic became the new policy of non-Jews in the Baum group.[6] Those unaffiliated Jews joined the non-Zionist *Ring* or the Zionist *Habonim* or *Haschomer Hazair*. Most Jews, however, including Baum, had been members of these legal Jewish youth movements for years.

In 1935, the Gestapo estimated that there were 5000 communists active in the resistance in Berlin alone and concluded that most of them belonged to one of two segments of the population: skilled members of the working class operating in factories, and unemployed workers living in the inner city. The main pursuit of the communist resistance was distributing flyers; much of this literature discussed the brutality of the Nazis against the working class. Throughout Germany, the Gestapo seized 1.2 million flyers in 1934 and 1.67 million in 1935.

Key posts in the German communist resistance were filled by paid KPD activists, who were supported by illegal subscriptions collected in factories and working-class neighbourhoods. They used false names and forged identification papers, but most were arrested by the Gestapo within six months. In January 1933, there were 422 salaried KPD officials. By 1935, 219 had been arrested, 125 were in exile, 24 had been killed by the Nazis and 54 of them had left the party. The year 1935 saw 14,000 communists arrested for resistance actions.[7]

In February 1936, an intensive two-day meeting took place. The underground KJVD were given the speeches and manifestos of the Brussels Conference to read and discuss. The young people were told to listen to illegal radio broadcasts from Moscow in order to get news about Germany and the world. The topic of how to infiltrate Nazi organisations in order to perform subversive work was dealt with in great detail; of course, anyone officially decreed a Jew or *Mischlinge* (part-Jew) could not engage in this assignment. Since it was very difficult for the young communists to contemplate being considered a Nazi 'comrade', their confidence had to be bolstered.

Wilhelm Bamberger, the Instructor of the Central Committee of the KJVD, had been attending the Lenin School in Moscow when he was sent to Prague in November 1935. In January he met with Herbert Ansbach, who briefed Bamberger on the situation of the KJVD in Berlin. In February he was in Berlin.

> My task was to help with organisation and tactics and with information about the Brussels Conference … I was aware of the rather small number of existing KJVD groups … Through him [Ansbach] I made contact with several youth groups in Berlin, amongst them Herbert Baum's in Neukölln southeast. His group was the largest that I encountered.

Bamberger met with Herbert Baum, Marianne Cohn, Martin Kochmann, Sala Rosenbaum, Heinz Birnbaum, Werner Steinbrink and Herbert Ansbach, all of whom were in Baum's KJVD cell. The discussions focused upon the following questions: 'What is the goal when the Hitler dictatorship fails?' 'What is the worldwide applicable validity of the Soviet experience in the construction of a socialist state in Germany?' And 'How can the KJVD group reach a larger circle of young people, mainly young workers?' Bamberger writes,

> …we decided to make use of the 1936 Olympics and infiltrate sports organisations. We also discussed how to counteract and overcome still existing tendencies to cling to religious and ideological divisions within groups or between individuals. We all agreed on a strong, sustained contact and interaction with the organisation [KJVD] in Prague.[8]

To that end, Baum group members visited Prague in order to develop political contacts and gather information for those who remained in Germany. Eric Weitz writes that:

> … the tactic of the 'Trojan Horse' inspired only confusion and dismay, and absolute hatred from social democrats. For many communists in Germany, contact with comrades, even in the small circles to which they had been reduced, was vital for their moral and material survival. Identification as a National Socialist was anathema, a violation of everything for which they had suffered so severely. In any case, many argued that no one would believe them if they joined Nazi organisations because their communist pasts were well known.[9]

Otto Wendt was one of the gentiles in Baum's KJVD sub-district southeast. Non-Jews were ordered by the KPD Brussels Conference to join Nazi sport and youth groups, which proved to be quite a dilemma for Otto, as well as the other non-Jews. However, Herbert Baum personally asked Wendt to join a Nazi group. Baum did not question KPD directives; he took them as direct orders and obeyed them to the letter. Otto and Herbert had a lengthy discussion on the subject, and Otto convinced him that he would lose all of his important contacts throughout Berlin if it was discovered that he had joined a Nazi youth organisation. It was easy for Moscow or the KPD-in-exile in Paris to order German communists to infiltrate Nazi organisations, but the reality of it was another matter altogether.[10]

The desperate 'Trojan Horse' tactic was promoted because it was so dangerous for communists to work in the resistance. The mass arrests of communists had brought about disillusionment in both the rank and file and the governing bodies of Berlin's communists. This widespread discouragement was due to the dismantling of the KPD's operational structure and policies and the departure of so many comrades from the anti-fascist struggle. The result was a climate of general suspicion. Who could one trust? Was the man sitting next to you at a cell meeting a Gestapo agent provocateur or a true comrade? How could one be really sure?[11]

10

POLITICAL AND INTELLECTUAL RESISTANCE (1936)

Lisa Attenberger was a non-Jewish communist in Neukölln. A native of the northern German city of Kiel, she moved to Berlin in 1933. Bit by bit, she built up a small resistance group/schooling circle which numbered no more than a dozen members, mostly via personal contacts through her sales clerk job at Woolworth's, striking up friendships with customers. It was in this manner that she met Herbert Ansbach, a comrade of Herbert Baum. Other comrades of Baum – Werner Steinbrink and Hildegard Jadamowitz – were also in Attenberger's small group. Werner and Lisa were romantically involved at the time.

Both Jews and non-Jews were to be found in Attenberger's circle. They rented a flat in Neukölln that was used only for their illegal meetings; nobody lived in the flat. Lisa's group was a heterogeneous mix; in addition to KPD loyalists, there were those who did not trust the party. Nonetheless the small group received guidance from the KPD and participated in communist-directed actions together. Attenberger collaborated with Herbert Baum on one KPD-directed assignment, picking up leaflets from his apartment to distribute in U-Bahn stations, cinemas after the lights had been dimmed, and other poorly-lit locations.[1]

As part of his activities with Lisa's group, Herbert Ansbach formed a rental car company as a cover for a courier system to distribute communist and anti-fascist propaganda throughout Germany. During the very first action, however, Lisa – who was transporting literature in one of the cars – was caught and arrested in her native city of Kiel. Tortured by the Gestapo, she revealed the address of the Berlin apartment in Neukölln and the names and addresses of eight members of her group. Nine people, including Ansbach, were arrested on 26 February 1936. All of them were brutally beaten and tortured. One person admitted knowledge of one 'illegal' newspaper that was found in the oven of the Berlin apartment. Six people were released, but Ansbach and two others remained in custody. Ansbach made what he felt was a convincing plea of innocence and his attorney tried to get him freed, but it was to no avail.

Sala Rosenbaum asked Alfred Eisenstädter to sit in on Anbach's trial and report on it to Herbert Baum. He was asked to attend because he was working night shifts and was available during the day. Alfred said, 'I guess she didn't trust me and also sent her mother ...' Eisenstädter remembers attending the same high school as Ansbach, the Karl Marx Schule in Neukölln. The trial lasted two days, 23 and 24 October, and he recalls feeling very bad for Ansbach and his comrades. Because one illegal newspaper was found in an oven in an apartment that did not even belong to him, Ansbach was sentenced to two-and-a-half years in prison.[2]

It was in 1936 that the Nazi Party forced the *Ring, Bund Deutsch-jüdischer Jugend* to change its name. It then became known as the *Ring, Bund jüdischer-Jugend* (Ring, Bund of Jewish Youth). The Nazis objected to 'Deutsch-jüdischer' (German-Jewish) being in the organisation's name.[3] Marianne Prager was one of many young anti-fascists in the *Ring*. The Prager family lived on the third floor of a tenement building at Belforter Strasse 12 in Prenzlauer Berg. Marianne's sister, Ilse, was four years younger than her. Their father, Georg, was a distributor who sold linen and other fabrics to wholesalers and retailers, while their mother, Jenny, was a housewife.

The Pragers were reformed Jews who attended the Rykestrasse synagogue around the corner from their house, which was also where the girls attended Hebrew school. Georg Prager was very traditional in his approach to Judaism and often told the story of the first Passover when he was not able to have matzo while he was recovering from injuries suffered while serving as a front-line soldier during the First World War. He was very proud of being Jewish, but was prouder of being a German who had faithfully served the fatherland. This became a sore subject for both Marianne and Ilse after the rise of Hitler. Ilse remembers the worried look on her parents' faces the day he took power. 'It will be bad for us,' they told the girls.

'[Marianne] always had to prove that she was never afraid,' recalls her sister. Her bravery may have been a result of an early battle with diphtheria. She was never short of friends, her closest being a schoolmate, Inge Gerson, who, together with Marianne, joined the *Ring* in 1936. They were in the *Dritte Zug*, which was led by Walter Sack, with whom they read and analysed Marxist-Leninist texts. Marianne wanted to know as much as possible about the political systems of other nations. She admired communism and was interested in Zionism, while Ilse preferred Zionism because of the ethnic music and gymnastic activities. Marianne had friends in Zionist circles, but never joined the movement. She never discussed what took place at her *Ring* meetings, but did talk about the plays and concerts that the group attended. One evening Marianne excitedly came home and acted out almost an entire Ibsen play for her sister. The *Ring* gave her an outlet that she sorely needed; Marianne was an exceptionally bright girl, the walls of her bedroom were covered with 'illegal' books that she read voraciously.[4]

In was during 1936 that Heinz Birnbaum became romantically involved with a gentile woman, Irene Walther, who worked as a secretary at Butzke and Company, where he was serving his apprenticeship as a tool and die maker. Not only did he convince her to leave the *Bund Deutscher Mädel* (BDM, the girls' division of the *Hitler Jugend*) and move out of her parents' home, but she also agreed to work with Heinz in the anti-fascist resistance, joining him as a member of an illegal KJVD cell at Butzke. Birnbaum must have been mature beyond his sixteen years to take the 20-year-old Irene as his lover and fiancée. 'I made her do all this,' he often said, 'I have a commitment to this woman.'[5]

Walter Sack, Ari Steinbach, Thomas Landau, Ellen Compart and a few others had gathered in Sack's father's shop one night in order to print anti-fascist flyers to distribute. Some flyers read: 'Read and pass on: Say no every which way you can. Say no to the ruin of Germany!' 'Read and pass on: Be a good citizen – think for yourself.' 'Read and pass on: Hitler, Germany's gravedigger.' 'Read and pass on: Love your country and think for yourself. A good German is not afraid to say no!' Sack and Steinbach assigned each member an area where they would distribute the flyers. They were placed under car windscreen wipers, under church doors, on park benches and in train stations.[6]

Walter and Ari led a *Ring* meeting on how to convince, relate to, influence and prepare younger members for the years ahead. The initial topic touched upon was education, more specifically the authoritative system that prevailed at the time. Steinbach told the group about an English boarding school where there were no grades and students developed their own learning programmes. Thea Lindemann proposed: 'It is important to teach about life and society, the social contract that we all have with one another.' Harry Oschinski, a young man with a desire to study medicine, spoke next: 'We all have ingested a lot of garbage and have to un-learn it – we must be de-schooled.'

'Give me specifics,' demanded Walter Sack: 'What do we have to free ourselves from? If I put this waste basket in the centre here, what "garbage" would you want to throw in?' The room exploded with 'garbage' to be tossed: 'Competition!' 'Tradition!' 'Convention!' 'Nationalism!' 'Patriotism!' 'Hypocrisy!' 'They are all holding us back!' declared Harry.

'Very good,' said Ari, 'but do we have new values to replace them with so the web will hold together? Do we have a premise to build upon – is the foundation firm in our minds?' Walter chimed in, 'We should empty the basket and see what we would throw in for a new way of looking at things.'

Oschinski was the first to respond: 'Enough birth control for everyone who wants and needs it.' Ismar Zöllner said, 'Equality regardless of achievement. Equal opportunity will raise the quality of life for everyone, which will even out the differences in the contributions one is able to make.' Eva Rumjanek, a young singer-guitarist, said, 'For happiness and fulfilment, stress the development of creativity in everyone.' Thomas Landau, an artist, added, 'Teach classes from Kindergarten on up in creativity so students can improvise and solve problems on their own. They must not be afraid of the unknown and must strive to make great strides instead of moving one little step at a time.' Ismar responded, 'Yes, we have to take risks in our thinking and in relationships with other people, and also learn to trust and be trustworthy.'

Etta, who worked with children, volunteered: 'From early on teach responsibility for actions and behaviour, and accept and deal with any consequences. Do not punish, but give incentives for doing what is good for everyone. Reinforce this and no punishment will be necessary. In time, we may no longer need prisons. Cooperation over competition, a win-win situation instead of winner over loser. We could be free and soar together, grow together.'

Walter stopped everything right then and there. 'Ah! Utopian fantasy, the opium of the oppressed! We must learn and teach defiance. In spirit. In thought. In action. Today – not tomorrow. The time is now. If you have ideas for the future, implement them now wherever you can.'

Ari had waited until this moment to make his point: 'But what about the other opium? The "opiate of the masses" as Karl Marx had called it. We forget about religion, but who amongst us can stand up and without looking over their shoulder proclaim, "I have no religion. I am a complete atheist. God has no meaning for me?" The room remained silent as Ari Steinbach the philosopher sat at the piano and began to play.[7]

11

COMMUNISM AS A CURE FOR NAZISM (1937)

'In 1937 I was a member of Ismar Zöllner's group of unaffiliated communists,' states Paul Friedlander. By that time, Zöllner had left Walter Sack's *Ring* troop and formed his own. Friedlander was promoted to lead a group of 10–15 Jewish boys and girls aged 12–14.

> They were taught to be politically aware and learn about Marxism-Leninism. We went on rambles and trips to nearby places. The older ones read social fiction and classic political and sociological works. This enabled us to familiar the youngsters with the aims of the KPD, and enlighten them about fascism.[1]

'The more the fascist regime excluded us as Jews from any cultural life, the more we turned to each other for sustenance,' writes Rita Resnik. 'The need and intent for resistance became intensified and very clearly necessary. As communists and Jews our position and existence was very precarious.' The lives of Resnik and the others became difficult in many ways. She was unable to secure training or an apprenticeship leading to a career, as 'Aryan' businesses could not employ Jews, and many Jewish concerns did not know how much longer they would be in business and so were reluctant to invest in new staff. Resnik usually worked temporary jobs, and received unemployment insurance benefits (3.90 Reichmarks per week) for a short time and she was able to make some money by reconditioning hats and clothing. It was in 1937 that Resnik married Herbert Meyer, a close comrade of Herbert Baum.[2]

On 15 January 1937 the *Ring, Bund jüdischer-Jugend* was banned; Schatzker cites a Gestapo report from Munich dissolving the organisation based upon the discovery that members wore uniforms and participated in military drill exercises, which was illegal for Jewish youth.[3] Ilse Held remembers that, as a member of the *Ring*, she always wore a uniform for large group rambles or formal occasions. She did not, however, partake in any military drills, nor did anyone else whom she knew in the *Ring*.[4]

Nonetheless, the non-militaristic Baum group was a small minority within the *Ring*. Henry J. Kellerman, its former national leader, writes, 'In 1934 I was elected head of the organisation which by then had 9000 members, a figure which later rose to 15,000 ...'[5] The Baum group did not participate in military activities and Kellerman and Baum were politically light years apart; however, they did share a similar cultural outlook. Kellerman writes:

> We never for a second accepted the Nazi verdict that expunged our German identity. We continued to consider ourselves as Germans ... we loved the country, the glorious landscape with its majestic mountains and forests, its idyllic lakes, romantic rivers, and picturesque towns ... This was our Germany, 'the other Germany,' where we could still read with impunity the plays by Goethe, Schiller, and Lessing ...[6]

'We were told that from now on we would meet in small groups at Herbert Baum's flat,' said Ilse Held. Her *Ring* group was led by Judith Kosminski, and included Inge Gongula, Hella and Alice Hirsch, Georg Varsanyi, Günther Prager and Gerd Laske. Judith's group often attended meetings with Walter Sack's troop of older children. Inge Gongula reports that, 'Walter told Judith what to do.' Both troops had names: Judith's was 'Steinadler' (Golden Eagle) and Walter's was 'Sioux'. Sometimes Felix Heymann would attend the combined meetings. Later on, Herbert and Marianne Baum also came along; the Baums had married the year before. During weekends or school holidays, the young people went on trips. Ernst Prager, Günther's older brother, would play the balalaika while the youngsters sang.

Herbert spoke to them as young adults, not children, and they discussed what they could do against the Nazis. Inge said, 'The idea was ... that we are Jews and they'll kill us anyway, so do something against them before we get killed ... He [Baum] was a communist, I knew that and I agreed with it.' She considered him very humane in his approach and never doctrinaire. Ilse

German-Jewish Anti-fascist resistance leader Herbert Baum c.1935. (Walter Sack)

Herbert and Marianne Baum (née Cohn) in the 1930s. (H. Christianson and H. Heymann-Wilsker)

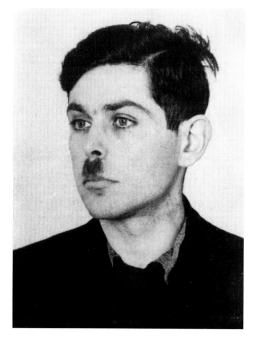

A photograph of Martin Kochmann, taken while in Gestapo custody, c.1942–43. (Margot Pikarski)

Sala Kochmann (née Rosenbaum), the de facto second-in-command of the Baum group. (W. Sack)

Herbert Baum (hanging on front right with canteen) and his DJJG troop c.1930–31. Walter Fuchs is hanging on the far left and Herbert Budzislawski is in the rear centre. (Rudi Barta)

Heinz Birnbaum (lying on the ground) and Herbert Baum during a ramble, c.1934–35. (Alfred Eisenstädter)

Georg Manasse – who met Herbert Baum and Heinz Birnbaum in 1933 – with his mother. He went to prison and suffered at the hands of the Gestapo, but did not betray Baum or Birnbaum. (George Manasse)

Rita Resnik – friend of Rudi Barta and Herbert Baum – photographed in the late 1920s or early 1930s. (Rudi Barta)

Herbert Ansbach, comrade of Baum in the KJVD who attended the same high school in Berlin as Alfred Eisenstädter. (V. Ansbach)

Werner Steinbrinck, friend and anti-fascist comrade of Baum in the underground KJVD (1933–36) and until the 'Soviet Paradise' action in 1942. (Margot Pikarski)

Hilde Jadamowitz, Werner Steinbrinck's half-Jewish fiancée and anti-fascist comrade. (Margot Pikarski)

Alfred Eisenstädter's passport photograph from the 1930s. (A. Eisenstädter)

Felix Heymann while in Gestopo custody c.1942–43. He attempted suicide shortly after his arrest. (G. Prager)

Felix Heymann working at the firm Steinrück in 1936, where he met Alfred Eisenstädter. (H. Christianson und H. Heymann-Wilsker)

Youngsters in the *Ring* during a ramble. Troop leader Judith Kosminski is second from right. (G. Prager/W. Sack)

A *Ring* outing; Gerhard Meyer is in the centre playing the guitar. (G. Prager/W. Sack)

Hella Hirsch, Ellen Compart's close friend and later wife of Felix Heymann. Ellen witnessed her arrest at Aceta-Werke. (A. Eisenstädter)

Alice Hirsch, sister of Hella. Sent to prison after the 'Soviet Paradise' action, she perished in Auschwitz. (Margot Pikarski)

Left to right: Martin Kochmann, Sala Kochmann and Amand Vasseur, 1939. (Alfred Eisenstädter)

Suzanne Wesse, the French-Catholic relative of Felix Heymann by marriage. (K. Sprittulla)

Ilse Held's U-Bahn pass. (Ilse Heller)

Edith Fraenkel, who met Herbert Baum at Elmo-Werke in 1939.

Edith Fraenkel, Harry Cühn and their son Uri in the winter of 1941. Uri died in hospital before he was a year old. (H. Cühn)

Rita (née Resnik) and Herbert Meyer c.1941. (Margot Pikarski)

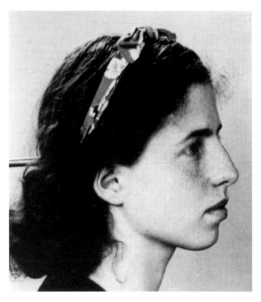

Hildegarde Loewy in 1941/42. (R. Biswas)

Heinz Joachim, who married Marianne Prager in 1941. (Manfred Joachim)

Ring member Marianne Prager. (Margot Pikarski)

Georg, Ilse, Jenny and Marianne Prager, c.1936.
(Ilse Kessler)

Joachim Franke, the controversial comrade of
Herbert Baum. (O. Barutzki)

Charlotte Paech in the 1930s. (E. Kürer)

Richard Holzer in 1945 after returning to
Berlin from Hungary. (B. Heimlich)

Hanni Lindenberger, c.1939–1940. (Manfred Lindenberger)

Gerd Meyer, who married Hanni Lindenberger in 1941. (Margot Pikarski)

Lothar Salinger, anti-fascist friend of Heinz Joachim, while in Gestapo custody c.1942. (Margot Pikarski)

Left to right: Ilse Prager, a friend, and Marianne Prager. (Ilse Kessler)

Postcards sold as souvenirs at the 'Soviet Paradise' exhibition in Berlin in 1942.

Poster advertising the 'Soviet Paradise' exhibition.

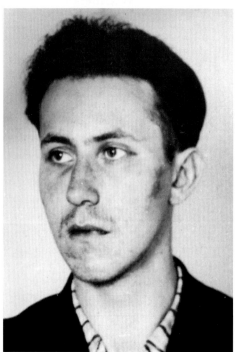

Heinz Birnbaum in Gestapo custody after the 'Soviet Paradise' action c.1942. (Margot Pikarski)

Siegbert Rotholz in Gestapo custody c.1942. (Margot Pikarski)

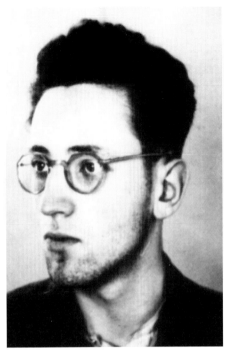

Heinz Rothholz in Gestapo custody, c.1942. (Margot Pikarski)

Hans Mannaberg, a member of the Franke-Steinbrinck group, who took part in the 'Soviet Paradise' attack. (Margot Pikarski)

Werner Schaumann, who tried to sever ties to Joachim Franke. He was executed on 11 May 1943. (Margot Pikarski)

Karl Kunger, who was executed for his anti-fascist activities on 18 June 1943. (Margot Pikarski)

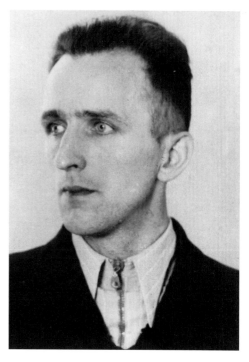

George Vötter, who was arrested along with his wife on 11 May 1942. He was executed on 18 June 1943. (Margot Pikarski)

Artur Illgen, who took part in a slogan painting campaign in January 1942. He was betrayed by Franke and executed on 18 June 1943. (Margot Pikarski)

Marianne Prager with forced labourers at Rathenow. She is in the middle row, right, wearing a white outfit. (Ilse Kessler)

Held has similar recollections of Baum, 'I knew that he was communist ... we were told that our whole group was ... communist led ... they wanted to train us as communists.' Since they had read the *Communist Manifesto* and parts of *Capital* with Judith Kosminski, the concepts were not new to the Steinadler group members. Just knowing that the Soviet Union existed was a morale boost.

'Baum gave us confidence and self-assurance,' said Inge Gongula. She remembers Herbert as 'a friend, a comrade ... He was very friendly and related to everyone personally.' Herbert became a much needed father figure for many of the youngsters. He taught the philosophy of communism, giving reading assignments which they would discuss. Ilse Held said, 'He drew us out. He made us all feel important ... He didn't let us fall asleep in class.' There were also social evenings; Ilse remembers hearing songs from the Spanish Civil War and Brecht and Weill's *Threepenny Opera*. Inge recalls hearing classical music and discussing it with Herbert.

Even though they were always aware of being Jews in Nazi Germany, they were all assimilated non-observant communists. Ilse said, 'Nobody seemed particularly Jewish to me.' The youngsters were told by Baum to attend Zionist meetings of *Habonim* and *Haschomer Hazair*, which were still legal at the time. These get-togethers, however, did not work out very well. According to Held, 'They wanted to convince us and we wanted to convince them.'[7]

Beginning in 1937, a small group that Ellen Compart belonged to spent much time grappling with the writings of Lenin and Trotsky, especially Trotsky's 1937 book, *The Revolution Betrayed: What is the Soviet Union and Where is it Going?* They considered both revolutionaries' theories as a shield to protect them from Hitler's Reich, analysing ideas, ideologies, theories, philosophies and systems. They knew that change was essential, and they had faith that a humane socialist system would replace the destructive National Socialist model. Compart writes, 'Under the existing situation one had to support the Soviet Union to combat Nazism and eventually liberate Jews and all other persecuted minorities.'[8] Rita Meyer writes, 'We grew up to look at the Soviet Union with respect and sympathy ... This position, this outlook, was strengthened by fascist terror and warmongering.'[9]

Most of the Baum group members had felt solidarity with the Soviet Union while part of the various youth movements they had belonged to during the Weimar Republic and early Nazi years. This strong loyalty was stressed by Baum and others in the DJJG, and continued after its dissolution in the *Ring*. It was certainly a major focus of those in the KJVD, both when it was still legal and during its underground phase. Many young people came to the conclusion that communism was the answer even before Hitler came to power. Others were convinced by the Soviet model after seeing what the Nazis were capable of. Fascism was seen as the arch rival of communism, a system that – in concept at least – treated people equally and did not engage in terrorising Jews or other minorities. The Nazis were creating a proletariat class of young Jews who had no hope of an education, a career or a future under Hitler. The writings of Marx and Lenin gave these Jews faith and something for which to strive.

The KPD (and KJVD) had organised an underground resistance that included many young people. The communists provided a system – fragmented though it might have been – that enabled them to work against National Socialism. Baum and a few others had direct contact with the KPD through the KJVD, and Baum, Sack and the others helped inspire a few hundred young people to not give up hope. Thus the emotional connection to the Soviet Union was shared by young communists, social democrats and Zionists alike.

They were further convinced of the merits of communism by the actions of the Soviet Union during the Spanish Civil War, as while Soviet involvement was not based solely upon ideological grounds, it did show Stalin and the Soviet Union taking the lead in European anti-fascism. After rebel forces led by Franco declared war on the duly elected republic in 1936, no 'democracy' came to its aid, but rather the Soviet Union and Mexico. After being approached by Spanish representatives in September 1936, the Soviets approved a plan to create companies in various countries in order to purchase weapons, supplies and combat materials and send it to Spain. This was despite there being no formal diplomatic relations between the two nations. Military specialists and advisors were also sent to teach Spanish republican forces how to use the equipment, as well as to help organise and train the army.[10]

From October 1936 until February 1937, over $130 million worth of combat equipment, weaponry and materials was sent to Spain from France, the US, Switzerland, the Netherlands and Czechoslovakia. The new aircraft, tanks, vehicles and guns not only helped the republican forces mount a formidable defence with up-to-date Soviet technology, but had the added benefit of allowing the Soviets to observe their equipment in combat conditions.[11]

Stalin carefully reviewed every single document concerning the war, allowing him to react promptly to all political and military developments. It could be argued that Stalin saw the Spanish Loyalist government as part and parcel of the government that was obedient to instructions from Moscow. Sarin and Dvoretsky document an example of a directive approved by the Soviet politburo in late 1937, which stated that 'it was necessary to remove all saboteurs and traitors from the army, to develop measures to mobilise industry for military production, and to clear rear areas of fascist spies and agents.' The directive also included 'laws regarding agriculture, industry, trade and transportation, and propaganda in territories occupied by the enemy.'

The chief Soviet military advisor, Marshall Meretshov, wrote that:

> In the Spanish Army, the situation was so bad that our advisors were required to perform both organisational and operational combat tasks ... Soviet advisors participated in organising and forming international brigades and a number of Spanish brigades. Later, they often led them in combat, especially in those first combat operations to show the officers how to command their units.

Both the Spanish Loyalist forces and the International Brigades (IB) were given ideological support through the Commissariat, which provided political commissars to every unit. Their people were not readily accepted and seen in non-communist groups as Stalin's attempt to establish total Soviet control over the Spanish military.

The Soviet Committee for State Security (KGB) made an impact during the war, specifically in penetrating and attempting to take control of the political and military institutions of the republic. Their stated purpose was to assist Spain in organising and implementing intelligence and counter-intelligence work, but this was not the case. The KGB specialists

> ... began to insinuate themselves into the political struggle itself, to recruit agents from the local people and soldiers of international brigades, and to conduct special operations against selected political parties and organisations. The most important KGB missions in Spain were like those in the USSR: provocations, shootings, persecution of people without trial or honest investigation, as well as torture ... KGB activities permitted favourable conditions for liquidating the various rivals of the Spanish Communist Party and the virtual 'Sovietisation' of the nation.[12]

It was the International Brigades in Spain and Soviet anti-fascism, however, that won the attention and admiration of the world at the time. Jews played a significant role in the defence of the Spanish republic by virtue of their high level of participation in the IB. According to Arno Lustiger, 6000 Jews volunteered to serve in the IB, 15 per cent of the total.[13] 500 of the 6000 came from German-speaking lands, many of them 'had already been persecuted, incarcerated in concentration camps and forced to take flight. Many have left no trace except for their index cards in the International Brigades' archives …'[14]

The first international combat unit of the Spanish Civil War was called the *Gruppe Thälmann*, as a tribute to the incarcerated German Communist Party leader. The eighteen members of this group, however, referred to themselves as the *Jüdische Gruppe Thälmann* because fourteen of them were either German or Polish anti-fascist Jews. The first elected commander of this group was Max Friedemann, a German Jew. Unusually there were women in the group, including Friedemann's wife, Golda, and together they took part in the street battles of Barcelona in the opening days of the war.[15] The later, expanded version of this group became popularly known as the XI Thälmann Brigade.

Georg Hornstein, a Berlin native who was raised in Düsseldorf, was an 'apolitical German Jew' who volunteered to serve in Spain. Upon his arrival, he was given an officer's rank and later became a company commander in the XI Thälmann Brigade. At the end of the war, Hornstein returned to Amsterdam where he had lived and worked before volunteering. He was arrested there in 1941 and brought 'home' to Düsseldorf, where he was interrogated by the Gestapo. Hornstein underwent weeks of interrogation and torture, which resulted in a written protocol of his anti-fascism. Gestapo file 31385 in the Düsseldorf city archive provides a rare anti-fascist testimony under terrible duress:

When I am asked the reason why I became an officer in the International Brigades … I have the following to say.

It is true that I possess German nationality and according to the letter of the law am a German national. But as a Jew I have lost practically all rights in Germany and I was therefore endeavouring to find a new home for myself. It was the nature of things that I used the special circumstances in Spain in that way.

I was aware that in Spain I was also fighting against German volunteer units recognised by the German Reich. As a Jew, I fought for my convictions and human rights. Under the prevailing circumstances I no longer regard myself as a German national and would use any opportunity given to me to obtain a new nationality, just as I would be ready as a Jew to fight for my rights at any time.[16]

Word spread throughout Berlin resistance groups about the *Gruppe Thälmann*, and many people got excited about the prospect of fighting the fascists. The fact that Hitler and Mussolini had both sent forces to fight alongside Franco's Spanish fascists made it even more appealing to German anti-fascists. Alfred Eisenstädter wanted to go to Spain, but Herbert Baum convinced him that it was more important to remain in Berlin in order to continue their anti-fascist work.

Eisenstädter got together with the Baums, Kochmanns and Lothar Cohn, Marianne's brother, on a weekly basis, to play the card game skat and socialise. Alfred remembers that Marianne was a friendly but argumentative person, and that she and Sala Rosenbaum had a number of petty spats. Eisenstädter became especially close friends with Sala, and felt that she and Herbert Baum were the true leaders of the Baum group. Unfortunately, he became involved in one of Marianne and Sala's arguments and took Sala's side. This cooled his friendship with Herbert somewhat, but they did remain friends and comrades.

According to Eisenstädter, there was an unwritten agreement amongst the leading Baum group members that no one would leave Germany. They truly felt that by remaining they could help bring an end to National Socialism. The group was expanding all the time and they felt they were giving the younger members an intellectual and cultural life that no Nazi could take from them. There was hope for the future.[17]

As part of maintaining a link with communist ideals, Herbert Baum told Gerhard Zadek that he should learn a trade, and said that 'a good communist must also be a good worker with a respected reputation. Then his political work will be even more effective.' In 1937 Zadek completed his apprenticeship in a machine shop, Apparatebau und Kesselschmiede, which was located in Berlin-Niederschönhausen, an outer district of Berlin. He was the only Jewish apprentice and later the only Jewish worker in the shop. Everyone knew that he was Jewish – he did not try to keep it a secret. He told his co-workers that he was born a Jew and not a religious one.

Zadek, who regularly listened to Radio Moscow, told his co-workers what he knew about the war in Spain and ventured his opinions on issues that were not covered in Nazi newspapers. The workers were suspicious about his source of information, which since listening to Soviet radio was illegal, was risky. He told them that he listened to radio stations from Strasbourg and London. He collected money for *Rote Hilfe* from his co-workers for imprisoned anti-fascists and for volunteers travelling to Spain to join the XI Thälmann Brigade; brigaders had to pay their own fare to Paris, which was expensive. Zadek felt strongly that some people at his factory were communists or former communists, but that they did not tell him for obvious reasons. He also knew that some of them had been imprisoned.

Upon completing his apprenticeship, Zadek received a document from one of the engineers at the shop confirming that fact, but the Nazi commission of artisans refused to grant him a diploma on the basis of his being a Jew; his name was written Gerhard 'Israel' Zadek on the application. German law dictated that all Jewish males were given the middle name 'Israel' and Jewish women were given the middle name 'Sara' in order to identify Jews more easily. Zadek spoke with the factory manager, who resubmitted the documentation but omitted 'Israel'; Zadek was awarded his diploma. The manager told him, 'I am giving you this document because even though some say that most Germans hate the Jews, this is an example that it is not always the case.'[18]

Another member of Baum's group was not faring so well. Herbert Ansbach had been sent to Brandenburg prison in October 1936 after being convicted of possessing an 'illegal' newspaper, and became extremely ill. He spent much of his time in the prison hospital, suffering from a heart condition. His attorney applied for Ansbach's early release, which was granted along with a suspended sentence. When Herbert's mother came to take him home, the doctor told her to give him all the food he wanted for two weeks in order to help him regain his strength. He later went to a sanatorium in Bad Kudowa and eventually became healthy enough to work again.

He returned to Berlin and secured work with the Jewish Winter Help, a charity for relieving hardship in the Jewish community during the cold season. It provided financial and material aid to the ever increasing number of Jewish people in need. Heinz Sachs worked there with Ansbach, and writes that the employees 'came from all walks of life and occupations, and were of all age groups between 20 and 60 ... The jobs were temporary, lasting from fall to spring in any given year.' Sachs worked in the Spiritual Aid department, which produced variety shows for both Jewish children and adults.

Ansbach worked in the archive, where newspaper clippings and documents were collected and organised. The head of this department was an older Russian or Polish Jew. Sachs occasionally had to gather data from the archive, and would spend lunch hours there talking with Ansbach and other workers. 'I was greatly impressed by his [Ansbach's] personality, his intelligence, and wide knowledge ... of course, we ... discussed politics, the most important topic those days.'

Ansbach was straightforward about his communist political convictions, and told Sachs that he had recently been released from prison. He did not breathe a word about his resistance work. After about three or four months working in the archive, Ansbach had to make a hasty exit from Germany.[19] He would not be the only one.

12

RESISTANCE IN ISOLATION AND KRISTALLNACHT (1938)

Ours was a double load of difficulties, dangers, complications of life … All dissenters, including communists, carried the risk and burden of stigma and terror, but to be a communist and a Jew made you an outlaw without any protection under the law … plus the fear and certainty that if caught in any act against the Nazis, not only the individual but the whole family could be subject to the harshest punishment – death.

Rita Meyer[1]

The dissenters, all of them, helped innumerable times any persecuted anti-fascist who needed food and shelter, a little bit of money, or moral support … there was a whole network of people who helped many, not organised in any way … Members of different groups freely participated in activities of other groups and cells, spanning the whole anti-fascist range … [the] Baum group and all anti-fascists made resistance their way of life 24 hours a day, everyday.

Ellen Compart[2]

The Baum group became increasingly isolated from the larger Berlin Jewish community both by choice and circumstance. By growing up in the youth movement, Herbert Baum and the others had developed a philosophy that stressed the primacy of youth.

Walter Sack, Sala Rosenbaum and Herbert Baum collaborated on political and educational work for the young people in the *Ring*, and after its dissolution did the same for illegal meetings, rambles and outings. Walter tells us that Sala, who married Martin Kochmann in 1938, 'was a remarkable woman. I will never forget her voice or her smile. Her voice had a special tone: soft, clear, expressive. We all admired her. And if people had troubles, they went to her.'

Sala's responsibilities included the weekly *Heimabende* that took place in the Jewish community house on Oranienburger Strasse. The attendees were Jewish schoolchildren from ages 12 to 16. Sala, Walter and others led these meetings, where political themes were discussed, literature was read aloud and analysed and songs were sung. A subject of constant discussion and debate was anti-Semitism and Jewish persecution. Sala believed that equality for Jews could only be realised after the fascist dictatorship was obliterated and replaced with socialism. This view was not universal; it was only held by the communists in the Baum group.

Sala also led Marxist political instruction; the young Jews read *Capital* with pages that were torn out of books. 'It was really crazy,' Walter Sack recalls, 'everything happened on Oranienburger Strasse.' They devised a cover just in case a Nazi decided to pay them an unannounced visit. 'We secured the entrance to the room – as well as having another book lying within reach on the table,' Sack tells us. They had ripped the relevant pages out of the study material so it would be easy to make it disappear if necessary.

Her creative talent led Sala to teach. She trained to be a Kindergarten teacher and secured a teaching position at the Jewish Kindergarten on Jerusalemer Strasse. Her training came in handy when she was involved in education and political work in the illegal KJVD as well as the *Ring* and the *Heimabende*.

'We were often at Sala's house,' says Walter Sack, 'we used to read Heine with her, *Germany: A Winter's Tale* and *The Harz Journey*.' Walter cherished those times of intellectual stimulation: 'We wanted to enjoy the beauty of life – fully enjoy it.'[3]

During this time, Ari Steinbach led his former *Ring* group in the reading of many esoteric books and articles. Amongst the authors were the Swedish sociologist Gunnar Myrdal, who wrote a series of essays on proposals to improve the living conditions of minorities in the United States. They read Werner Illing's *Utopolus*, a science fiction novel about a socialist utopia that was written in 1930 by a social democrat. Ernst Toller's *Memoirs From Jail* (aka *Look Through the Bars*) was discussed and dissected. The group could relate to Maxim Gorki's *The Lower Depths*, about a place where homeless people find shelter. Edward Bellamy's *Looking Backward* began in the year 2000 and worked backwards to 1887, the year it was published. The focus of the book was that a better world would come if people helped make it so.

The group also read an article from the United States about an association called Technocracy, Inc., that wanted to further production and distribution of abundant physical wealth using a governmental body called the 'Technate,' which would implement behaviour modification though an engineered environment. Group sessions focused on finding alternatives and imaging the future. Some questions brought up at the time were: 'How would a world food production and distribution administration be created?' 'Does man build his environment or does the environment build the man?' 'How participatory can we make society?' Ellen Compart recreates a troop leader's lecture:

> In any good society everyone has a stake in the scheme of things, so let's aim for a very democratic, egalitarian, classless system with as few divisions as possible. Education should aim for cooperation – not competition. This will result in one striving to be a team member of a system that will work well for you and me. A guaranteed income covering basic needs – housing, food, medical care, education – is also something worth striving for. Does this all call for behavior modification? Education, religion, law, and prescribed codes of ethics all use it. Coercion does not really convince, but positive reinforcement will. It can replace punishment.[4]

The anti-fascists saw their cause as important, a means to beat Nazism, which is why Herbert Baum, Alfred Eisenstädter and the others remained in Germany, rather than leaving for safer lands. Then Walter Sack took a trip to Sweden – and did not return. Alfred vividly recalls that some people, including himself, condemned Sack for running out on those left behind; Eisenstädter felt that Sack's organisational abilities would be sorely missed. Herbert Baum, on the other hand, was quite understanding.

Other members were also considering flight. Herbert Ansbach, who had only recently been released from prison, discovered that the Gestapo was planning to arrest him. Upon hearing this news, he decided to flee to Czechoslovakia. Herbert Baum wanted to help his old comrade and friend, and sent Alfred Eisenstädter to Prague as a courier to announce Ansbach's circumstances and planned date of arrival. Alfred was chosen for this task because he still possessed a valid German passport. He left for the train station directly from work at 3.00pm on a Friday. While on the train, a young woman approached him to ask whether or not Alfred was Jewish. He told her that he was and she said, 'They are arresting all of the Jews at the border.' Since Alfred did have a valid passport, he was not concerned. Upon reaching the German-Czech border, an SS man asked him a few cursory questions and let him through.

The one problem was ironically with a Czech border guard, not an SS man. The Czech confiscated his German-language paper, which was to be folded in his back pocket as identification for his contact. Eisenstädter had to wander around an empty train station for an hour before someone approached him. He was then taken to an abandoned building, which was the home of his hosts. Eisenstädter was told that because they were German citizens they not allowed to work in Czechoslovakia, and therefore never knew where their next meal was coming from; the KJVD-in-exile was in a sad state in 1938. That evening an old mattress was dragged out of the rubbish for Alfred to sleep on.

The next day Alfred was taken to an open area in Prague to meet another contact, a member of the central committee of the KJVD. He explained to him that Herbert Ansbach had been released from Brandenburg prison early due to illness, and that he was going to be arrested again by the Gestapo and had to leave Germany. The contact knew nothing of Ansbach and became suspicious of both him and Eisenstädter: 'Why was he released? Why were you sent from Berlin to announce his coming? Why couldn't he just come across?' The contact became quite unpleasant and even accused both Alfred and Ansbach of being Gestapo spies. Alfred wanted to punch him, but was able to keep calm. Upon returning to Berlin, Alfred briefed Herbert Baum on his meeting in Prague; Baum was shocked by the conduct of the contact man. Nonetheless, Herbert Ansbach was safely in Prague within a few days.[5]

In early November a German diplomat in Paris, Ernst von Rath, was shot and killed by a young Jew named Herschel Grynspan. He had been distressed over the conditions under which his parents were living while in a displaced persons' camp at the German-Polish border after they were deported to Poland from Germany. His parents and he were Polish nationals who had lived for many years in Germany but had not become citizens. A Nazi law expelled all such Polish Jews to Poland, who did not want them either. Thus they lived in the border region in terrible conditions.

Hitler used this act to unleash a wave of terror and destruction through-out the Reich against the Jews. *Kristallnacht* (9/10 November 1938), or the Night of Broken Glass, was meant to appear to be a spontaneous reaction to the murder of von Rath. In actuality, it had been planned in advance and the Nazis had been waiting for the right moment to carry it out. Jewish busi-nesses and homes were vandalised, synagogues were burned to the ground, over 100 Jews were killed, and 30,000 Jewish men were arrested and sent to concentration camps. In addition, the Jewish communities were fined one billion Reichmarks to pay for the damage. It was now clear to many Jews that their only option was to leave Germany as soon as possible.[6]

On the night of the attack Sigi Rotholz was returning to Berlin from *Hachshara* and was at the Weissensee Jewish cemetery. Rotholz and several friends used nearby pay telephones to warn Jews in Berlin not to sleep at home that night.[7]

The KPD responded with great emotion to the persecution in short-wave radio broadcasts from Madrid:

To all Germans!
Solidarity with the persecuted!
Take heed!

The Communist Party speaks to you, it turns to every decent German. Down with the vile Jewish pogroms, which bring dishonour upon Germany.

Down with the vile Jewish pogroms, which the National Socialist dic-tatorship is using to try and make people forget its own crimes against the German people …

Workers! Upright Germans! Turn against these shameful pogroms! Help the persecuted and tormented Jews. Remember that the great German workers' leader Bebel called anti-Semitism the socialism of fools. Remember that Karl Marx, one of the greatest Germans, who showed the working class of the whole world the way to liberation, was of Jewish descent. Always consider that all great Germans have seen in anti-Semitism only regression and barbarism. Anti-Semitism is the weapon which the National Socialists use against the interests of all decent Germans. Do not allow the name of Germany to be dragged through the dirt.

Communists, Socialists, Catholics, Protestants, and all who are oppo-nents of the regime, hold together! Offer common resistance to the National Socialist regime …[8]

The unwritten rule about remaining in Germany was renounced by Herbert Baum after *Kristallnacht.* 'It is now clear that we are too exposed as Jews and limited in what we can do,' Baum told his inner circle. 'You should all try to emigrate.'

Alfred Eisenstädter and Felix Heymann both lost their jobs at Steinrück at this time. Heinz Birnbaum heard about their trouble and arranged a job for Alfred with him in the tool room of Norman Lager, a Jewish-owned concern. As they worked together on semi-automatic machines making nuts and bolts, Alfred noticed that Heinz made friends very easily. The two young men frequently went drinking with a group of young co-workers who belonged to the Nazi Party. Once when they were all pretty drunk, one of the Nazis slapped Alfred on the back and told him, 'You know, you guys are all right even if you are Jews!' But the camaraderie did not help when the firm fell into German hands; Alfred and Heinz were to lose their jobs in January 1939.[9]

Shaken by the events of *Kristallnacht*, the Jewish community of Berlin had purchased telephone books from around the world which were passed from family to family. Marianne Prager's family leafed through the Amsterdam, Buenos Aires and New York phone books searching for the name 'Prager'. There were quite a few in New York, so they had a family friend compose a letter in English that read, 'Quite by chance, I came into possession of your name. I think we must be related…' The letter went on to describe the desperate situation the Pragers were in and begged for help in getting them out of Germany. A few people responded but no one was willing to provide any assistance. Marianne was training to be a governess at a Jewish children's home, one of the few employment opportunities left open to Jews, but her father lost his job. The family was forced to sell off many of their possessions in order to survive.[10]

13

RENEWED ACTIVITY, ATTEMPTS TO FLEE AND THE NAZI-SOVIET TREATIES (1939)

'This is ridiculous – we are not doing anything about it!' Alfred Eisenstädter told the group at a meeting right after the occupation of Czechoslovakia on 15 March 1939. He brought a rough draft of a flyer that he had written describing the anti-fascist view of the situation. He told Baum and the others that 'waiting for directives is useless – the time to act is now.' And act they did. Baum realised that since the Nazis were now occupying Prague, there was no longer a KJVD centre in exile that could issue directives on behalf of the KPD. Herbert, Alfred, Felix and the others rewrote the copy and prepared it for printing. Irene Walther typed the flyer and 500–1000 copies of it were run off on a primitive machine that was kept hidden in the basement of Baum's apartment building.

Alfred and Felix created a device to disperse the flyers. Alfred describes the process:

> We created little catapults on a lever. On one end was a punctured tin can filled with water. The water would slowly drip out. The leaflets were to be placed on the other end. The devices were to be secured on window sills. When the water level falls, the weight of the paper puts too much pressure on the catapult and the flyers will spill onto the street.

They spent a long time finding buildings with staircase windows facing the street. Finding quite a few near the Alexanderplatz, they began to mount the catapults. Alfred was working and Felix was the lookout. In one of the buildings, Alfred was placing a contraption into a window when suddenly he felt a hand press down hard on his shoulder. He almost passed out, but it was only Felix warning him that someone was walking up the stairs. Ten people were involved in this action, which went smoothly. Hundreds of flyers littered the streets telling Berliners the anti-fascist version of the German occupation of Czechoslovakia.[1]

Two young men visited the home of Marianne Prager one evening in May. Dressed casually and sporting large caps, one of them went by the name of Ariel Rosenberg. After explaining that they were Jews from Palestine who were helping Jewish children leave Germany, the Pragers invited them into the apartment. 'How many children do you have between the ages of ten and fifteen?' one of them asked.

Marianne was sixteen but Ilse was only twelve. The two men explained that they could get Ilse safely out of Germany within the next few weeks, but they were unable to provide any further information. Jenny Prager listened, but Georg became violently angry and said that he would never let his younger daughter leave Germany alone. Jenny told the young men that they would discuss it, and asked them to return in a week for a definite answer.

Marianne wanted Ilse to go. She saw it as a way for the family to continue if the unthinkable happened to the rest of them. Her mother was sad about it, but also felt leaving was the right thing to do. Her father, however, was stubborn and deluded himself until the very end. He was a 'German' and was going to 'stick it out.' Jenny tried to discuss the subject with him, but he refused even to consider the possibility of Ilse's departure. 'Germany cannot do anything to me,' he declared. 'I have the discharge papers and the medal for my injury while serving the fatherland.' How could they not guarantee his little girls' futures? Somehow he resigned himself to the fact that Ilse would indeed leave Germany, and he wrote to a cousin in London who agreed to care for her.

The night before Ilse was to leave, the two sisters had their last private talk together. Marianne handed her a leather-bound diary with a lock on it and told her not to open it until after she arrived in London. There was a special inscription written on the frontispiece. Marianne made Ilse promise to write in it every day as if she was talking with her. Ilse was, of course, very nervous about leaving her family, but Marianne tried to make the trip sound exciting. The talk ended on a serious note.

'Look,' she said. 'You are what would be bar mitzvah age for a boy and you are going away. You should express your gratitude to your parents for raising, educating, and spoiling you.' Ilse listened intently as her sister continued: 'I am being very serious now. I want you to promise me that you won't make a scene. Don't shed one tear on that train platform tomorrow morning. Get a hold of yourself and don't fall apart.' Ilse promised.

The next morning, 21 May 1939, the Prager family went to the train station. Ilse had packed a large brown suitcase full of clothing, family photos and her favourite possession – a heavy set of steel roller skates. On her jacket was pinned her name and she was carrying an identification card.

After arriving at the platform, Ilse saw dozens of children – some of whom she knew from school – crying their eyes out. Ilse remained strong but when the train pulled up her father broke down and cried like a baby – she had never seen him cry before. Soon the entire family was weeping as they held each other tightly. As she waved to her family from the moving train, Ilse felt deep in her heart that she would never see them again.

While on the train, Ilse peeked at the inscription Marianne had written to her in the diary. It read:

Beloved sister,

I believe that two sisters have never understood each other as well as we have. We have had no secrets from each other. In this diary, you should write all of your experiences just as you would tell them to me. I hope that I will be able to read your diary when it is finished, because my greatest wish in this life, whether you believe it or not, is to see you again. Where there is a will on both sides of a matter, then there is a way to realise it.

No day will pass that I will not think of you. Stay well.
We have to see each other again!

With love,
your Marianne[2]

At this time Herbert Baum and a few other communist comrades joined *Haschomer Hazair*, the Marxist-oriented Zionist bund that propagated a classless Jewish state in Palestine; the Nazis tolerated *aliyah* camps for German Zionists who wanted to emigrate. Perhaps Baum saw Zionist camps as fertile ground for ideological schooling of sympathisers, people who could spread socialism in Palestine.

Baum's comrades Alice Kronheim and Gerhard Zadek went to an *aliyah* camp in April called Gut Winkel, near the town of Spreehagen outside Berlin. Over 200 young Zionists were there learning to work the land, raise poultry and grow crops. Gerhard, Alice and a young woman known only as 'Spinne' (Spider) travelled around Germany to visit other *Haschomer Hazair* camps, creating anti-fascist cells in Essen, Bremerhaven, Bremen and Hamburg. A large children's Zionist camp was set up in Poschendorf near Dresden and they got to know many Zionists during their three-week stay there. All the contacts were initiated by Herbert Baum.[3]

Baum's young comrade Günther Prager, the brother of Ernst, became a group leader at Gut Winkel. He writes:

> The activities in these Zionist groups and their meetings did not vary greatly from other youth movement groups. Herbert Baum, of course, tried to stress the importance of working against Hitler and for socialism. Under his guidance, a great number of youngsters came to important insights about the current political situation in Germany, Russia, and beyond. They learned to recognise aggression and oppression.

Baum asked the young Zionists never to forget: 'In whatever country you find yourself, be on the right side, support communism and the Soviet Union.' He spoke with as many people individually as possible, urging them to join with other left-wing forces in their new countries to do battle against fascism, militarism and imperialism. He pleaded for a socialist regime in Palestine, and hoped that the young, idealistic Zionists would work towards that goal.[4]

It was in 1939 that, while in Berlin, Günther Prager was captured by a group of *Hitler Jugend* members and brought to the police. They claimed that he was a member of an illegal Jewish group. He then spent two days under interrogation at Gestapo headquarters. They let him go, but told him, 'If you are sent back here again, you won't go home again.' Prager had to figure a way to get out of Germany.

This was not Günther's first run-in with the Gestapo. During 1936, both he and his brother Ernst were arrested and interrogated separately. A traitor had given the name 'Prager' to the authorities. Günther was prepared to keep quiet about the activities of his group, but they did not ask about that. What they wanted to know about was his brother's work, which he honestly knew nothing about. After six or seven hours they let Günther go home. He asked if he could wait for his brother, and was told that, 'we have more questions for him. He will go home later.' Günther had a gut feeling that this was not true. He was right. Ernst was charged with 'Preparation for High Treason,' and, since he was only 19 years old, was given one and a half years in prison, even though the prosecutor wanted to give him a stiffer sentence.

During Ernst's prison term, the Gestapo came to the Prager home at least three times to rummage through the apartment. Günther was told by his group leader to keep a low profile: 'Being associated with you can be danger-ous because of your brother being in prison.' They did not take him to many activities because that would have placed them all in danger. Family members of imprisoned anti-fascists were at times followed by the Gestapo.

Prager states that proletarian solidarity was stressed. 'There was a sup-port fund [*Rote Hilfe*] to assist imprisoned anti-fascists, Christian and Jewish alike.' Donations came from all troop members, including Günther. He worked odd jobs – such as plumbing and carpentry – and put the money he received into the fund. Since his brother was in jail, this money also helped his own family. Günther states:

> Considering the situation, it was only natural that Jewish persecution and its causes were often on our minds and in our hearts. So discussions ensued, often led by Herbert Baum and Sala Kochmann ... they had a most convincing, clear teaching style and pedagogic abilities. They taught us to search for causes, to delve into the past to understand the present. They made us see anti-Semitism and race politics in the light of history, an old weapon in the arsenal of exploitative societies needing a scapegoat ... As during the nineteenth century when Jews in Germany became quite assimilated, living in all classes of society. But when the people in power tried to cover up for their failures or wanted to instigate willing-ness to go to war, out came anti-Semitism ... To realise this was important in the development of the political consciousness of these young people.

Shortly after Ernst Prager was released from prison, he discovered that he was going to be sent to a concentration camp. Fortunately, he was able to flee to the Netherlands. By this time, his brother Günther was the leader of his own group of about a dozen youngsters. He was teaching them about socialism the same way Herbert Baum, Rudi Barta, and the others had educated him.

It was fortunate for Günther that while he was at Gestapo headquarters, the connection with his brother was never discovered, otherwise he would probably have been sent to a concentration camp. People in the underground told him that he had to get out of Germany fast. There was no longer any choice in the matter. Somehow he was able to get a visa for Britain, and left for London as soon as he could. His father had recently died and he felt badly about leaving his mother and younger sister in Berlin, but he had to go. On his way to London, he stopped in the Netherlands to see his brother, Ernst. They had an emotional reunion before Günther continued on to Britain.[5]

A pair of treaties signed by Germany and the Soviet Union in August 1939 took most of the world by surprise. The German–Soviet Credit Agreement of 19 August and the Ribbentrop-Molotov Pact of 23 August (officially the Treaty of Non-Aggression between Germany and the Soviet Union) shocked leftist political circles. Many communists were totally disorientated. The one consistently anti-fascist nation had become a political and economic ally of Nazi Germany.[6]

Why did the Soviet Union make deals with Nazi Germany? Sarin and Dvoretzky write that, 'Stalin was doing anything possible to give up any friendly alliances with Western nations in the 1930s in order to get closer to Fascist Germany.' The authors believed that Stalin had plans to dominate Europe with Hitler's military help and then push Germany aside to gain total control of Europe. In his report to the Eighteenth Party Congress of 1939, Stalin 'made it clear to Hitler that their interests in a future European war were identical.' He wanted Hitler to believe that the United States, Britain and France wanted to foment a war between them.

Stalin ignored every warning from the democracies that Hitler intended eventually to go to war with the Soviet Union. The Ribbentrop-Molotov Pact gave spheres of influence to both Germany and the Soviet Union. This treaty completely isolated the Soviets from Western Europe and thus gave Hitler free rein to invade them.[7]

The German–Soviet Credit Agreement – which was disadvantageous to the Soviets and which they signed in order to secure the Ribbentrop-Molotov Pact – left them extremely vulnerable. It provided Germany with Soviet sugar, oil, butter and meat, raw materials that benefited the German war effort.[8]

Considering the Stalinisation of the KPD, it is not surprising that the party reacted positively to the treaties. Weitz writes that 'the 'Nazi-Soviet Pact, the KPD claimed, lay in the interest of the German people, while … the British and French desired a war that would destroy Germany.' Walter Ulbricht, the leader of the KPD-in-exile in Moscow, along with various Comintern officials and communists in Germany, felt that one result of the non-aggression pact might be a newly legal KPD in Nazi Germany. Weitz writes:

> [o]nce again the KPD failed to grasp the central dynamic of the regime – the drive to create a racial utopia, which necessitated aggressive expansion and a panoply of murderous policies. Since in Nazi ideology communism blended inextricably with Judaism, there could never be an easing of the repression against the KPD …

German communists suffered terribly because of the treaties. No arrangements were made by the Soviets to relieve the repression of communists in Germany, thousands of whom languished in concentration camps and prisons. While the German military machine marched westward in 1940, the 'KPD's main western exile points now came under Nazi control, breaking the last links between the border secretaries and the underground. Hundreds and perhaps thousands of German communists (and other anti-fascists) were captured and sent off to concentration camps.'[9] Arthur Koestler reports that the Soviet secret police (GPU) handed over to the Gestapo, in 1940, at Brest Litovsk 'a hundred-odd … Austrian, German, and Hungarian communists.' amongst them were communists of Jewish heritage.[10]

The Nazi-Soviet pact sent shock waves through the Baum group. Many people, including Alfred Eisenstädter, condemned it. He was a socialist who had considered himself a communist fellow traveller up until that time. Thereafter he totally rejected communism in disgust, however, as did others. Baum, on the other hand, supported the pact. He told Alfred and the others: 'It was born of necessity and we must live with it.' Baum carefully explained to both his group and the young Zionists that Hitler would not feel bound by any agreement and that Stalin was buying time before a possible future German attack. Alfred remembers that the Unter den Linden, the main boulevard of Berlin, was decked out with Soviet flags and military bands played the *Internationale* in honour of Molotov's visit. Eisenstädter was revolted by the entire charade.

While their political world was being shaken, the Baum group members were working out ways to get out of Germany, as Herbert had advised. Alfred Eisenstädter and Felix Heymann put Amand Vasseur, a relative of Felix's by marriage, on a train for Paris on 28 August. It was no longer safe for him to remain in Berlin since he was a French citizen. Alfred and Felix also devised a plan for their own escape: they would take a train to the German–Danish border and walk across the 'green border' (the forest) to freedom. The two young men went to a local park and hid all of their money under a bench. It was illegal to take money out of the country, and if they were caught trying to flee with it they would be arrested. 'If we ever come back to Berlin, we will go back to the bench,' Alfred told Felix.

They boarded a train en route to the border, and got out near Flensburg. Heading for the forest, they began a hike to freedom, and, after walking through a thick forest, assumed that they were in Denmark. However, they were arrested by German border guards and placed in 'protective custody' at Flensburg prison. One of the guards confided to Alfred: 'I cannot understand it. The Jews are supposed to leave Germany, but when they try they are put in jail.'

Since Flensburg was a prison rather than a concentration camp, they were not treated brutally. Their arrival doubled the Jewish population in the prison, and Alfred was placed in command of the four Jews. This angered the oldest Jew, a Russian First World War veteran who had moved to Germany without becoming a citizen. He denounced the other three to the prison authorities, which resulted in all four men being placed in isolation cells for a while.

Both young men had paying jobs in prison. Alfred made paper bags and wove holsters for saddles, while Felix's job was to repair looms used to weave the holsters. With the money he made, Alfred was allowed to subscribe to a newspaper. Since he was not receiving it, he went to the warden to ask about it. The warden became furious and began to berate Alfred: 'You are very lucky that I don't beat you up! What Jewish nerve you have!' A few days later, he began to receive his newspapers.

Alfred had to get up each morning at 5.00am to wax the floor and make his bed in Prussian army style – 64 checks had to show and the bed had to be as flat as a board – which took two hours every morning. The men were allowed to receive packages and mail from family and friends. One day, when they were marching in the prison yard in single file, they exchanged an apple and a newspaper between them. A guard with a terrible reputation saw the exchange, but after seeing what they had exchanged he let it go. Felix's father came to visit them and was upset to see how pale they both were. Alfred recalls that the food was terrible and there was never enough of it. But they decided to eat everything given to them no matter how bad it tasted. When they became sick, they ate twice as much watery cabbage soup as usual.[11]

14

WAR, FORCED LABOUR AND RESISTANCE (1939–1940)

A few days after Alfred Eisenstädter and Felix Heymann's aborted escape attempt to Denmark, on 1 September the Second World War started when German forces invaded Poland. The Poles fought valiantly, but their courage was no match for Hitler's powerful Wehrmacht, which swept through the country in a few short weeks.

One could argue that the war had started in 1936, when Germany remilitarised the Rhineland, which was forbidden by the Treaty of Versailles. France mobilised but did not attack, allowing Hitler to win the first 'battle'. This success was compounded by the Spanish Civil War, when Germany supplied Franco with men, arms and supplies. Spain was an excellent testing ground for the Luftwaffe and Wehrmacht, preparing them for the future conflict. The western powers opted for an embargo on arms and supplies, which doomed the democratic Spanish republic. Hitler had flexed his muscles twice without any interference from Britain, France or the United States. In March 1938, German soldiers occupied Austria, and a short time later it was annexed into the German Reich, the Anschluss. Of course, warnings were issued through diplomatic channels, but this did not stop the Führer.

A major focus of Hitler's foreign policy was to bring 'persecuted' German minorities from neighbouring countries into the Third Reich. His next target was Czechoslovakia, which had a concentration of Germans in the Sudetenland. Hitler wanted this area, and negotiated with Britain and France – rather than Czechoslovakia – to get it. He had neutralised the entire country by March 1939, when a puppet leader was installed.

The western nations thought they were following a successful policy of appeasement by giving Hitler whatever he wanted in order to prevent a war. In fact they were increasing his popularity at home, which strengthened his stranglehold on Germany. His next goal was the ethnic German in Poland, who were to be 'liberated' from Polish 'oppression'. Even though France had a treaty with Poland, the French did nothing to assist the Poles when Germany invaded.

How did the Soviet-controlled KPD react to the German invasion of Poland? It showed itself to be an extremely flexible political party. The KPD rhetoric shifted from the call for anti-fascist unity to claiming that the war was a rivalry between the imperialist nations.[1] In the Soviet Union, the media took a similar line and excused the German attacks, explaining that Germany was defending itself against aggression.[2]

Herbert Baum and the other members of his group continued their political work under increasingly difficult conditions, and Baum intensified political and ideological schooling. Listening to short wave radio broadcasts kept them apprised of the military situation, but since Jews were not allowed to own radio sets, it was extremely difficult to gather information on a regular basis. By combining what they heard on the radio with information from German newspapers, the Baum group managed to develop a broad knowledge of political, military and economic affairs, which they distributed through opposition leaflets to the Berlin populace.

These activities were extremely dangerous. Leaflet campaigns, listening to short wave broadcasts and possessing illegal literature all fell under the 'crime' of 'preparation of high treason', which was punishable by death. But the Baum group members were able to balance their political work with more relaxing pursuits. They went on picnics and enjoyed music, poetry and swimming, allowing them to briefly forget the strain of living under the Nazis.[3]

In early 1940, while Alfred Eisenstädter was still in Flensburg prison, he received a letter. Opening it, he found it unusual that it was on red paper. Reading it made his heart sink: 'You are hereby ordered to be transported to Buchenwald concentration camp.' He fell into a deep depression. A short time later, however, he received a letter from Herbert Baum, who had arranged to get both him and Felix Heymann out of Germany. They would board a ship in Romania bound for Palestine. Herbert's Zionist connections had saved them, as Baum, in addition to being a Jewish and communist (KJVD) functionary, was also a Zionist functionary in *Haschomer Hazair*.

Upon his release, Eisenstädter was taken to the Flensburg Gestapo office and told that he was free to go, but that he had to report to the Berlin Gestapo upon his return. He was given no money, and only had light summer clothing for his trip back to Berlin in the middle of winter. He could not afford a ticket for the express train, and had to take a series of local trains, a journey which took 24 hours. He sent money to Felix, who was to be released a few days later; his trip on the express train took only eight hours. Together they went back to the park where they had hidden their money under a bench months before. Not only was their money gone, but so was the bench![4]

As ordered by the authorities in Flensburg, Alfred Eisenstädter reported to the Berlin Gestapo. Told to leave Germany, he was given a date to return to Gestapo headquarters if he had not emigrated by that time. The plan for him and Felix to emigrate to Palestine via Romania collapsed, and he went back to Gestapo headquarters where an officer screamed at him: 'God damned Jewish pig! Didn't I tell you to leave? I do not want to see you again!' This scenario was repeated fortnightly – by the same Gestapo officer – with the same dialogue.[5]

Meanwhile the Baum group engaged in resistance work under extremely difficult circumstances. Amongst these was the forced labour programme which placed all able-bodied Jews at the service of the war production industries as virtual slaves. The prioritisation of material interests, however, was the only way to reincorporate Jews into the German economy, which would slow down the deportations and thus give Jews with skills more of a chance of surviving the war.[6]

A decree of 20 December 1938, was used to place unemployed Jews who were fit enough to work into jobs that were 'politically important projects'. Racial doctrine came into play and these Jews were to work exclusively with other Jews and were to be isolated from the 'Aryan' workers. Konrad Kwiet writes that these people were generally given hard manual labour jobs: 'Building sites, road and motorway work, rubbish disposal, public toilets and sewage plants, quarries and gravel pits, coal merchants and rag and bone works were seen as suitable.'[7]

The armed forces supported the employment of Jews in the war industries. Military experts in Berlin claimed that 29,400 workers were needed in the metal trades alone, and said that the shortage of skilled labourers was about 15,700. They wanted Jews to fill these positions. At this time – October 1940 – both public and private industries were demanding Jewish workers.

Jewish forced labourers were paid the lowest possible hourly wage and were taxed at the highest rate. The Siemens-Schuckert-Werke in Berlin paid women assemblers half a Reichmark per hour. Many of these workers found that their pay was not enough to cover basic living expenses. This included rent on small, squalid rooms in which they were forcibly quartered. Jews continued to seek extra sources of income, which included illegal work in small firms in the big cities. The result of working so many hours was profound exhaustion.[8]

The Jewish forced labourers had to abide by many rules, three of which were:

1. Jews must be collected by the gate-keeper before starting their work, be taken by security to their changing room and handed over to the foreman of their work crew.

2. The Jews may only move about the works property under supervision. They may never stay within the works alone. Work will be undertaken by them in self-contained crews which must be under the leadership of an Aryan member of the company.

3. After the end of work, the Jews are to be taken by security in the same way, as a self-contained group to the exit of the works property.[9]

Hunger was a constant amongst the Jewish forced labourers as food rations were cut little by little. Jews were not allowed meat, fish, eggs, fruit, chocolate, cake, coffee, tea, wine or other alcoholic beverages. The office in charge of food rations issued directives such as

Jewish workers may no longer receive extra [ration] cards for long, heavy and very heavy labour. Non-Aryans also may not receive the same food as the Aryan workers in ammunitions firms … Special cooking facilities can also be made available to non-Aryans. However, it is not permissible for Jews to eat in the same canteen or mess halls as the Aryans.

On top of everything else was added the strain of travelling to and from work, which could add hours onto the work day. Jewish forced labourers needed a special pass to use buses, trams, the S- and U-Bahn or the municipal railways. They could receive this pass only if the distance from home to work was over an hour's walk. Jews had to wait until all Germans had found a seat before they themselves could sit down. Every Jewish forced labourer had to work a ten-hour day.[10]

Electrician Herbert Baum was assigned to work at the Electric Motor Works division of Siemens (Elmo-Werke), where there were around 500 Jewish forced labourers. It was a heterogeneous mix of people from all strata of society, including academics, professionals and housewives; there were very few skilled mechanics or electrical workers. Baum wanted to create anti-fascist cells amongst them, and was assisted in this by KPD functionaries Hans Fruck, Karl Kunger and George Vötter.[11]

Baum attempted to improve the overall working conditions but only small advances were possible. He tried to get a subsistence minimum wage for all workers. Since Baum was a skilled electrician, he was allowed to pick up work instructions in different parts of the building, enabling him to learn about the other departments of Elmo-Werke, including finding out about the different salaries paid to the Jewish workers.

Herbert discovered a Siemens company rule: if a quantity of work was not completed by anyone for a three-week period, then the quantity had to be reduced. If this could be applied to the Jewish workers, then their lives would be a little easier. A Miss Joseph was selected to represent them, and she spoke with the room supervisor, department master, engineer, department manager, assistant director and even approached the director of Elmo-Werke. The director refused to speak with a Jewish woman. Miss Joseph officially requested the following day off from work so she could bring up the labour issue in court. That same day the department master told her that she was going to get a raise in salary and promotion to group leader. The same thing happened to Ilse Haak, who also worked at the factory and had known Herbert Baum in the KJVD. The Nazis were trying to foment conflict amongst the Jewish workers over the issue of money.[12]

Ellen Compart worked with Hella Hirsch as forced labourers on the late shift at Aceta-Werke at IG Farben in Berlin. Ellen remembers Hella as being wise and serious beyond her years. They met every night after midnight in the basement locker room, where they ate cola tablets to stay awake and keep alert. During their ten-minute break they huddled close to each other and didn't say a word. They weren't allowed to talk and there were stiff fines or punishment for any breach of discipline. Hella smiled but never laughed; Ellen remembers her saying, 'Progress in history seems to come about only through human suffering. Terrible events have to happen and great destruction has to take place for the Phoenix to rise from the ashes. In our situation only a complete German defeat could lead to a new beginning, but we might be vanquished and wiped out in the process.'[13]

Shortly after returning to Berlin from prison, Alfred Eisenstädter met Suzanne Wesse, the French Catholic wife of Felix Heymann's cousin, Richard Wesse. Her father was a wealthy man who owned a factory in Calais that manufactured window curtains. Suzanne was able to travel often and attended school in England, Spain and Germany, learning each nation's language in the process. In 1935 she returned to Berlin where she had previously met her future husband and found work as a translator. Suzanne, Richard and their daughter lived with Richard's mother; Suzanne's brother, Amand Vasseur, had also lived with them until Alfred and Felix got him out of the country. Not long after they met, Alfred and Suzanne were taking a stroll when an air raid began. They ducked into an 'Aryan' air raid shelter to wait for the bombing to stop. A drunk stumbled over to them and proceeded to insult and harass Suzanne for being with a Jew. She began to cry and Alfred felt utterly helpless because he could not fight or chase the drunk away – he could have been arrested for simply being there.[14]

In preparation for their possible emigration to Palestine, the Gestapo sent Alfred Eisenstädter and Felix Heymann to work for a German farmer in a small village near Jüterbog in southeast Germany. The farmer had to pay the Gestapo for the services of six Jews, for whom he put piles of straw in a barn to serve as beds. A local man visited the farm to show the young Jews how to chop down trees. After three months Alfred developed a painful sore throat and a very high fever. The farmer's wife brought him noodle soup to help him recover. Alfred wanted to leave, but Felix felt it was too dangerous to return to Berlin. Besides, Felix was in charge of the Jews on the farm and felt responsible for them. The two friends had an argument; then Alfred rode his bicycle 20km to the nearest train station. Finding it strange that there was still snow on the ground in May, his fever broke as he rode through the countryside. He boarded a train and returned to Berlin.[15]

Alfred reported to the labour office and was assigned a job in a coal yard. He had a ten-minute walk to work in the morning but it took a half hour to get home. He was so weary from carrying coke into cellars that his knees shook. However, it paid relatively well – 50 Reichmarks per week – and the foreman was a likeable man. The Gestapo discovered, however, that the foreman let the Jews shower with the 'Aryan' workers. The Jews were dispatched to a different coal yard where they were paid piece work; Alfred was paid 2 Reichsmarks a day, not enough to live on. He and the other Jews complained to the inspector: they wanted to be put on salary and would file a labour grievance if they were not. This display of Jewish 'nerve' angered the inspector, who fired them on the spot. They were told to report back to the labour office.[16]

Waiting in the reception area of the labour office, Alfred realised that he had a love letter from a young Christian woman whom he was dating. The Nuremberg Laws of 1935 made sexual relations between Jews and non-Jews punishable by concentration camp confinement or possibly death. He sat there for almost three hours wondering what to do with the letter. He and the other Jews were then arrested and escorted to the police station. The police did not handcuff them, letting the young Jews walk in from of them, and Alfred was tempted to toss the letter into a trash can on the street, but couldn't find the courage to do it. If the police saw him toss it, they might check it and then Alfred would be on his way to a camp or worse. After reaching the police station the young men were called in separately to be searched.

Alfred had a sandwich in his briefcase and asked a policeman for permission to eat it. He told him to go ahead. Alfred ate the sandwich and then took the letter out of his pocket and crumpled it up in the sandwich paper. All he had to do was throw the paper into the waste basket next to him but he was too frightened. He stuffed it into his briefcase which was then taken away from him. Alfred and the others were taken to police headquarters on the Alexanderplatz where he was given back his briefcase. It was sealed and had a sticker on it that read: 'Searched by Patrolman Müller.' Then it was taken away from him again and tossed into a corner.[17]

Alfred and the others slept on hard wooden benches in the police station before being sent to a forced labour camp on the outskirts of Berlin. For four weeks he was part of a crew building a circular railroad around the city. Amongst the workers on the crew were labourers from the Ukraine, Poland, Denmark and France. They had to get up every morning at 4.00am, walk for one-and-a-half hours, and begin work at 6.00am. They were each given a hunk of bread with margarine smeared on it in the morning, which Alfred would carry all day, taking a bite every few hours to keep his strength up. He worked a twelve-hour shift and was given two half-hour breaks. Alfred spent most of his time worried about the letter in his briefcase. He was certain that he would wind up in a concentration camp after his work assignment was completed.

After four weeks he was sent back to the Alexanderplatz police presidium. He was shocked to learn that he was being set free – all he had to do was wait for his briefcase. While he was waiting, he struck up a conversation with a young man.

'Why were you brought in?' asked Alfred.

'High treason. They accused me of being a member of a communist cell.'

'What's your sentence?'

'I've been condemned to death.'

Alfred lit and shared a silent cigarette with the doomed man. After his briefcase was given back to him, Alfred walked down the street and opened it. The letter was still there! He tore it into tiny pieces and dropped it into a rubbish bin.[18]

Back at Elmo-Werke, Herbert Baum met and became friends with Edith Fraenkel. They spoke often and Herbert invited her to a group meeting. She asked if she could bring along her fiancé, Harry Cühn, who was politically active before 1933 and had been an active anti-fascist since. Herbert was happy for her to bring him along. Edith and Harry had met in 1937 at an ice cream parlour on Olivaer Platz in Charlottenburg called Balsam-Eis. Located just off the stylish shopping street Kurfürstendamm, it was near Harry's flat on Lietzenburger Strasse.[19]

Heinz Joachim, a promising young musician who had a Jewish father and non-Jewish mother, was also assigned to work as a forced labourer in the Elmo-Werke division of Siemens. Heinz was an aspiring jazz musician, playing both the saxophone and clarinet, and had studied the latter at the Jewish Private Music School Holländer in Charlottenburg until it was closed down in 1938. His bedroom closet was packed with jazz records by Benny Goodman and Artie Shaw. Considered the intellectual of the family, according to his brother Manfred, Heinz cut a dashing figure with his jacket and tie, long coat and fedora. Heinz's good friend, Lothar Salinger, lived with his parents at Rosenthaler Strasse 41 in the Hackescher Market neighbourhood of Mitte. Lothar enjoyed photography and had his own darkroom at home; he hoped to become a photo-journalist. He studied photography when possible, and took a course offered by the Jewish community in retouching and colourising.

Heinz met Marianne Prager as she was finishing her training at the Jewish children's home, and they began dating. Unfortunately Marianne was soon dispatched with other Jews as a forced labourer at a farm outside Berlin in Rathenow. In June 1940, Heinz, Lothar and Lothar's then girlfriend went to Rathenow to fetch Marianne and bring her back to Berlin. Upon his return, Lothar had his camera repaired and then spent two days photographing Heinz and Marianne. The result was a jokey and irreverent album; one memorable shot has Heinz wearing women's clothing while Marianne wears a man's suit.[20]

It was around Easter 1940 that Hildegard Loewy graduated from the last remaining Jewish high school in Berlin, which was on Wilsnacker Strasse in Moabit. She was the only girl in a class of ten boys who had trained for the *Abitur* exam, the final test after 12 years of schooling, also used as an entrance exam to university. One of the boys in her class, Ernst Ludwig Ehrlich, describes the graduation: '[it] took place under relatively normal circumstances. A Nazi commissioner, Schulze, arrived and behaved quite correctly. We were welcomed by our Jewish teachers and examined in his presence. And he signed our high school diplomas. My diploma has a swastika stamp under his signature.' Ehrlich also tells us that Hilde had made the best grades of them all and that she was equally good in all subjects. 'She was determined, strong and intelligent,' says Ehrlich, 'and perhaps more mature than we boys.'

A devoted Zionist, Hildegard Loewy had been a member of *Haschomer Hazair*. However, she had lost an arm in a tram accident as a child and wore a prosthesis, so had not been confirmed on Youth *aliyah* in 1938. That dashed all hope that she had of studying medicine at the University of Jerusalem. Georg Israel was the friend and lover of Hilde, and they took the *Abitur* together. She made sure that he had no idea whatsoever of her anti-fascist activities.[21]

In 1940 Charlotte (Lotti) Paech (née Abraham) was working at the Jewish Hospital on Iranische Strasse in Mitte. 'I was an unwanted child,' she told an interviewer. Her mother was in a loveless marriage and wanted nothing to do with Lotti. As a little girl she suffered from rickets and later survived tuberculosis. By the time Lotti was a teenager, the family's connection with Judaism was crumbling, as was the family itself.

Lotti first joined the Jewish youth movement (DJJG) when she was thirteen; she had always been interested in social and political issues and knew Herbert Baum, Marianne and Lothar Cohn and Sala Rosenbaum when they were teenagers. She visited the *Roten Falken* youth movement of the Social Democratic Party, but did not join. Upon graduation from high school, she studied to be a baby nurse at the Jüdisches Säuglingsheim (Jewish Children's Home) in Berlin-Niederschönhausen. Since her mother did not want her at home, Lotti lived in the nurses' quarters from the age of seventeen. Every two weeks she would visit her mother, who was divorced and living alone. After finishing her exams she got a job at the Jewish Hospital and was again able to devote time to politics. She was drawn to the communists, and joined the KPD in 1931. Thereafter she spent her free time studying at the *Marxistischen Arbeiterschule* (Marxist Workers' School).

While marching in the May Day Parade on 1 May 1931, she met the non-Jewish radio technician Gustav Paech, who lived in Wedding. Paech, who had recently been released from prison, worked closely with nurses agitating for the Red Trade Union Opposition (RGO).

Gustav had a miserable childhood and a long criminal record, having served time for fraud, theft and possession of weapons. When they met Paech had given up drinking and was quite a charming fellow. This was Lotti's first relationship; she loved having a man want and pay attention to her. Finally, the love she never had from her family would be hers. But it was not to be. Gustav pressured her, saying 'If you do not stay with me, I will begin drinking again.' She caved in to his demands and married him. It was a loveless marriage, just like that of her parents.

They became comrades in a communist party cell on Badstrasse in Wedding. In late August 1933, a few days after the birth of their daughter Eva, Gustav was arrested in relation to a railway worker strike. He was sentenced to sixteen months in prison, leaving Lotti alone with the baby. She was unemployed and they lived on welfare payments. She also received a few marks here and there from *Rote Hilfe*, the illegal anti-fascist support network.

Upon his release in 1935, Gustav couldn't work for a year due to the brutality of the Gestapo. His personality had changed so drastically that living with him was simply unbearable for Lotti, and he was drinking again. Gustav moved out in 1936 and she was again alone with her daughter. They divorced and Lotti remained in the apartment that was in Gustav's name. She then had Eva registered as a *Volljude* (a full Jew) despite the fact that her father was a gentile and therefore she had the 'elevated' status in Nazi race law of Mischling of the 1st degree. She went back to work as a nurse in the Jewish Hospital. At that time she felt that any political involvement – considering her being a Jew, her husband's arrest and incarceration, and having to care for her daughter – would be completely out of the question for a very long time to come.[22]

One day in 1940 Lotti Paech was making her rounds and recognised a patient from her younger days in the Jewish youth movement. He remembered her also. It was Herbert Baum, who was there for minor surgery due to renal colic. She confided in him, describing her loneliness and how she missed her comrades. After a few conversations, Baum invited her to attend a group meeting.[23]

Richard Holzer, an active anti-fascist, had been in the Baum group for a few months when Herbert became reacquainted with Lotti Paech. A member of the *Schwarzer Haufen*, Holzer had joined the KPD before 1933. *Schwartzer Haufen* was a small group whose members were anarchists influenced by both Marxist theory and the left-wing Jewish subculture from which many of them emerged. The group's name came from a song from the German peasants' uprisings of the 1520s. Richard's brother, Gerhard, who was a dedicated communist, had been sent to the Soviet Union to train for espionage work in Germany. However he was caught by the Gestapo shortly after returning to Germany. Arrested and convicted as a Soviet spy, Gerhard Holzer was executed.[24]

Lotti took some weekend trips to a farm in Kummersdorf with the Baum group and brought her daughter Eva with her. There she met Richard Holzer and they fell in love. Her life was getting better despite the growing threats against the Jews. She saw the worst of the Jewish persecution while at work at the hospital: Jews beaten by the Gestapo or bullet-ridden after being released from a camp, as well as those who had attempted suicide. Additionally, the hospital was looted by the Nazis on several occasions. But the Jewish Hospital became her home, the place she felt most secure. She also came to feel confident about her relationship with Richard Holzer, and shared those feelings with a few close friends, including the lawyer Hilde Benjamin, who was a forced labourer in the confectionery industry, and Edith Brück, who was the head of the Jewish nursery school on Auguststrasse. She confided that she had met Richard in a 'group', but they dismissed this as either 'a provocation or a frivolous gimmick' and they didn't ask her about the group again.[25]

By this time Alfred Eisenstädter had a job at a division of Siemens where he worked at a machine on which powdered metal was compressed. He recalls that the Jews were treated decently. Herbert Baum asked Eisenstädter to tutor Irene Walther (Heinz Birnbaum's non-Jewish girlfriend, see Chapter 10) in Marxist ideology and he visited her regularly to discuss the *Communist Manifesto* and other works. Alfred usually disregarded the 8.00pm curfew but after one meeting he missed the last train. He walked home on a night when Berlin was lit up by a full moon but was not stopped. If he had been caught he could have been sent to a concentration camp.[26]

In October 1940, the father of Rudi Arndt told Ilse Haak (who worked at Elmo-Werke and was an old KJVD comrade of Baum's) that the Gestapo had notified him that his son had died and then sent an urn containing his ashes. Ilse told Herbert about Arndt and he wanted to honour this fallen comrade with a public memorial service. Rudi Arndt, a communist by persuasion and Jew by decree, was arrested in autumn 1933 and sent to Brandenburg prison. Afterwards he was imprisoned in Dachau, Sachsenhausen and finally Buchenwald concentration camp, where he was made Kapo of the Jewish Quarter. He saved the lives of hundreds of Jews by procuring medical supplies with the help of a non-Jewish campmate. After the quarter was dissolved Arndt was made the head of Block #22. He organised a communist cell and meetings were held under his leadership.

Shortly after the war began, a large group of Polish Jews were crammed into Buchenwald. The Nazis wanted to starve them and gave them only half the typical 'hunger ration'. Arndt managed to find more food for them and did what he could to oppose Nazi policy by trying to bring out the best in those confined with him. He encouraged friends to write poetry and compose music, and inspired musicians to form a string quartet to play Mozart, Haydn and Beethoven for the inmates.

On 3 May 1940, however, his activities were discovered. Arndt was called up to the camp gate early and was received by commandant Schobert, who shouted, 'Here comes the king of the Jews!' It was claimed that he had organised the Jews and given them easy jobs. He was stripped of his Kapo rank, beaten and sent to the rock quarry. Interrogation sessions began shortly afterwards, and Arndt realised that he was finished. He feared that in a weakened physical state he might be pushed to give away his secrets, so one day in the late summer of 1940 at around 3.00pm, Rudi Arndt calmly walked past the guards, ignoring the shouts of the SS men. He was dead by the second shot.

The memorial service was held at night in the Jewish cemetery in Weissensee. The compulsory wearing of the yellow Star of David was disregarded. It was significant that the memorial service for a communist Jew was held in a Jewish cemetery, as even though the young people there were far removed from the Jewish community, they chose a religious site to honour Rudi Arndt. Ilse Haak writes, 'We managed to go to the memorial service with as many comrades as possible. I assured his legacy in a short speech, saying that we feel obligated to continue in his footsteps and will work together to reach the goal.' There were eight attendees, including Herbert and Marianne Baum, Heinz Rotholz, Richard Holzer, Lotti Paech and Rudi Arndt's father.[27]

In the autumn of 1940, an eighteen-year-old émigré from Grinsmark, Ellen Lewinsky, received a postcard telling her to report to the National Employment Office in Berlin for a specific work assignment. The card stated the name and address of her future employer, Schubert-Werke, but she had to pick up documentation before reporting there. Her initial reaction was fear; she had no idea what was in store for her. At the employment office she met a young woman, Gerda Marcus, who was also assigned to work at Schubert-Werke. Ellen was comforted by the fact that she was not alone. They struck up a conversation and decided to report to work together. When they did, a foreman looked at their cards and told them, 'OK, girls. You start tomorrow. You'll be working the night shift – that's from 3.00pm until midnight. See you then.'

Schubert-Werke was an aircraft parts factory in the Reinickendorf-Ost section of Berlin. It was a large, flat building with two areas separated by a long walk through the mid-section. About 100 people worked in the two sub-divisions: one for small, intricate parts and the other for creating different types of screws. In the area where Ellen worked, machines were lined up in rows with shelves that served as benches on occasion. When a job ran for a while, one could sit on a shelf until it was finished. The owner of the plant, Schubert, was a high-ranking SS officer who rarely visited his factory. When he did it was with Luftwaffe officials to give them tours of the operation and show off his product line. The Jews did not have much supervision after 5.00pm when there was only one German foreman on duty; the Jewish sub-foremen were in charge during the late shift.

Shortly after Ellen began working at Schubert-Werke, Heinz Birnbaum was assigned there. About a week later Heinz approached Ellen and offered to walk with her after work since they both took the same train home. It was an attractive offer since there were several bars along the way to the train station and she hated walking there alone.

The foreman had started Heinz out on one of the machines but soon realised that he was what he claimed to be – a trained toolmaker who had completed an apprenticeship; he was then made one of the Jewish sub-foremen. Ellen remembers that Heinz seemed different from anyone she had ever known. He was able to relate to everyone, man or woman, no matter their age or political beliefs. He even joked around with one of the Nazi foremen who was a communist troop leader before 1933. At one time the men in the shop voted him the 'Men's Man'. Nobody said anything bad about Birnbaum and many people found him very easy to talk to. He and Ellen became close friends in a short time, travelling to and from work everyday, as well as spending their lunch hours together.

They both lived in Charlottenburg and Ellen would visit Heinz at his flat on Wilmersdorfstrasse before they took the train to work in the afternoon.

Heinz's landladies were a mother and daughter with whom Ellen had taken sewing lessons when she first arrived in Berlin. Before moving there, Heinz had lived with Herbert and Marianne Baum for two years. He had a tiny room with a small bed, a chair, a bookcase and a window. It was so small that one had to enter the room sideways.

There were many 'illegal' books on his bookcase, mostly the writings of Marx, Engels, Lenin and Trotsky. Ellen recalls that amongst Heinz's favourite authors was the Jewish philosopher Martin Buber. Heinz spoke a great deal about communism with Ellen, telling her why he believed in it. He wanted her to know that there was another way to live besides National Socialism. Birnbaum tried to win Ellen over to the communist camp but she remained apolitical. Her philosophy was simple: 'Let's kill Hitler!'

Heinz's job was that of a set-up man, which gave him the freedom to move around the plant whenever he wanted to. He worked directly from the blueprint on the jobs he was responsible for. Heinz would take the blueprint, set up the machine, and tell the workers their individual jobs for the project. He then walked through the rows of machines asking if anyone had a problem or question. If the tool bit didn't cut correctly, Heinz would sharpen it and double-check the dimensions.

In actuality he didn't care about the work. He trusted that Ellen and a few others would commit acts of sabotage. He taught them how to pour sugar into a machine's transmission to make it freeze up; the sugar would melt and was undetectable. A banana could also work wonders. 'Oh, if only we had some nice ripe bananas!' Heinz would say. Ellen's favourite ploy was to change the measurements of a given job and then call Heinz over to tell him they were incorrect. He would say, 'The test piece came out fine. Try it again.' She then knocked the measurements off again and he had to redo so in that way one machine could be idle for up to two hours.

One of the other Jewish sub-foremen, Fred Cassel, was against any kind of sabotage and spoke to Heinz about this on occasion. Cassel was given a letter warning of the consequences of any sabotage in the factory. Birnbaum cautioned Ellen in private: 'Girl, if you want to fool around on your machine, it's all right, but just a little at a time. Remember: not too often, not on the same machine and definitely not on the same job. If it's too much, you get in trouble, I get in trouble and we get absolutely nowhere.'[28]

Since Herbert Baum was trying to help people get out of Germany, different contacts needed to be established for this purpose. One contact was Bernt Engelmann, a young Luftwaffe officer who was deeply involved in anti-fascist resistance and helped whenever possible. One day Engelmann received a postcard written in metaphors telling him about three young men who needed help getting to Spain. The contact was arranged to be at the Hotel Blanche on the Rue Banquier in Paris. Telling the proprietress a password, he was directed to a room on the second floor where he met three young men in their early twenties. He remembers that they were sturdy looking men with a determined air about them. One kept his hand in his pocket at all times which suggested that he was carrying a pistol. Engelmann handed them the special passes.

'You have to fill them out in old German script or with a typewriter, but not a French one. Do you know the script?'

The tall, blond one said, 'We went to school in Berlin until '36 so that's no problem.'

'Do you have uniforms?' the young Luftwaffe officer asked.

'Not yet, but we will…'

Engelmann explained how they should fill out the forms and then told them to go to a small hotel on Rue Othaz in Hendaye on the French-Spanish border. 'When you get there ask the proprietor for Madame Ondarraitz and then say, "Marie la Basquaise from Rouen." She'll take care of the rest.' He then asked if there was an active resistance movement in Berlin. One of them hesitated for a moment and then said, 'Yes, there is. We're a small group because most of the younger Jews left long ago or they're in concentration camps. A few non-Jewish comrades from the Communist Youth League [KJVD] and from the Socialist youth movement [SAJ] are involved and we have contact with a number of groups, but for the most part we're on our own.'

'Do you have weapons?'

He was evasive, 'We confine ourselves to pamphleteering, especially in the factories—' He broke off and looked at his two comrades. The man with his hand in his pocket told him, 'It's important to do something and not just wait to see what the others are going to do – do you see?' Continuing, he said, 'If you ever want to link up with us, ask your Uncle Erich about 'the Baum."

'Uncle Erich' was Erich Elkan, a Jewish Berlin lawyer who lived underground using various guises after the Gestapo got on his trail. He had arranged for 180 young Jewish boys and girls – and 60 more children from an orphanage – to escape to the United States. His first cover was 'Major von Elkan,' a retired Prussian career officer, followed by an actual assignment as a major in the Luftwaffe for a short time. He then reappeared as a

Berlin proletarian, holding down a working class job. Even though his life was in constant danger he worked in the resistance and was even able to help the Baum group.[29]

Near the end of the year 1940, Alfred Eisenstädter learned that the American visas that he and his mother had applied for in 1934 would come through in a few weeks. In order to celebrate his departure, a farewell party was arranged at Sala and Martin's apartment on 31 December 1940. It was a sad occasion. Alfred recalls that, 'Nobody was saying that we would meet again. We all assumed that those who stayed in Germany would not survive the war. That's one thing Herbert always did say. We believed that the Nazis would kill us either for our activities or because we were Jews.'

Sala was very sad Alfred was leaving; she was losing one of her closest friends. She asked him to contact a relative in New York to try to get her and Martin out of Germany. Herbert was very happy for him, saying, 'Good for you. You're getting out!' Herbert told Alfred that he shouldn't do anything for him. Eisenstädter was sure that Baum would have remained in Germany even if he were handed a visa. Alfred felt badly about leaving his friends behind, but there was nothing he could do about it.[30]

15

ANTI-FASCISM TAKES CENTRE STAGE AND TROUBLE BREWING (1941)

In early 1941 Siemens-Halshe-Werke in Berlin demanded 400 female Jewish workers for a special communications project on behalf of a General Fellgeibel. At this time, around 30,000 Jews had been conscripted as forced labourers, approximately 20 per cent of the remaining Jews in Germany. Shortly thereafter all Jews between 15 and 65 who were able to work were conscripted, when on 4 March 1941, general forced labour was formally introduced. This made an additional 73,000 Jews available to work in the important war-related industries.[1]

In the department of Siemens Elmo-Werke where he worked, Heinz Joachim came to know many young people who shared his intense hatred of Nazism, and he formed a resistance cell of around fifteen members. This cell, which later became a part of the Baum group, included Herbert Meyer (husband of Rita Resnik) and Heinz Rotholz. Other young people from different factories either continued their anti-fascist work or joined Joachim's cell at this time. They included Lothar Salinger, Marianne Prager, Hildegard Loewy, Helmut Neumann, Ellen Compart, Ursula Ehrlich, Harry Oschinski, Willi and Gerda May, and Siegbert Rotholz and his wife Lotte.[2]

'If the circumstances were different and they would give me a salary, a living wage, I could enjoy this work,' Helmut Neumann told his friend Ellen Compart. They had first met at Siegbert Rotholz's flat at a meeting back in 1935; Ellen recalls that Helmut was both 'sensitive' and 'physical', and that he was 'very creative ... we all learned improvisational games, but he was truly a master of them.' Ellen and Helmut lived close to each other so they travelled to work together. Helmut's job was that of a transport worker at the Kodak-Rohfilmfabrik (raw film factory) in Köpenick, where he operated a forklift, and Ellen worked at Aceta-Werke, a division of IG Farben. Ellen remembers that Helmut was fascinated by machines and technology. Helmut's father had been arrested by the Gestapo without warning or cause, and it was Helmut – rather than his older brother – who took responsibility for the Neumann family, which included his mother, brother and younger sister, whom he called 'little mouse'. It was important that his family know nothing about his anti-fascist activities and connections, and he made sure that his girlfriend, Erna Dorffmann, did not suspect him of resistance work.[3]

Two other members of Heinz Joachim's cell, Willi and Gerda May, had been introduced to each other by Siegbert Rotholz in 1932. They fell in love on the youth group rambles and married the next year. Mixed marriages such as theirs – Gerda was born a Jew (Gerda Fichtmann) and Willi was a Catholic – were relatively common until the introduction of the Nuremburg Laws in 1935.

Gerda was raised by dedicated communist parents; her father's name appeared on numerous blacklists due to his political work. She was always politically and socially active, which led her to join the KJVD in the late 1920s; it was there that she met Herbert Baum in 1932. Gerda and her comrades often talked with KJVD, *Roten Falken* and Jewish groups, without ever asking their name or the name of their organisation. Even though she was born Jewish, Gerda never belonged to any Jewish youth groups, only communist ones.

Willi, on the other hand, was raised in a middle-class family in Berlin, but he was young and in love, so he moved closer to Gerda's politics and away from his own family. Willi's sister felt that he could have found a 'better catch' – a girl with more money. She would not have minded him marrying a Jewish girl if she was wealthy, but Gerda was no such thing. Around this time, Willi was unemployed for a long spell. He drifted further towards socialism as a result of being unemployed and spending time with Gerda and her friends.

Gerda May maintained a loose connection with Herbert Baum and other anti-fascists during the late 1930s. She met people on rambles with Baum or at his apartment, at the home of Sigi, or her sister's apartment. They always discussed resistance. Siegbert Rotholz gave Gerda leaflets and small stickers backed with glue, which were either distributed or hung on walls. One time Herbert Baum told her to keep all illegal materials out of the apartment so she could give shelter to anti-fascists on the run when needed.[4]

Beginning in 1941, Herbert Baum's communist comrade and friend Werner Steinbrink belonged to what later became known as the Franke-Steinbrink group. This was a significant development in the history of the Baum group. This group also included Hilde Jadamowitz, who was Werner's fiancée, Hans Mannaberg, Joachim Franke and Georg and Charlotte Vötter.[5]

The non-Jewish Hans Mannaberg was born and raised in the Kreuzberg district of Berlin. His father ran a printing business, and after finishing school Hans took an apprenticeship with him. He was involved in the Communist Party of Germany from a young age, when he joined the KJVD. Working in the resistance from 1933, he designed, printed and distributed anti-fascist material whilst working along side Werner Steinbrink and Hilde Jadamowitz. In 1935 he served a four-month sentence in prison for his communist activities. The Gestapo caught up with him again in 1938, when he was sent to Sachsenhausen concentration camp for eighteen months.[6]

Joachim Franke and George Vötter had known each other since the early Nazi years, when they both belonged to the organisation *Internationale Arbeiterhilfe* (International Workers Help, or IAH).[7] George Vötter, a gentile who worked as a typesetter, was born in 1901. As a teenager, he belonged to the *Wandervogel* youth movement and later joined the SAJ. He joined the KPD in 1920. Moving to Berlin in 1925, Vötter held several leading communist party positions after Hitler took power in 1933. In June 1935, however, the Gestapo discovered a branch of IAH and George Vötter was arrested. Tried in court in December, he was found guilty of subversive communist activities and sentenced to five years in Luckau prison in Berlin.[8]

After her husband was arrested, Charlotte Vötter began to hold meetings in her flat. Attending the meetings were Werner Schaumann, his estranged wife Hilde Schaumann, Werner's girlfriend and future wife Elfriede Topp, who rented a room in Charlotte Vötter's apartment, Erich Korvey and Karl Kunger. Hilde left the group for personal reasons and the others joined a schooling circle led by Werner Schaumann. They read classic Marxist-Leninist works, especially Lenin's treatise of 1920, *'Left Wing' Communism: An Infantile Disorder*, as well as daily Nazi newspapers.[9]

Werner Schaumann's father had a business distributing flower and plant seeds. After finishing school, Werner became a trained gardener in order to be ready to run his father's business. He and his father worked together until 1931, when Werner began attending Fredrich-Wilhelm University in

Berlin. At the same time he attended a Marxist school for workers, where he took classes in Marxist philosophy and economic theory. This led to his joining the KPD in 1932. Beginning in 1935, Schaumann held a series of jobs with a Berlin construction firm where he earned steady promotions. His communist political work included volunteering with the KJVD and doing what he could to fight the abuse and falsification of labour legislation under the National Socialist regime.[10]

Werner's comrade Karl Kunger was only able to complete eight years of schooling because his family was poor, and his career consisted of a series of unskilled labour jobs. In 1931 he became involved with the IAH and joined the KPD in 1932. Karl performed different functions for the party, mostly working with George Vötter. One important assignment was to take communists being sought by the Gestapo safely over the border into Czechoslovakia; he did this regularly from 1935 to 1938. Kunger attended schooling sessions in Prague sponsored by either the KPD- or KJVD-in-exile on the Brussels Conference of 1935. He took the 'Trojan Horse' policy to heart: in 1937 he joined a Nazi workers' group at his job at AEG Treptow and organised an anti-fascist cell. He also reached out to French forced labourers who worked there. Kunger and his cell engaged in sabotage as well as the production and distribution of anti-fascist flyers.[11]

Werner Steinbrink and Hildegard Jadamowitz had belonged to a second schooling circle led by Werner Schaumann from 1938 until the summer of 1940. Werner and Hilde became close friends and were a couple while Werner's former girlfriend, Lisa Attenberger, was in prison. They were engaged, but since he was an 'Aryan' and she a 'Mischlinge first grade' (half-Jew), marriage was out of the question. The schooling group began shrinking considerably after September 1939 due to the military draft. This smaller group had included, in addition to Werner and Hilde, Hans Mannaberg, Hilde Schaumann and Charlotte Vötter, amongst others. In July 1940 George Vötter was released from prison and there was fear of having him in the group because it was believed that the regime kept tabs on those who had recently been incarcerated. Thus several people left the Werner Schaumann schooling circle, which had ceased to be by the spring of 1941.

While Vötter was still in jail, his wife Charlotte began associating with Joachim and Erika Franke. Franke then met Werner Steinbrink, Hilde Jadamowitz and Hans Mannaberg in his flat. While others had refused to speak with Vötter, Franke and Steinbrink did not shun him. These talks developed into regular meetings at the apartments of the Vötters, Frankes and Hans Mannaberg.[12]

It was in August 1941 that Marianne Prager and Heinz Joachim married. Her friend Inge Gerson received an invitation and attended the service at the Neue Synagogue on Oranienburger Strasse in Mitte. Marianne's parents did not seem pleased by the whole thing, but the religious ceremony seemed to mollify them. Inge remembers that 'they were so much in love, like there was an aura of happiness around them.' Marianne wore a pretty dress with puffed sleeves and Heinz wore a dark suit. The interior of the hall in the synagogue, recalls Inge, was long and narrow with marble walls.

Afterwards everyone went to the couple's newly-rented furnished flat on Rykestrasse in Prenzlauer Berg, which was near Marianne's parents' apartment on Belforter Strasse. Heinz's father, Alfons, had written a *Tafellied*, a traditional song sung at German-Jewish weddings about the bride and groom set to a popular melody. This one was set to the tune of *Stimmt an mit hellem hohen Klang*, a popular patriotic song from the nineteenth century. Marianne and Heinz sat together beaming on the love seat while their families and guests sang it to them.[13]

It was also during the summer that closer ties were formed with French and Belgian forced labourers at the Siemens Elmo-Werke factory where Herbert Baum and other group members worked. Suzanne Wesse, Felix Heymann's multi-lingual cousin by marriage, acted as translator and liaison between the Baum group and the foreign workers. The foreigners were given information translated by Suzanne, including news about the world beyond Germany. Meetings between the two groups took place in town, and Suzanne, Herbert Baum and Richard Holzer arranged the purchase of French, Belgian and Dutch ID cards. The price was steep at 150 Reichmarks each.[14]

During an afternoon outing, Ursula Ehrlich told Lothar Salinger and Ellen Compart that she had to go home to help her mother prepare for a Jewish holiday. Even though Ursula's family were quite assimilated, they did observe the high holy days. Lothar strongly objected to the practicing of Jewish rituals.

'Hitler made me a Jew,' he asserted, 'and I will remain one as long as anti-Semitism exists. For that time only will I be a Jew – by loyalty, by affinity. But this Jewish god has been thumbing his nose at us. What does it mean to be the 'chosen people'? Does it mean being singled out for special misery?'

This angered Ursula, who said, 'If we let go of our religion we will have nothing. We will feel cast off from the anchor which gives us a place in the scheme of the human family. If I am not a Jew I am nothing.'

'I do not feel cast off,' said Lothar. 'I know who I am and who I want to become – if they let me, that is.'

Ellen took Lothar's side. 'Yes, religion is a security blanket, a crutch. Belonging to a religion or nationality is a false illusion of community. Every man and woman is born alone and dies alone. Pain and feeling cannot be shared. But commitment can be shared. We have the freedom to become involved in the everyday world. That will be our salvation.'

'So we have 'freedom'?' Lothar sneered. 'To freedom condemned, is that what we are?'

After further discussion they compromised. Ellen and Ursula agreed that they had some degree of choice to behave in one way or another.

'That's right,' said Lothar, 'until they kill us very, very dead.'[15]

At this time Gerda and Willi May were being required to provide rooms for foreigners who were brought to Berlin to work in the armaments industry. This was because they had a 'non-Aryan' household, as well as a large three-and-a-half room apartment on Wat Strasse, so the workers were given one and a half rooms of the flat. Gerda had no idea who these people were, but she soon discovered that they felt the same way about fascism as she did. The foreigners worked at Allgemeine Elektricitäts-Gesellschaft (German Electric Company, or AEG works) and told Gerda and Willi about their work and the layout of the plant, which Gerda in turn revealed to Herbert Baum. Two of the men were from Czechoslovakia, and one of them had fought in the International Brigades during the Spanish Civil War. The other was Robert Lüth, a Swiss-German.

Apart from taking in foreign labourers, Gerda also provided illegal forms of hospitality, hiding resistance fighters sent to her by Herbert Baum. She also arranged for others to take in 'illegals' for a night or two, including Hans Krause, who hid people in his flat. He was aided in this activity by his adopted Jewish son Heinz; Hans, a non-Jew, had taken Heinz in during the early Nazi years. Max Kronbosch, a Jewish cobbler, also took in people who needed a place to stay, and helped many Jews by crafting hollow, removable soles for their shoes so they could hide money and other valuables from the Gestapo.[16]

In the wider world, the Nazis were mounting a large scale attack on non-German communists. Operation *Barbarossa*, named after the medieval German leader Frederick Barbarossa, was the invasion of the Soviet Union by Nazi Germany that began on 22 June 1941. Over 4.5 million troops opened up a 2900km eastern front, supported by 600,000 vehicles and 750,000 horses.[17] *Barbarossa* changed the political landscape; since Hitler and Stalin were no longer 'allies,' anti-fascism became the official communist party line once again.

Within a few months of the attack upon the USSR, the Baum group's activities displayed a confidence and perhaps a recklessness that foreshadowed its last action in the spring of 1942. John M. Cox writes that, 'This audacity was inspired by more than simply an implicit duty to defend the Soviet Union; it was also spawned by a combination of hope and misplaced optimism.'[18]

The Baum group members were also spurred into action by further attacks on German Jews. On 15 September 1941 a new police regulation went into effect that required Jews to wear the yellow Star of David with the word '*Jude*' (Jew) printed upon it. Then on 14 October the systematic deportation of German Jews began. Berlin Jews began to be deported on 18 October, their first destination being Lodz (Litzmannstadt) in Poland. Notices detailing deportation dates were sent to Jews' homes with forms to fill out declaring their valuables.[19]

Ellen Lewinsky, the young woman who was a forced labourer at Schubert-Werke (see Chapter 14), recalled that they had a lot of fun with the star. 'We took it off, we pinned it on – then they started pulling on them to make sure you had it sewn on. So then we sewed it on the pocket and made the pocket removable.' Heinz Birnbaum told Ellen that his mother and sister had immigrated to London before the war. She never asked why he didn't go with them. They never discussed Zionism because by 1941 immigration to Palestine was practically impossible.

Ellen and Heinz became very close friends, and she also came to know Irene Walther, Heinz's non-Jewish girlfriend, who was also in the Baum group. Irene would meet Heinz and Ellen on the U-Bahn and travel with them to the last stop. They would walk as far as Heinz's flat on Wilmersdorfer Strasse and then Ellen would continue alone to her apartment. She once had to walk home during an air raid – Irene did not invite her into the shelter. Perhaps she did not want to risk bringing a second Jew in with her, which would have made it more difficult to protect Heinz in the future.[20]

Ellen Compart remembers that Harry Oschinski, a member of Heinz Joachim's cell at Siemens Elmo-Werke, was a colourful character. One time – after the introduction of the yellow star – Ellen and Harry were berated by a uniformed Nazi on the street after they had allegedly scratched his car with their bicycles in traffic. Harry, who was very tall, drew himself up to his full height and became very threatening. The Nazi backed off and left them alone. Harry had a passion for medicine. 'I'm going to be a doctor, a physician, if they let me live long enough,' he said. He studied on his own and worked in Jewish outpatient clinics and hospitals. While working at the Jewish Hospital, he met Charlotte Paech, and the two of them became friends. Ellen spent several weekends with Harry and Lotti at Lake Prendener outside Berlin at a secluded spot where a friend of Harry's had a small cottage in the woods. Ellen recalls that Harry loved life and had more self-confidence than most people. However, once Ellen visited his apartment and saw a different side of him. On his bedroom wall there was a neatly coiled rope hanging on the wall as a decoration. Under it was a sign that read, 'Eat and Drink and be Merry – for Tomorrow it Might Be Time to Die.'[21]

In autumn 1941 a paper called *The Situation* was making the rounds of anti-fascist cells in Berlin. Written from a social democratic viewpoint, it was studied in the Franke-Steinbrink group, and was almost certainly read by Herbert Baum. *The Situation* analysed the power relations between the Axis and Allied nations in international and military terms. It stated that the German leadership had made several decisive errors since September, particularly in respect to British war preparedness and the potential duration of the Eastern Front campaign in the USSR; that the Axis powers had growing conflicting interests, with those countries collaborating with Germany having little support from their people; that war with Russia would end in a German victory but with very heavy losses; and that the United States had entered the war with no domestic geopolitical or economic interests.

The Situation predicted the weakening of the Soviet Union during the war, and discussed a world-revolutionary process that could involve an 'an alliance of intact Russian socialism with the struggling of the German people for its existence under a new socialist leadership.' Concerning the situation in Germany, the paper stated that 'One policy which builds up on the illusions of the insane reactionary circles in Germany, is naturally against the industrial workers and the intelligentsia without the least understanding.' It presented a prophetic warning to the Baum Group: 'a depressing spring 1942 is approaching.'

The Situation concluded:

For clear-sighted Germans there is a final decision to make! To show the world, that the German people is not identical with the tragic farce of fascism. That fascism was an international disaster – and not typical German meanness. That the German people in its best parts are courageous and fearless [and] fights for freedom in the Reich and the world like the other peoples. The German soldier must know, that the propaganda is lying to him, when [it] whispers to him that the Russian people live in misery and had to be freed. All comparisons between the Russian and the German way of life is absurd; comparisons are only possible between the current Russian state and the former. The Christian must know that there is only one possibility, to demonstrate that religion is not the opium of the masses: that is clearly to refrain from the bogus Crusades. And every German patriot must know, that there is only one thing [that must be done in order] to secure the future of the German people: to put an end to mass murder and prove to the world, that the real Germany is still alive and will be shoulder to shoulder with the other peoples [of the world] for the future rights of life.[22]

When not discussing the international situation, the members of the Baum group had more immediate concerns. After they had known each other a while, Heinz Birnbaum asked Ellen Lewinsky to sew buttons on his coat and shirts, mend torn clothing, and do other simple domestic chores; it turned out that he was completely unable to take care of such things. She did it gladly, feeling sorry for the helpless Heinz. He had a hotplate in his room but she never saw him cook anything on it. Ellen 'didn't think the poor thing could boil water.' She cooked extra food and would bring it to his flat or invite him over for a meal. He was easy to please and ate everything she prepared.

They had long discussions about the food they loved but couldn't have. Heinz had an insatiable sweet tooth and enjoyed eating or talking about any form of chocolate. The continuous food shortages helped make Ellen a creative cook. She taught herself how to make cake with non traditional ingredients. Heinz absolutely loved pudding, telling Ellen, 'This girl I know makes the best pudding. She puts eggs in it – do you put eggs in it?' Heinz called everyone he knew 'girl' or 'buddy' either directly or if he referred to someone in conversation.

There were many times that he couldn't get together with Ellen and told her that he was seeing someone without mentioning names; he didn't want to put her at risk by telling her about his resistance work. On one occasion, however, she did meet a friend of his. They went to the Jewish Hospital on Iranische Strasse to visit a co-worker who was a patient there, and Heinz introduced Ellen to Charlotte Paech. 'Lotti's the one who makes the egg pudding,' he confided to her later.[23]

The Baum group began distributed pamphlets again in autumn 1941. The first of these was called *Der Weg zum Sieg* (The Path to Victory) and was subtitled 'Central Committee of the KPD'. Written by official KPD propagandists, this document appealed to readers to join in the anti-fascist 'revolutionary' struggle, employing Marx's famous command to change and not just interpret the world. The text repeated pleas for a revolutionary spirit: 'It is not difficult to be a revolutionary when the revolution has already broken out.'

Production values were poor; the KPD's intent was just to fit as many words on each piece of paper as possible. Cox writes, '*Der Weg* was notable for its failure to recognise, at this late date, the magnitude suffered by the working class after 1933; its analysis and prescriptions assumed a much stronger working class ... than had existed for many years.' The publication had an air of unwarranted optimism about the impending defeat of Hitler's military machine.

> Attention all German workers! The KPD always sounded the warning. Fascism means war. Hitler is Germany's gravedigger. Your fathers, your sons, your brothers, are dying for Hitler ... Germany is one big concentration camp where the death penalty is given for thinking independent thought ... Be aware of the never ending stream of propaganda falsification. Be aware of Gestapo methods. Be aware of human suffering caused by the Nazis. An ocean of blood and tears is left in their wake, and Russia suffers most ... Dehumanised Nazi beasts murder Russian POWs. More and more becomes known about Nazi bestiality in the treatment of Russian soldiers and civilians; cannibals seem like angels in comparison ... Guilty is the Hitler regime, its disciples and everyone who does not work in the anti-fascist resistance, and does not declare in word and deed their dissent. The grim school of Nazi terror through which we all went has hardened us. Our comrades, closest friends, mothers, fathers, and children were victims. We will know no mercy at the moment of truth.

Der Weg zum Sieg also indulged in some parody, claiming that Wehrmacht soldiers had been writing enthusiastic letters home about the glorious 'Soviet Paradise' they had seen first hand. This was a direct satirical response to a booklet published in 1941, called *Soviet Paradise*, of excerpts of letters from German soldiers in the Soviet Union. In the booklet, soldiers described the horrible conditions they found in towns and cities on the Eastern Front. This booklet formed the concept of the massive propaganda exhibition 'Soviet Paradise' that Goebbels and his ministry created in 1942 that was shown to crowds in Paris, Vienna and Berlin.[24]

Another pamphlet, *Der Ausweg* (The Way Out), was published in November and was also distributed by the Baum group. Its authors, who used 'German Anti-fascist Action' as their byline, presented a wittier and more spirited publication than *Der Weg zum Sieg*. Using the popular Nazi word *Untermenschen* (subhuman) against the regime, they referred to the 1933 Reichstag fire as the 'dreadful comedy of the National Socialist *Untermenschen*.' *Der Ausweg* has an 'irreverent spirit,' says Cox, and in 'comparison to other publications of the leftist underground ... provided a stronger and more concrete analysis of the war and the diplomacy amongst the various powers...' *Der Ausweg* presented a scenario in which Hitler and Göring attempted to liquidate Rudolf Hess before his embarrassing journey to Britain in 1941. Additionally, the pamphlet expressed the KPD's traditional viewpoint that Hitler was a tool of German finance capital.[25]

Edith Fraenkel wrote in her diary on 15 November: 'Amongst us Jews is now very much havoc. There are deportation notices and then cancellations being sent out. We have as yet been spared.' Two days later she wrote: 'We were today at the Baums. Herbert reported to me. How is it possible that Herbert is in such good spirits? Should I follow his example or not? Isn't Baum taking the whole matter too lightly? Well, regardless, by all means I must become a littler firmer and tougher!'

Edith Fraenkel raises a good point. What are we to make of Baum's positive attitude in November 1941? Her diary entry is the only surviving contemporary testimony of Baum and gives some insight into his state of mind. Michael Kreutzer sees the development of the Baum group at this time being strongly influenced by 'the escalation of the persecution of the Jews, that measures of the hitherto unimaginable would only be exceeded in time, contrasted with the optimistic, burning desire and willingness to become more active communist-oriented resistance fighters after the attack on the Soviet Union...'[26]

Meanwhile there was a problem brewing that would eventually spell tragedy for the Baum group. It seems that Joachim Franke, anti-fascist and communist comrade, was not at all what he seemed. Gunter Schulz was an anti-fascist who knew Franke very well. At the time he began to associate with Werner Steinbrink and Hilde Jadomowitz, Franke's behaviour was seen as a dangerous breach of conspiratorial rules. His apartment, reports Schulz, which looked like a KPD office before 1933, was where all of his anti-fascist work was conducted. 'The apartment was noisy,' he writes, and Franke's 'neighbour [was] an SS man, who knew that Franke was an anti-fascist.' If that was the case, why did Franke conduct 'all of his anti-fascist work' in his flat? 'Where previously the accordion sounded,' continues Schulz, 'now the typewriter clatters late into the night. Comrades came and went.'[27] What does this tell us about Franke? Why would he place his comrades in such danger?

Gunter Schulz was scared, truly frightened. Franke's comrades were in danger. Didn't Franke realise that, or did he just not care? Schulz set up a meeting with Werner Schaumann and two other comrades to discuss Franke and described his working methods. Schaumann and the others were completely dumbstruck; they all worked with groups that had regular contacts with Franke. Schulz writes that '...we decided, after consultation of different groups, that Franke [in all probability] will be hanged.'[28] But would Schulz, Schaumann and the others be hanged along with him?

Around the time that Gunter Schulz began sharing his grave concerns about Joachim Franke, in November 1941, Robert Uhrig severed all connections to Herbert Baum.[29] Uhrig was a Berlin toolmaker and KPD member, who, beginning in 1940, led one of the largest communist resistance groups in Germany. One of the few groups to receive periodic courier reports from the exiled KPD leadership, the Uhrig group had an extensive network in Berlin factories and residential areas; 80 members of his group were in the German Weapons and Armaments Works AG of Borsigwalde alone. Ulrig also had contacts with other resistance groups in Berlin, such as the Baum group, as well as groups in Hamburg, Mannheim, Leipzig, Essen, Munich, Vienna and the Tyrol.[30]

Their first contact was in 1939 shortly after the outbreak of war when Baum attended a small meeting led by Uhrig. The contact was though Hilde Jadamowitz, and she, Baum, Werner Steinbrink and three others connected to Hilde attended the meeting. A possible reason for Uhrig's break from Baum may have been due to his connection to Karl Kunger and his factory group. Kunger had connections with the Franke-Steinbrink group, to which Hildegard Jadamowitz belonged. Duplicate connections were to be avoided for security measures.[31] Another possible reason for the Uhrig-Baum split was that word got around that any association with Joachim

Franke was political and personal suicide. Werner Steinbrink was one of Herbert Baum's closest friends and comrades. Did he know about the controversy over Joachim Franke?[32]

In December 1941 the Baum group distributed a second edition of *Der Ausweg* created by 'German Anti-fascist Action'. The issue included several letters written by soldiers on the Eastern Front, including one that stated, 'I am ashamed to be a German!' in response to witnessing the abuse and murder of Russian prisoners. Most of the letters quoted in *Der Ausweg* described atrocities against Russian civilians and POWs and the hardships experienced by the soldiers themselves.

> Whatever manoeuvres these criminals engage in we anti-fascists are not duped. Peace with Hitler – never! The Nazis are over the hill … These enemies of humanity must be put on trial. Long live the anti-fascist battle for liberation … Don't believe … that it is better to die on the battlefield than to be taken prisoner … Soldiers, don't harbour illusions. While you are able-bodied they will use you as cannon fodder. But wounded and crippled you are only good for the dung heap … Sentences from letters: 'No warm meals for days … only bread … eating from the emergency rations is punishable by death … the partisans have cut off our transportation lines … we have no water … influenza … typhoid … lice … damn it!' Save Germany! Form anti-fascist cells and circles. Refuse orders, shoot Nazi officers, have no mercy.

The pamphlet also included stories from Germany describing the growing impoverishment of the German population and deepening discontent with Nazi leaders. *Der Ausweg* had a broad-based appeal and featured substantive articles blaming the suffering of Germans on Hitler's domestic and foreign policies. It ridiculed Nazism's obsession with 'Jewish-plutocratic-Bolshevik presumptuousness,' which was the only reference to anti-Semitism. This issue concluded with the popular communist slogan that 'the best Germans' are the 'deadly enemies' of Hitler.[33]

Great care had to be taken during every step of production, duplication and distribution of such anti-fascist materials. In order to do this the Baum group worked in concert with the Franke-Steinbrink and Hans Fruck groups. Both paper and envelopes had to be purchased in small quantities so suspicion would not be aroused, as did stamps; the Gestapo monitored large purchases. Irene Walther and Suzanne Wesse did the typing; their typewriters had to be effectively soundproofed. George Vötter procured the ink, while the material was run off on the duplicating machine in Herbert Baum's basement that Heinz Joachim had acquired.

For mailings within Berlin, names and addresses were taken from the phone book. Some mailings targeted front line soldiers; military addresses were more difficult to gather and group members had to procure them from soldiers' families. George Vötter and a few others were responsible for the mailings. Vötter, Hans Fruck, Hilde Jadamowitz, Karl Kunger, Werner Steinbrink and others donated small amounts of money to help cover costs. Different envelopes and handwriting had to be used, as did different post boxes. Hans Fruck had a motorcycle, which made it a lot easier to drop a few pieces of mail in boxes far from one another. Both mailing and in-person distribution was generally a two-person operation: one person was the look-out while the other mailed or distributed the material. Escape routes were planned in advance. Anti-fascist material was also distributed to workers in armament factories; Karl Kunger worked at AEG and did so regularly.[34]

On 5 December 1941 Charlotte Paech was arrested, having allowed a Dr Loboschin to perform an abortion in her kitchen. The woman's 'Aryan' husband had threatened to divorce her if she did not have the procedure, leaving her other children vulnerable. However, all three of them were denounced and taken into custody. Lotti was not well at this time; she had had an operation a month before, a consequence of her labour intensive work at the Jewish Hospital. After her surgery she needed care, and Baum group members Gerd Meyer and Hanni Lindenberger – who were married a month later – brought her to their small flat on Georgenkirchstrasse in Mitte near the Alexanderplatz. Lotti was not in prison for long, and was free by Christmas. The woman, her children and Dr Laboschin, however, were all deported to a concentration camp.[35]

On 31 December 1941 Gunter Schulz had a meeting with Joachim Franke and Werner Schaumann. Werner 'brought up the errors of his [Franke's] actions, but [that] ended fruitlessly.' Schaumann tried to get Vötter, Steinbrink, Jadamowitz and Mannaberg to 'break away' from Franke, but failed. Schaumann had done everything that he could to shield his comrades. There was nothing else he could do.[36]

16

LIVING ON THE EDGE AND 'SOVIET PARADISE' (1942)

It was February 1942. Herbert Baum sat down one night after work at his kitchen table with an 18-page pamphlet, 'Organise the revolutionary mass struggle against fascism and imperialist war!'

The historic certainty that the fascist military power will be defeated by the Red Army, and soon, is also believed with an ever growing conviction throughout Germany. While in Moscow every threat is posted publicly to enhance the initiative of the Soviet people to the utmost, total terror and the excesses of propaganda suffocate the knowledge of the German people. This is due to fascist fears in the face of the real situation and the political development…

Now Hitler is caught in the millstone of the two-front war. The inevitable victory of the Red Army will make the revolutionary character of the struggles in Europe more visible. In the Red Army, the European working class has the guarantor of their social and national liberation…

The war is lost for German finance capital. It must also lose its power over the German working class – and in no way be allowed to find a political 'solution' with the aid of cowards and opportunists. The imperialist war places the civil war on its agenda. Fascism must fall. With it, its base must be destroyed – capitalism.

As long as the proletariat itself is not the ruling class, it has no other avenue open to anchor the achievements of its political and trade union struggles, short of the consequent revolutionary activity that leads to the elimination of capitalism.…

The army, sacrificed senselessly by Hitler, can be radicalised quickly. Army post addresses can be collected and supplied with material, the kith and kin can be discreetly influenced, and contact with tourists and the wounded is on the increase. The comrades at the front are forming cells, in which they discuss defeats, losses, bad food, inadequate clothing, arrogance of the officers, the SS terror ... promoting defeatism, mass insubordination and switching over to the Soviets and the essential aim of reversing the guns...[1]

It was a 'religious' moment for Baum; it was a sign to carry on his work. Thus he used 'Organise the revolutionary...' as a tool, a framework upon which to base all future resistance work in the Baum group. However there was a problem with that approach which Baum did not consider. The pamphlet was just propaganda, a rallying call to strengthen the resolve of communists in Germany who had been living under the Nazis for nine long years. The first line probably inspired and misled Baum the most, stating that the Red Army would soon defeat Germany. He was grasping at straws, looking for something to motivate him to continue the struggle. Every Jew Baum knew had either emigrated, worked as a force labourer, been sent to a concentration camp or deported to Auschwitz. By early 1942, Baum and the others knew all about Auschwitz and other camps in Poland.

Herbert Baum's character must be taken into account here. He was brave and fearless without a doubt, and, as stated throughout, was charismatic and forceful as a political leader, teacher and friend. But he also had his flaws. He was known to be dogmatic and stubborn and when he got an idea in his head, woe to anyone who disagreed with him or attempted to convince him otherwise. Because of the situation in Germany at the time, there was no central KPD leadership issuing directives to anti-fascist cells. Thus Herbert Baum was a 'freelance' communist and anti-fascist. If there had been party leadership in Germany at the time, however, Baum would likely have followed the party line to the letter with no question. Based upon testimony of several people, Herbert Baum can be reliably categorised as a Stalinist.[2]

Despite the growing strain as more and more Jews were deported, many Baum group members were able to alleviate some of the pressure by regularly hiding their Jewishness, allowing them to feel like 'normal' Germans. Some of them disregarded the 8.00pm curfew by ignoring the compulsory wearing of the Star of David. By taking it off, a Jew could once again use public transportation, enter a restaurant, a telephone booth or any other public place. Ellen Compart turned the avoidance of this law into a fine art. She would always come out of her apartment wearing her star while holding a book or magazine. About a block away she would cover the star with the book, then enter a building and take it off. She could then return to the street a freer woman, although she had to be on the lookout for street or metro checks.

On a Saturday afternoon in early 1942, Hella Hirsch, Sala Kochmann and Ellen removed their stars and went to Zuntz Coffeeshop on Breitenbachplatz in one of the nicer neighbourhoods of Berlin. At the time they still served one cup of hot chocolate without a ration card. It was a pleasant place where the three young women could sit and talk. Ellen remembers the trio on that day, 'we could be described as children of Job, the biblical figure who argued with God. Accepting nothing without protest. Until they put a muzzle and handcuffs on us we would joke, knowing full well that the joke was on us.'

In the coffee shop was a newspaper with the headline, '40 Dead in Calcutta.' Sala reacted to it by saying, 'the distance in miles makes the death of these people irrelevant to us. If it was next door, we would feel with them.' Hella then questioned the value of empathy, 'It's useless unless you effect change or give immediate support. It does not have meaning for the person suffering.' She then quoted a philosopher, 'I carry my own death from the day I am born. It weighs me down. I cannot carry yours as well.'

'In these times we are trying to make ourselves tough and unfeeling,' said Sala. 'But don't try to fool yourselves – or try to fool me. I know your hearts and only too well.' The three young women then agreed that 'we must not be all negating but loving and strong.' And Hella said, 'Yes, and end the evil and injustice ... make sure in whatever small way we can that our idea of a better world is not complete illusion.'[3]

The Baum group also railed against their lot while working as forced labourers. The Jewish departments at Siemens where Herbert Baum and others worked saw repeated acts of sabotage. Ilse Haak organised the sabotage in her area – making armature coils for small motors used in submarines and battleships – but did not meet with Baum and the others outside of the factory.[4]

The workplace was also used to circulate anti-fascist literature. The communist group at AEG Werke-Treptow led by Karl Kunger and Maria Puff distributed handbills that read, 'Work Slow,' 'If we get food we will work,' and 'Down with the war.' These flyers made the rounds at many factories throughout Berlin, both Jewish and non-Jewish. Joachim Franke did similar work at AEG Werke-Oberschönweide. One night Franke, Werner Steinbrink and Artur Illgen went on a slogan painting action, covering the outer walls with 'Hitler step down'. Hans Mannaberg and George Vötter created leaflets that read, 'Hitler leads us into a mass grave' and 'Hunger and Death, Misery and Lies, How Much Longer?' At this time the Baum group intensified their contact with the French, Belgian and Dutch workers at Siemens, even going so far as to teach one of the workers to speak German so they could communicate better.[5]

In the spring of 1942, Herbert Baum and Werner Steinbrink collaborated on an 'Open Letter to the Centre'; it is one of few contemporary documents surviving from the Baum group. Somehow Baum was able to make contact with people who had connections to the central organisation of either the KPD of KJVD, but he never mentioned any names to Steinbrink. Baum explained that these people were of the opinion that a central organisation was not necessary, that it was sufficient to have loosely formed communist groups. According to Steinbrink, the reason for writing the 'Open Letter' was to get clarification on doubts as to whether or not a strong centre was needed or even desired. The letter was last in the possession of Joachim Franke, who was to revise and review it together with Baum and Steinbrink before it was forwarded on.

Michael Kreutzer explains that the handwritten letter opens with a few paragraphs outlining communist policy in Germany from 1933 until 1941. Then the paper bares a striking similarity to 'Organise the revolutionary…', paraphrasing the pamphlet's claims. The transition from imperialist war to civil war and thus a revolutionary situation is explained more pointedly by Baum and Steinbrink: 'by increased activity, by centralising all forces exploiting the favourable situation and prepare for Hitler's defeat in the summer.'

Baum was forceful in his writing: 'Conspiracy can only be associated with revolutionary work. The stronger our resolute revolutionary determination, the better and clearer the assurance of the work.' A very telling phrase is 'We are going on the offensive,' demonstrating the powerful influence 'Organise the revolutionary…' had upon him. It also shows a cockiness in regards to 'Hitler's defeat' which Baum declares will occur 'in the summer,' only a few months away. What evidence did he have, besides the pamphlet, upon which to base such an overly optimistic claim?

Hans Fruck led a communist cell in Berlin and was in contact with Baum around this time; he took issue with his comrade's approach. Fruck writes that after the invasion of the Soviet Union it was accepted that Germany could not win the war, but the timescale was debatable.

> Herbert's group arrived at this position but also expressed that it was imperative to enter into political campaigns and actions directed at the public. So that it would be visible from afar that the German communists were helping the Soviet Union to end the war against the fascists and be victorious … They did not realise at the time that the internal situation for such actions was not yet ripe.

Was Herbert Baum reckless or just deluded?[6]

Two major pamphlets were created by the Baum group in early 1942. One of these was called 'To the Housewife' and was a direct response to an article by Goebbels, published in the Nazi newspaper *Das Reich*. The pamphlet discussed the poor rations available to civilians and soldiers, as well as Nazi propaganda lies. Another brochure called 'To the Medical Profession' was written by Heinz Birnbaum and two others; it was sent to physicians in Berlin and at the front. It was based on Nazi medical publications procured by Hilde Jadamowitz, who worked in a doctor's office. It discussed the high rate of disease at the front, the lack of proper medical supplies and tried to encourage doctors to become part of the anti-fascist resistance.[7]

Several Baum group members took part in a big action in April 1942. The participants included Helmut Neumann, Ellen Compart, Ursula Ehrlich, Lothar Salinger, Hella Hirsch, Felix Heymann, Siegbert and Lotte Rotholz and 'Unke'. Their aim was to cover all of Berlin with the slogan 'No to Hitler's Suicidal Politics! No! No! No!' Unke pointed to a section of town on a map. Then he said, 'If there is enough time to spell out the sentence then do so. If not then just write, 'No! No! No!' Paint on everything in reach. Use whatever paint, chalk, grease pencil you can get a hold of. Anything that will make a line or form a letter. We want Berlin covered in one night!'

Helmut Neumann always make a joke in even the most dangerous situations – and this was one of them. He said: 'We must appear harmless. Go as a couple and if anyone walks by, take cover – or just disappear into the nearest building or just leave. Put your paint can under the girl's coat and then hug and kiss – moan loud – make it look and sound real. Anyone need to rehearse?'

Ways to avoid capture were discussed. The group was told to wear dark clothing and to work in pairs: one would paint while the other acted as lookout. The city was blacked out which helped cover the action. 'Ede', a friend of Unke, went with his girlfriend. All together there were ten of them; none of whom were caught.

The next day the slogans were everywhere and homeowners, business-men and street cleaners were busy cleaning up the mess. The action greatly angered the Nazi authorities. People either shook their heads or smiled when they saw the group's work. Helmut's suggestion ('make it look real') worked. One couple announced their engagement the next day.

The group had a meeting to discuss the effect of the action; they were elated.

'How much good did it do?' asked Willi May. The group agreed that sowing discontent and protest would have an effect. 'It's impact and value cannot be measured but every show of defiance brings us a step closer,' said Ellen Compart.[8]

Joachim Franke received two visitors in early May: Gunter Schulz and his wife. According to Gunter they went to him because 'he had still not returned to me a volume of Lenin, and I wanted absolutely nothing from us in his apartment. He made on us a frightening, even dangerous impression. He nonchalantly told us that he still received comrades in his apartment.'

'Franke, what about your conscience?' said Schulz. He could barely keep his temper in check. 'Even if you don't give a damn about what happens to you, what about the comrades? What about Kunger?'

Sitting there looking at Schulz with a calm expression on his face, Franke lit a cigarette and took a deep puff. Schulz was incredulous; he just couldn't believe that Franke was so noncommittal. He was worried about Karl Kunger, who trusted and worked very closely with Franke. Schulz scooped up his Lenin volume, glared at Franke, and stormed out with his wife. That was the last time Gunter saw Joachim Franke.[10]

The Baum group needed money; their situation was dangerous and they needed to purchase French and Belgian worker ID cards and to be able to live underground without having to be reliant on income from employ-ment, which would be hard to find. They came up with a plan to approach wealthy Jews who were going to be deported, and request that they sell some of their belongings to support destitute Jews. The property would end up in the hands of the Nazis anyway. These requests, however, fell on deaf ears, so they decided to help themselves.[11]

An 'expropriation action' was conceived by Baum, Heinz Birnbaum, Richard Holzer and Werner Steinbrink. They decided to play the roles of

Gestapo officers, enter the apartment of a wealthy Jewish family and confiscate their possessions, then sell them on. They picked a family in Charlottenburg through a Jewish comrade Baum knew in the 1930s; she had lived with her mother as lodgers of the Freundlich family at Lietzenburger Strasse 43.

It was in Baum's apartment on 6 May that Baum, Holzer and Birnbaum had a serious discussion in which they planned how the 'expropriate action' would go down. Afterwards they all went to Joachim Franke's flat and waited for Werner Steinbrink to arrive. Werner was told about 'an important matter' that would occur the following day. Given instructions on how to dress, he was asked to arrive at Baum's between 5:30 and 5.45am.

The two 'Gestapo' men – Steinbrink and Birnbaum – arrived early the next morning and were impeccably attired: Heinz sported a light summer jacket and hat while Werner was nattily dressed with sunglasses for added effect. They both wore light brown leather gloves. Baum gave Heinz a briefcase containing a folder with writing paper and the official seal of a Nazi financial authority. In tense whispers, Herbert, Heinz and Richard briefed Werner on the details of the action. The four men then left Baum's apartment building at Stralauer Strasse 3/6 and took the S-Bahn to the Bahnhof Zoo station in Charlottenburg and walked to Lietzenburger Strasse 43.

Rosetta Freundlich and her daughter Margarete were fast asleep at 6.30am when they were awakened by a loud knocking and ringing at the door. Upon opening the door Rosetta was greeted by Birnbaum saying, 'Gestapo!' He asked about the residents and demanded to see their identification cards. Then the 'Gestapo' men inspected the apartment with Heinz leading the way as the 'senior' officer. Birnbaum asked about valuables, specifically paintings by Liebermann and Defregger, which were owned by the Freundliches but were not in the apartment at the time. Heinz and Werner spoke quietly about the objects that they had gathered together and decided upon which ones to take. Steinbrink jotted down a list on a piece of paper: an oil painting, a typewriter, two cameras and an opera glass. The 'Gestapo' demanded to see the contents of a large bag. It contained 14 small carpets, which Werner added to the list.

After an attempt to find another painting at an apartment of another Jewish family in the nearby Kaiserallee failed, Birnbaum returned to Lietzenburger Strasse 43 and told the Freundliches to expect a return visit. The following day Birnbaum and Steinbrink removed the goods, carrying them outside to where Herbert Baum and Richard Holzer were waiting. They took the carpets to Harry Cühn's room in the Pension Lau on Lietzenburger Strasse, just down the street from the Freundlich family. The four men then got a taxi and travelled back to Baum's apartment in Friedrichshain, where they stored the 'expropriated' goods in the basement. They went up to Herbert's apartment briefly, where they reassured each other that the action went smoothly. Then Baum and Steinbrink rushed off to work.[12]

Harry Cühn reports that the painting from the heist 'went to a sympathiser, an art dealer, Ludwig Wisnet, in the Uhlandstrasse.' He had an antique shop and the artwork was stored in his cellar. Wisnet then brought the rolled up painting to Harry late one evening. 'Herbert [Baum] came with his bike,' says Cühn, 'and rode to a glazier in Mitte to whom he gave the picture for framing.'[13]

On 13 May the news of the 'expropriation' appeared in the Berlin papers: 'Three Bogus Detectives – Insolent Swindle in Charlottenburg Flat' and 'Bandits Play as Fake Detectives. They "confiscate" 20,000 Marks Worth of Valuables.' The reports contained descriptions of the suspects and the stolen valuables, specifically the oil painting, 'Landscape with Fishing Village' by Heffner. The next day it was reported in the *Völkischer Beobachter*, the leading Nazi party newspaper.

Harry Cühn went to the ice cream parlour on the Olivaer Platz and sat with a group of acquaintances. Amongst them was a Greek who had his nose buried in the pages of the *Völkischer Beobachter*. Noticing Harry, he put down the paper.

'Listen,' said the Greek to Harry, 'did you read the headline?'

'No,' said Harry. 'Why?'

The Greek pointed at the newspaper. 'Well, here. Lietzenburger Strasse. Bogus Gestapo in the Lietzenburger Strasse. And oddly enough, they took a painting that you had offered me for sale!'[14]

On 9 April 1942, the opening of an expansive anti-communist propaganda exhibition called 'Soviet Paradise' had been announced in *Völkischer Beobachter*. It was to be presented in the Lustgarten, a large park next to the cathedral on the main boulevard of Unter den Linden. The purpose of 'Soviet Paradise' was to expose Soviet deficiencies and the horrible conditions of life under communism. It was probably more than coincidental that it opened when the war with the Soviet Union was taking a turn for the worse. It was also likely motivated by a desire to draw attention away from food shortages, air raids and other hardships.[15]

The official opening of 'Soviet Paradise' took place on 8 May to a crowd of 20,000. With great fanfare a captured Soviet KV-2 self propelled gun was driven throughout the city and parked at the entrance of the exhibition, which was housed in 9000 square feet of tents. High-ranking Nazis and representatives of Italy and Spain were invited to the opening and there was even a postage stamp issued to commemorate the event. A total of 250,000 people visited the show during the first week.

The basic concept of 'Soviet Paradise' was, according to one Nazi newspaper, to show that Bolsheviks, communists, socialists, Jews and the Devil were one and the same, out to conquer the world and destroy the racial superiority and uniqueness of the German people. There was a model of the Byelorussian city of Minsk, as well as a 'Farm Hut,' a makeshift structure made of mud and straw. Photographs of SS men posing as Russian citizens and soldiers were displayed, the Russians depicted as little more than primitive brutes.

All anti-fascists in Berlin saw 'Soviet Paradise' as a slap in the face. The 'Red Orchestra' resistance group hung a flyer at the exhibit that read, 'Nazi Paradise. War, Hunger, Lies, Gestapo. How much longer?' Countermeasures had to be taken, but what could be done? Jews were not allowed to visit the exhibition but five Baum group members removed their yellow stars and saw it for themselves; five non-Jewish comrades also attended. Amongst the attendees were Charlotte Paech, Richard Holzer, Herbert Baum, Martin Kochmann, Suzanne Wesse and Rita Meyer. [16]

The exhibition had an accompanying brochure: 'Everything that had been said about Bolshevism before the outbreak of the war with the Soviet Union has been thrown in the shadows by reality … Words and pictures are not enough to make the tragedy of the Bolshevist reality believable to Europeans.'

Attendees entered the exhibition past the captured Soviet KV-2. They probably waited in a long line, as Goebbels' propaganda shows were always very popular. The first thing one saw – and smelled – upon entering was a large, fresh dung heap. Next was the 'Farmer's House' a dismal representation of life in the Soviet Union. Window panes were smudged with grime or missing altogether, and the wallpaper was dingy, poorly applied and torn. Chairs were rickety or broken, the table functional but messy and the oil cloth flooring was stained and cracked. The two small beds had rusted frames and dirty blankets, pillows and linen. A wooden bulletin board standing on two legs had a few torn propaganda pictures upon it. There was dust and soot everywhere.

There were panels illustrating the Bolshevik revolution of 1917, the November Revolution of 1918 in Germany and the revolution of 1919 in Hungary. The panels depicted many anti-Semitic caricatures; the Hungarian panel showed a Jew holding a gun, looking over his shoulder, with a dead Christian woman below him. In the German panel, a white-bearded Karl Liebknecht and a buxom Rosa Luxembourg were shown facing outward, their arms entwined, with him holding a hammer and she a sickle, the symbols of the Soviet Union.

Next to these was a large panel devoted to 'Marx-Mordochai' (Karl Marx), depicted holding his book *Capital*, resting his foot upon a city in flames. In Marx's shadow were caricatures of several well-known Jewish socialists. The brochure explained, 'The inventor of Marxism was the Jew Marx-Mordochai ... the present Soviet state is nothing other than the realisation of that Jewish invention ... The Jews exterminated the best elements of the East to make themselves the absolute rulers of an area from which they hoped to establish work domination.'

Another part of the show presented shabby, crumbling homes with huge, seemingly luxurious buildings behind them. The pamphlet declared that the 'prestige buildings' were 'built only for propaganda.' 'Model streets in the American style are filled with huge buildings with a thousand deficiencies, which mock the miserable workers beneath who are forced even after 25 years of Bolshevist culture to live grey and joyless lives.'[17]

The Baum group tried to decide what would be an appropriate response to 'Soviet Paradise'. Even before any of the members had seen the exhibit for themselves, a meeting was held at Herbert's apartment, attended by the Baums, the Kochmanns, Suzanne Wesse, Gerhard Meyer, Heinz Joachim and Irene Walther. At that point it was decided to distribute leaflets to visitors at the exhibition, but this fell by the wayside after Baum, Steinbrink and Franke attended 'Soviet Paradise'. It was then that Baum announced to his inner circle that there would be no leaflet campaign; they would plan an arson attack instead. The later interrogation reports reveal conflicting accounts as to whose idea it was to implement the arson attack, but it seems that either Baum or Franke came up with it on their own or discussed and decided upon it together.[18]

Martin Kochmann was Baum's oldest friend from school. He respected and loved his friend Herbert, but he did not agree with the plan. But Martin was a friendly, outgoing fellow and it was not in his nature to be disagreeable, so he kept his mouth shut. Sala Kochmann was much more politically astute and charismatic that her good-natured husband, and was a leading figure of the group. It was Sala who was looked up to by the younger group members, who would ask her opinion or share an idea with her. Martin was in Herbert Baum's 'inner circle', but his role was to provide support and encouragement to Herbert and Sala – who supported the plan – not to contradict them. Martin never told Herbert how he really felt about the planned arson attack; he justified it in his own mind that it was a continuation of their illegal work, but at a higher risk level. But he would not participate in its implementation.[19]

Richard Holzer was similarly horrified by the plan. He was a year older than Baum and was not under his influence like the younger members. He respected and understood Herbert's motives, but was not afraid to disagree strongly with him. Holzer felt that such an action would have terrible consequences for all Jews and anti-fascists in Berlin, that only a bloodbath could result from such an attack on the establishment. Felix Heymann was also against the attack, possibly as the result of an argument put forth by Holzer at a meeting.[20]

In contrast Heinz Birnbaum supported the proposed arson. A protégé of Baum since first meeting him in 1933, Heinz was a convinced and dedicated communist; he was thoroughly under Baum's spell. He also lived with Herbert and Marianne for two years (1938–1940), which probably made his devotion to Baum and the communist cause even stronger. The non-Jews in the Baum group and those connected to them – Irene Walther, Suzanne Wesse, Joachim Franke and Werner Steinbrink – also supported the attack. Franke and Steinbrink were involved in the initial planning with Baum, while Irene Walther was Heinz Birnbaum's lover, who was a strong supporter of the action. Suzanne Wesse and Sala Kochmann were best friends, which may explain Suzanne's support of the attack.

Late one night at Schubert-Werke Ellen Lewinsky noticed that Heinz Birnbaum had started making a device she had never seen before. This made her curious because all they every worked on were large quantities of a given part. A few nights later she found the courage to ask him about it. 'Are you making something for a friend?' He cautiously replied, 'Yeah, a friend...' After work they got on an empty metro car and Heinz whispered to Ellen, 'You know that exhibit at the Lustgarten, the one against Russia?' She nodded her head. 'There's a group that's going to blow up the exhibit to show that they are against that kind of propaganda. What they show is a lie; that's not how it is in the Soviet Union.' He told her that the group was planning to escape to France after the attack and asked if she wanted to join them. She accepted his invitation and later they had photos taken for false French passports. 'Look, you got to give me a hand; we've got to get stuff out of there [Schubert]. Will you help me?' She said that she would.

What Ellen had seen Heinz making was a detonator with a firing pin, working from a small blueprint. The next night Heinz gave Ellen the detonator and she put it in her bra. When she left the plant, she opened her coat as usual and the guard waved her out. After boarding the metro together, she gave it to Heinz who hastily stuffed it into his coat pocket. Ellen had a good feeling about what she had done, for she strongly believed that it was her duty to engage in any activity that would hurt the regime. She never considered refusing Heinz's request for help.

The success with the detonator did not mean all of the necessary elements for the bomb were acquired. Heinz had to get a long wire out of Schubert and asked Ellen who she thought he could trust. She chose a young man in her work area who Heinz took aside and asked for help, telling him the wire was for a light fixture in his apartment. The young man agreed.

There was a locked room at Schubert filled with baskets of fresh apples. Nobody knew why the apples were there, but a few people, including Heinz, could force open the lock to get a snack. Heinz opened the apple room and brought his unwitting collaborator in with him. He closed the door, turned on the light, and made him take off his jacket, shirt and undershirt. Heinz then wrapped the wire around the young man's abdomen, across his back and around his shoulders. It was taut enough to avoid detection when dressed and loose enough for relatively comfortable movement. Heinz then helped him get dressed. After passing the guard at the end of their shift, they entered an empty S-Bahn car where Heinz removed the man's top clothes and spun him like a top to remove the wire.[21] The Baum group was a step closer to their goal.

17

ARSON, ARRESTS AND REPRISALS (1942)

'I had already emerged as taking a position against the plan of the attempted attack,' wrote Richard Holzer, 'because it was clear that this action – even if it were to be successful – would have resulted in severe reprisals against Jews and anti-fascists … when I heard the final plan I again strongly advised against it. It came to a confrontation between Baum and myself, one that could clearly be seen as hostile. The influence of Herbert Baum, however, was much stronger than mine and the execution of the plan had been decided. I took no part in the attack.'[1]

Werner Steinbrink and Joachim Franke had been working on the technical preparation of the attack before most of the Baum group even knew of the plan. Finding a manual for the production of gunpowder in the city library, Werner brought it to Joachim's apartment. He managed to make the gunpowder with saltpetre, sulphur and charcoal – as well as a solution of carbon disulphide and phosphorus – at the Kaiser Wilhelm Institute where he worked as a technician. Back at Franke's flat both men were convinced of the incendiary properties of the chemicals. Franke had been working on a way to replicate a spark based on British incendiary bombs, and he built a simple detonator with cardboard and a torch battery.[2] Heinz Birnbaum's contribution was the detonator he had made and the long wire stolen from Schubert-Werke.[3]

Steinbrink visited 'Soviet Paradise' again and walked around the exhibits in order to select a suitable target for the arson attack. He decided that the *Speisehaus* (literally 'eating house') in the 'Soviet Village' was the best location. A few days later Franke and Steinbrink met and went over all the details.

Then Werner met with Herbert Baum and briefed him about the discussion. Steinbrink told Hans Mannaberg and Hilde Jadamowitz that they should take part in order to cover up 'any action'. Neither of them knew the true nature of what was to transpire; they both assumed they would be leafleting the exhibition as had been discussed at previous meetings.[4]

The last Baum group meeting took place on the planned day of the attack, Sunday, 17 May 1942, at the flat of Martin and Sala Kochmann on Gipsstrasse 3 in Mitte. Heinz Rotholz, Irene Walther, Heinz Joachim, Richard Holzer, the Kochmanns, Herbert Baum and possibly others were there to discuss the plan. Holzer's sole purpose in attending the meeting, however, was to attempt to dissuade Baum from carrying out the action. When Baum told those assembled the planned attack devised by Franke, Steinbrink and himself, Holzer was quick to speak up.

'Herbert,' said Holzer, 'You simply cannot go through with this plan. It is just too dangerous. Nothing good can come of it. All it will do is bring terrible reprisals against Jews and anti-fascists. Think about it. How will the Nazis respond to such an affront, especially if they find out that Jews were involved?'

Baum was incensed by Richard's remarks. It led to an exchange between the two men that escalated from a heated argument into a shouting match, but Holzer was not able to sway Baum from his position. In his anger Herbert threw Richard out of the group. The wheels were set in motion; nothing would prevent Herbert Baum from going through with his plan. Shortly thereafter Joachim Franke arrived and met some of the others who would be taking part in the action. Critically for what was to come, he learned their first names.

At 4.00pm members of the Baum group and the Franke-Steinbrink group broke up into smaller assemblages and met at the Soviet KV-2 self-propelled gun that sat at the entrance to 'Soviet Paradise'. Herbert and Marianne Baum, Sala Kochmann, Gerd Meyer, Heinz Joachim, Suzanne Wesse and Irene Walter represented the Baum group. The Franke-Steinbrink group participants were Joachim Franke, Werner Steinbrink, Hildegarde Jadamowitz, Hans Mannaberg and Walter Bernecker.

Steinbrink arrived before Franke, who was accompanied by his wife, Erika, and Walter Bernecker. Mannaberg purchased too many entrance tickets at the cashier and had to sell the extras to patrons waiting in line. Franke passed two fire platelets to Steinbrink. There was a huge throng of visitors that day and the groups were separated; Steinbrink found himself running back and forth between them. Dismayed by the mass of people in the exhibition hall, Herbert Baum decided to postpone the action, and Franke agreed. They would return the next evening at 8.00pm. [5]

On 18 May the group members once again met at the exhibition; it was a cool 10 degrees Celsius and a slight breeze dispersed the fragrant aroma of the linden trees on the Unter den Linden as they arrived at the KV-2.[6] Everyone from the previous day was there with the exception of Erika Franke. Her husband, Joachim, had the incendiary devices in a briefcase, while Werner Steinbrink had the two fire platelets in the breast pocket of his jacket. Shortly after arriving in the exhibition hall, he surreptitiously handed one of them to Herbert Baum.

Baum, Steinbrink and Franke headed directly towards the *Speisehaus* that Werner had earmarked for the action, but found it to be closed to the public. Scrambling for a different location, Franke and Steinbrink happened upon an exhibit – the 'Farmer's House' – in which there was a bed. Before Werner knew what was happening, however, Franke had placed an incendiary device, smashing the glass tubes and thus setting the firing mechanism in motion. At around this time, in the 'Farmer's House,' Jadamowitz and Mannaberg both noticed that Herbert Baum was adjusting a pillow on the bed.

Then things started to go seriously wrong. Franke told Steinbrink that his briefcase was on fire. All twelve activists started to leave the exhibition hall, either on their own initiative or because they were told to do so by Herbert Baum. Steinbrink took the fire platelet from his breast pocket and tossed it into a gully. Then Herbert Baum noticed that his hand was getting hot. Looking down, he saw that the fire platelet had started to burn and that his jacket was singed. He threw it away and hurriedly left the building. By carelessly discarding their explosive materials without a second thought, they left valuable evidence for the Gestapo.

Finding each other on the way out, Hildegarde Jadamowitz and Marianne Baum left the exhibition hall together and looked around outside for Herbert, but he was nowhere to be found. Hans Mannaberg then joined the two women outside. He told them that he had not seen Herbert either. Hilde and Hans had previously made plans with Werner to go to his mother's flat for a late Mother's Day visit, so they left while Marianne continued to look for her husband. Werner arrived at his mother's after Hilde and Hans had been there for a while.

The three left Werner's mother at around 11.00pm and headed toward the Baums' apartment on Stralauer Strasse in Friedrichshain. It was on the way there that Hilde and Hans asked for details about the action at 'Soviet

Paradise'. When told about the firebombs, both were outraged that they were not properly informed about it beforehand. It was the possibility of injuring or killing visitors that upset Hilde. Werner reassured her that according to his calculations the devices were in no way powerful enough to risk lives.

Joachim Franke took his time leaving the Lustgarten area. In fact, he sat on a bench enjoying a cigarette in front of the exhibition to soak up the aftermath. Visitors poured out of the entrance after the fire brigade and a large contingency of police arrived on the scene. Franke heard several visitors comment that 'it was next to nothing'. After that, he made his way to the Börse train station.[7] Eleven people were taken to the hospital with superficial wounds. The Nazis prevented the media from reporting the attack, but news of it soon began to spread around Berlin. The Gestapo saw to it that the damage was repaired immediately and 'Soviet Paradise' opened the next day as scheduled.[8]

Propaganda minister Goebbels wrote about the attack in his diary:

Late in the evening I was told that a fire, probably the result of sabotage, broke out at the anti-Soviet exhibit. It can be extinguished in a timely manner. One notes again that in our big cities a communist opposition, small but still not to be ignored, has established itself. At the moment it obviously poses no danger to us, but one would do well to observe this development very closely.[9]

No group meetings were planned for the week following the 'Soviet Paradise' action. Since Baum and the others assumed that no one had seen them enter or leave the exhibit, they continued going to work as if nothing had happened. They needed what little money their jobs paid in order to survive.

The following day, 19 May 1942, a secret report was received by the security police:

Acts of sabotage against the anti-Bolshevist exhibition 'Soviet Paradise' in Berlin. At about 8.00pm on 18 May 1942, as yet unidentified perpetrators attempted to set fire to the exhibition. A wad of cotton soaked in phosphorus and placed on a wooden post covered with cloth was set aflame at the site of the first fire. An incendiary device with two bottles of phosphorous carbon disulphide exploded in the Farmer's House. Eleven people were injured. A sabotage committee of the State Police office in Berlin has begun necessary investigations without delay.[10]

Four days after the 'Soviet Paradise' action, on 22 May, the Gestapo went to Department 131 of Siemens Elmo-Werke and arrested Herbert and Marianne Baum, Gerhard Meyer and Heinz Rotholz. Their arrests were witnessed by Ilse Haak.[11] Heinz Joachim, who worked in a different department at Siemens Elmo-Werke, heard about the arrests and spoke about them to Irene Walther and Suzanne Wesse later that day.[12]

The same day saw the arrest of Werner Steinbrink at the Kaiser Wilhelm Institute where he worked, as well as that of Joachim Franke at his job at AEG Werke-Oberschönweide. Karl Kunger, George Vötter, Charlotte Vötter, Erika Franke, Hildegard Jadamowitz and Hans Mannaberg – all members or comrades of the Franke-Steinbrink group – were also arrested either on 22 May or a few days later. Work colleagues of Joachim Franke – those who contributed money to the cause as well as participant Walter Bernecker and anti-fascist Artur Illgen, who participated in the 'Hitler step down' painting action of January 1942 – were also arrested.[13] On 23 May the Gestapo came for Sala Kochmann at the Jewish Kindergarten on Jerusalemer Strasse, and Irene Walther and Suzanne Wesse were also arrested.[14] Suzanne was taken from her apartment along with her husband, Richard Wesse; after three weeks, however, Richard was released from prison.[15]

Jacob Berger was the Kochmanns' lodger at Gipsstrasse 3, a building which also housed a Jewish children's school. After hearing of Sala's arrest, Berger told Mrs Debra Bahnmüller, the director of the school, and a Jew married to an 'Aryan' who also lived in the same building, about the arrest.[16] Bahnmüller immediately called Martin Kochmann at his job and told him that he should not come home,[17] that his wife was 'ill' and that he should go directly to a specific address on Auguststrasse.[18] Arriving at Auguststrasse, Kochmann found Bahnmüller and Berger waiting for him. Martin asked Jacob to get clothing, food and money from his flat. He also asked him to burn a box of books by 'illegal' authors. Berger agreed and went back to the flat, returning a short time later with Kochmann's belongings.[19] He also gave Martin 350 Reichmarks. The books were burned the following day.[20]

Rushing over to Charlotte Paech's flat on Zechliner Strasse, Martin informed her and Richard Holzer of the arrests. She in turn told Heinz Birnbaum. It is not known, however, who told Felix Heymann, but he found out through some means.[21] Heinz and Felix immediately went underground.

On 24 May, six days after the counter-propaganda attack, it is clear from Goebbels' diary that the Gestapo had discovered more about those who took part in the sabotage.

We have now discovered a club of saboteurs and assassins in Berlin. Amongst them are [those] who undertook the bombing of the anti-Soviet exhibit. Significantly, amongst those arrested are five Jews, three half-Jews and four Aryans. An engineer at Siemens [Herbert Baum] is even amongst them. The bombs were manufactured partly at the Kaiser Wilhelm Institute.[22]

At around midnight on 24 May, Martin Kochmann, Charlotte Paech, Richard Holzer, Heinz Birnbaum, Felix Heymann and Heinz Joachim met at Alexanderplatz in Mitte. During what could be considered the only post-arson Baum group meeting, the six activists discussed what they should do next, tension and cigarette smoke filling the air.[23] They stood beneath the Berolina statue, damaged and covered with scaffolding.[24]

They were worried about the evidence that was sitting in the cellar of Herbert Baum's apartment building: the duplicating machine, paper, ink and other equipment of their illegal work.[25] Felix mentioned a pistol, which he had been given by Alfred Eisenstädter in 1941 before he left for America.[26] Heinz knew that there were the small carpets from the Lietzenburger Strasse 'expropriation action' of 7 May in the basement; they could help raise money to cover some of the cost of living underground. They arranged a time and place to meet in order to deal with the items, both illegal and profitable.

At 11.00pm on 25 May, Kochmann, Heymann and Birnbaum met at the corner of Spindlerstrasse and Neue Friedrichstrasse. Under cover of the blackout, they silently walked to Baum's block of flats at Straulauer Strasse 3/6. Prepared with tools to jimmy open the cellar door, they were surprised to find it unlocked. The three men went downstairs and began to clear the cellar of incriminating material and valuables.[27] They packed everything in sacks, then carried it to the Waisen bridge on Rolandufer.[28]

Waiting for them at the bridge were Richard Holzer, Heinz Joachim and Hella Hirsch. The carpets were stuffed into three suitcases and given to Heymann, Kochmann and Birnbaum. Additionally, a wad of 1000 Reichmarks was split between Felix and Richard, and Holzer took custody of a few hundred cigarettes. After splitting up the valuables, they dumped the duplicator, paper, flyers and the pistol into the murky Spree river, throwing them into the water at different points at the foot of the bridge's stairway.[29]

The next day, 26 May, Felix Heymann visited his old friend Heinz Overbeck. They had become friends when the two men worked together, and at the time Heinz had told Felix that he believed in communism and had nothing whatsoever against Jews. Felix felt he could trust Heinz, and carrying a suitcase stuffed with the small carpets, Felix confessed to Heinz that he was fleeing from the police for political problems and begged him to hold onto the contents of the suitcase. Overbeck agreed at first, but had second thoughts when Heymann left. He was worried about keeping Jewish possessions and so passed them on to a Jewess named Gertrude Schmidt.[30]

Martin Kochmann, who was now homeless, took his suitcase, containing more of the carpets, to the luggage storage area of the Gesundbrunner train station in Wedding. The next day, he travelled to Spandau in outer Berlin and went to the aircraft manufacturing factory. He purchased a Belgian identity card in the name 'Alfons Buys' for 150 Reichmarks from a contact made through Suzanne Wesse. Then he returned to central Berlin to meet with Heinz Joachim and Heinz Birnbaum. Martin told them of the desperate plan he had hatched: to escape to Belgium via bicycle with his new ID. Later that day he went to Charlotte Paech's flat on Zechliner Strasse and told Richard Holzer his plan, asking Richard (Charlotte's lover) for his bicycle.[31]

Heinz Birnbaum was being sheltered by Harry Cühn at this time; Harry called him 'Buber' because the Jewish philosopher Martin Buber was one of Birnbaum's favourite authors. 'Buber' took his share of the 'expropriated' carpets to Cühn's room in the Pension Lau on Lietzenburger Strasse, the same street from where they had been stolen on 7 May. Cühn was an organiser, one who could make deals with the most unsavoury people if necessary; at this time he was receiving goods from Paris – hairstyling products, perfume, hair tonics etc. – and selling them on. Harry sent three people to different hair salons around Berlin to sell the products, including Birnbaum. The proprietors were happy to buy the items at any price and Heinz and the others were paid for their efforts. Heinz had been selling the French goods before the 'Soviet Paradise' action and continued to do so after the arrests began on 22 May. Cühn said about his friend, 'He probably would have found his own accommodations. At that time he had money.'[32]

On the morning of 27 May Martin Kochmann took Richard Holzer's bicycle from the hallway of Zechliner Strasse 6 and wheeled it onto the street. His Belgian ID card and a German bicycle card were tucked in his pocket, Martin rode to the nearest train station and boarded a train to Potsdam. From there he began his trip to the Belgian border, cycling to Brandenburg, where he took another train bound for Hanover. He escape was foiled in Magdeburg when he had a run-in with a railway policeman.

Martin was arrested as 'Alfons Buys' because he could not produce a leave pass from Berlin, and he had also lost his bicycle card; bicycles could only be taken 100km from their documented home. Thus the 'Belgian' Kochmann was taken to a prison in Magdeburg.[33]

At this time Martin's wife Sala, who had been arrested on 23 May, was being held in a cell at the Alexanderplatz police presidium. The Gestapo were trying to get her to talk, and tried to break her psychologically as well as physically. Two officers walked back and forth in front of her cell saying, 'Thank God the Jew Kochmann is dead. We sure killed him good!' Unbeknownst to her, he was still alive and was being transferred from Magdeburg to the same building where she was being held. But she had no way of knowing this, and being sleep deprived, physically weak and terribly anxious, she believed the officers. The next time her cell door was opened, she rushed past the guard and bolted towards the air shaft, jumping over the banister and down the shaft head first in order to take her own life.[34]

Ellen Lewinsky was worried about her friend Heinz Birnbaum when he stopped showing up to work at Schubert-Werke. One day the foreman took her aside and said, 'I found out why your friend hasn't been coming to work. Did you know the Gestapo has been looking for him?' She replied that she had no idea. She thought to herself that the detonator she smuggled out of the plant must have worked well and wondered if she would ever see him again.

She was therefore very surprised when she found Heinz waiting for her on the staircase of her apartment building. He seemed very tense and anxious; he had always smoked cigarettes but now he was chain-smoking. 'What's going on?' she asked. They spoke in tense whispers.

'I've got to get out, I've got to run. I hope it works because if they get me it's the end!' He told her that he hoped to get out of Germany, perhaps to France. 'The courier was caught, but maybe it'll still work out,' he said. 'I still have papers in the apartment – on the bookcase. If they find them there, it will absolutely nail the case shut. They have to be taken out. Will you do it?'

Ellen nodded her head and Heinz told her what to take from his room. He told her an address as she fumbled for a pen in her purse. 'Don't write it down – you have to memorise it.' He smiled at her and said, 'With a little luck we'll see each other again.' Then he disappeared down the stairs.

Ellen went directly to Heinz's apartment and asked his landladies for permission to collect some of Heinz's possessions.

'Is he in trouble?' one of them asked.

'I think so.' she replied.

She stuffed the papers into a shopping bag and caught the U-Bahn. Then she walked to an empty car and removed her yellow star. She went to the address Heinz gave her and rang the bell.

'I was told to give you this,' she said to the young man who answered the door, holding out the shopping bag.

'I know,' he replied. 'Thank you very much.' Ellen left quickly and rushed home.[35]

In May 1942, Charlotte Paech had been working as a nurse in the Jewish Hospital for fourteen years. Even though she was connected with Baum and the others, the Gestapo were not yet on her trail. One day one of her friends from the Baum group was brought to the Jewish Hospital on a stretcher. It was Sala Kochmann.

Sala's suicide attempt had been unsuccessful; there was netting near the bottom of the air shaft which had broken her fall slightly, but she had a fractured skull and spine, as well as several other wounds. She was unable to move and was in agonising pain. There was a police station at the hospital so Sala could be kept under close watch. Since Paech was a nurse and no connection between her and Sala was made by the Gestapo, she was able to visit and communicate with her stricken friend.

Sala, who according to Charlotte was lucid, once whispered to her: 'The plot was conceived by a spy. The people who were arrested and tortured gave no information to the police, but others have been arrested.' The name of the alleged spy was Joachim Franke.[36]

It was on 22 May, the day of his arrest, that Franke 'spilled his guts' with such unbridled gusto that it must have bemused his Gestapo interrogator. There was no anti-fascist solidarity from 'comrade' Franke. Interrogation minutes from 22 May 1942 include a list of fourteen names – mostly complete and correct – of Franke-Steinbrink group members and the schooling circle led by Werner Schaumann. Seven of these people were arrested that very day, while the others were tracked down and brought in within a day or two.

According to Michael Kreutzer, Franke was no Gestapo agent provocateur and 'was certainly in the years 1941/42 not in contact with the Gestapo.'[37] There are survivors of the Baum group, however, who have accused Franke of being a Gestapo collaborator, or at the very least a traitor.[38]

It was during Franke's first confession that he named some of the Baum group members: Herbert, Marianne, Suzanne and Irene. He did not know their last names, but how did he know their first names? What happened to communist security tactics and codenames that effectively prevented the arrest of Herbert Baum, Heinz Birnbaum and others in earlier years? The Baums were arrested on 22 May – the same day as Franke – and Suzanne Wesse and Irene Walther the following day. Was it Franke's 'enthusiasm' that led to their arrests or was it just coincidence that these four were amongst the first to be arrested? Considering his behaviour once in prison, one could concur with Herbert Ansbach who wrote that the group was 'betrayed' by Joachim Franke.[39]

The 'Soviet Paradise' action gave Goebbels an excuse to step up the terror campaign against the Jews of Berlin. He wrote in his diary:

> Now I'll accomplish … my war against the Jews of Berlin. I've ordered the preparation of a list of Jewish hostages, which will be followed by many detentions. I don't fancy catching a bullet from a 22-year-old Jew from the East, as an example of the murderers who are amongst the types in the anti-Bolshevik attack. Ten Jews in a detention camp or under the ground are better than one of them who is still free.[40]

The same day that Martin Kochmann began his failed attempt to flee, 27 May, a confidential list circulated through Nazi security offices, containing the names of people associated with Herbert Baum and Joachim Franke, including those people already in custody. Amongst those listed were the Baums, Gerhard Meyer, Werner Steinbrink and Suzanne Wesse. Significantly, Joachim Franke's name appeared at the top of the list, which was made up of 22 names and details of each individual: full name, maiden name, profession, birthdate and birthplace.[41] The list included all the names and other information provided by Franke during his interrogation sessions on 22 May and later.

While many of the Baum group were being held in prison, an event far away in Prague made the situation worse both for them and Berlin Jews in general. On 27 May an assassination attempt was made on Reinhard 'the Hangman' Heydrich, Deputy Reich Protector of the Protectorate of Bohemia and Moravia, the section of Czechoslovakia incorporated into the German Reich on 15 March 1939. Two Czech nationals, trained by the British Special Operations Executive, carried out Operation *Anthropoid*, ambushing Heydrich in his open car on a hairpin turn in the Prague suburb of Liben. When one man's machine gun jammed, he threw a bomb at the rear of the car. Gravely injured, Heydrich was taken to a hospital in Prague.[42]

This attack on one of the Nazis' own heightened anti-Jewish feeling in Berlin, and there were dire consequences for Berlin Jewry as a result of it and also directly because of the fire at the 'Soviet Paradise' exhibition. The same day that the confidential Baum-Franke document circulated through the intricate web of Nazi security (27 May) an indeterminate number of Jews – none of whom were involved in the arson attack – were arrested and sent to the assembly camp on Levetzowstrasse. After a short time a number of them were released. The next day, 28 May, however, 154 of them were transported north of Berlin to Sachsenhausen concentration camp where they were immediately shot. At evening role call an additional 96 Jews were chosen and they too were shot. Relatives of the first 154 Jews were deported in a series of transports to Thereisienstadt. Yet another 250 Berlin Jews were shipped off the Sachsenhausen. They were either killed there or dispatched to Auschwitz.[43]

Also on 27 May, Norbert Wollheim, who knew Herbert Baum and several other members of his group as children and young adults in the Jewish youth movement (DJJG and later the *Ring*) in the 1920s and 1930s, was working at his forced labour job at a firm in Lichtenberg. While there, an 'Aryan' foreman told him of the arrests of hundreds of Jews in Berlin. When his shift was finished he took the U-Bahn to the office of the *Reichvereinigung der Juden in Deutschland* (Reich Association of Jews in Germany) at Kurfürstenstrasse 115–116 in Tiergarten, intending to speak to Dr Paul Eppstein about the arrests, whom Wollheim knew from his work in youth immigration.

Upon his arrival, a colleague of Eppstein named Meyer told Wollheim that something terrible had happened. That morning Eppstein, Rabbi Leo Baeck and Philipp Kozower had been called to the office of Adolf Eichmann, the head of the Nazi Jewish Department. After a very long wait, Eichmann bellowed at the trio, telling them that on 18 May there had been a Jewish arson attack, and that 'any attempt to throw a wrench in the works' would be met with unrelenting harshness by the Gestapo. In retaliation, continued Eichmann, 250 Jews had been arrested and killed. In the excitement of the meeting, Eppstein and his companions wrongly concluded that some of the Jews who had participated in the arson had been amongst those killed.

Wollheim instinctively knew who was behind the 'Soviet Paradise' attack. He asked Meyer: 'Please ask Herr Dr Eppstein whether or not the names Herbert Baum or Martin Kochmann were mentioned by Eichmann.' Meyer left to pass on the message, then returned, telling Wollheim that Eppstein had confirmed that both Baum and Kochmann had been mentioned and that he should come in and see him. In a telephone interview conducted in 1993, Wollheim stated:

> Through conjecture my guess is that Dr Eppstein learned which circle was involved in the attempted attack on the Lustgarten ... I had heard ... that Herbert Baum worked at Siemens. And it was ... talked about – that he was involved in active political resistance ... There were plenty of friends of mine who worked at Siemens. And as brave as Baum was, he was not always very careful. So more people knew than should have known, what he was thinking and what he was likely to do.

Paul Eppstein, Leo Baeck and Norbert Wollheim discussed what could be done to prevent a possible act of revenge by the Baum group, having no idea that its members were on the run and had no thought of retaliation. Wollheim had known Richard Holzer and his family quite well in the past, and he told the two older men that he would meet with someone connected with Baum and express their concerns about any reprisal.[44]

Norbert Wollheim located Richard Holzer through his family and arranged to meet with him. Under cover of blackout, the two young men met at the market at Alexanderplatz. Wollheim told Holzer that the Gestapo had struck hard against the Jews as a result of the 'Soviet Paradise' attack, and that any act of revenge would mean more bloodshed.

'What you're telling me is not of interest to us,' Wollheim recalls Holzer saying. 'We're just not interested. If we think we should retaliate we will. We're not interested in what the Jewish leaders think. Our only consideration is what will serve our cause.'

Wollheim reported the conversation to Leo Baeck, who was angered by Holzer's comments. 'Frankly,' said Baeck, 'I didn't think that in these circumstances reason would prevail. What they did was folly in the first place. Now, at least they are aware of it.' He added, 'There is nothing more we can do.'[45] Richard Holzer himself recalls telling Wollheim that the Baum group was already destroyed.[46]

Richard's lover, Charlotte Paech, reports that around 28 May, Dr Lustig, the director of the Jewish Hospital, told a meeting of employees that 500 Berlin Jews had been arrested by the Nazis in response to the arson attack at 'Soviet Paradise'. The fear that Richard Holzer had raised at a Baum group meeting a few short weeks earlier had come to pass. Meanwhile Martin Kochmann had arrived back in Berlin after being transferred from the prison in Magdeburg.

Held in a large hall for foreigners in the Alexanderplatz police presidium, he didn't dare speak for fear that he would give away himself as a German and not the Belgian 'Alfons Buys,' the name on his ID.[47]

Goebbels spoke with Hitler on 30 May about deporting the Berlin Jews without delay. His diary recorded that the Führer was to speak with Albert Speer (the Minister of Armaments) about replacing Jews with foreign workers 'as soon as possible.' Leaving the Jews in Berlin was, according to Goebbels, 'an invitation for murder'.

> The fact that 22-year-old *Ostjuden* should be participants in the latest firebomb attempts speaks volumes. I thus plead again for a more radical Jewish policy, an opinion with which the Führer is in full agreement.[48]

On 1 June, Heinz Birnbaum, who was still staying with Harry Cühn, told him that he had to meet a 'buddy'. Cühn knew without hesitation that 'Buber' was walking into a trap and warned him not to go, but Birnbaum did not heed him. Instead he went to the Kaiser Wilhelm Institute, thinking he was going to meet Werner Steinbrink. Unbeknownst to him, Steinbrink had been arrested on 22 May. When he arrived the Gestapo were waiting for him.[49]

On 2 June Reinhard Heydrich – who had appeared to be recovering from the assignation attempt of 27 May – slipped into a coma.[50] Goebbels was told of Heydrich's condition and wrote in his diary:

> We still don't know the background on the attack … in any case we will retaliate against the Jews. I've fulfilled my plan to imprison 500 Jews in Berlin and to let the leaders of the Jewish community know that as a reaction to any Jewish plot or attempted revolt 100 or 150 Jews that are held by us will be shot. As a result of the attempted assault on Heydrich, a large group against which we had proof has been shot dead in Sachsenhausen.[51]

Some members of the Baum group were still on the run; Felix Heymann and Hella Hirsch used French ID cards which had been obtained for them by Herbert Baum, and under the names 'Pierre Rappaud' and 'Genevieve Sauteurs' rented a flat in Fredersdorf. They spend the last week of May there laying low. They also had an illegal apartment in Gleinicke, which they gave to Hella's sister, Alice, in June.[52]

During the first week of June, Felix began to look for an 'illegal' job to make some money. He remembered Wolfgang Knabe, a non-Jewish co-worker of Heinz Birnbaum's whom he had met in 1938 and befriended. Felix and Richard Holzer went to see Knabe at his apartment at Friedenstrasse 1 in Schönow bei Bernau. Felix waited outside while Richard asked Wolfgang to come out.

Knabe remembered Heymann right away and asked about Heinz; Felix, who had lost contact with Birnbaum, told him that it was more than likely that he had been apprehended by the Gestapo. Felix told Wolfgang that he was living underground and asked if he knew of anyone who could give him a job; he said that he could claim to be a foreigner and that he had false ID papers. Knabe told Heymann that he knew a Hungarian who might have a position for him. They arranged to meet again with the Hungarian and Felix was offered a job in Kreuzberg. The job only lasted two days, however, because the Hungarian wanted to advise the Labour Office to keep things in order, and Felix had to disappear.[53] Knabe told Heymann that if he needed anything he could be found every afternoon at a certain time at the Gesundbruner train station.[54]

It was around this time that Hanni Meyer, who was still in a state of shock over her husband Gerhard's arrest on 22 May, went to see her in-laws Rita and Herbert Meyer at Neanderstrasse 7 in Mitte to seek their advice. Using her illegal papers she had rented a summer cottage in Petershagen with Gerhard. After his arrest, however, she gave it to Heinz and Marianne Joachim. She told her in-laws that she wanted to go underground and live using her false ID. Warning her that such conduct would be equal to an admission of guilt, Rita suggested that she wait and see what happened.[55] Unfortunately on 3 June Hanni Meyer was arrested by the Gestapo and sent to Charlottenburg prison.[56]

Felix Heymann and Hella Hirsch resurfaced after living underground only since 23 May. Felix had been unable to find illegal employment and they didn't have enough money to remain in hiding. It seemed to them that the arrests had ended, so in the second week of June they felt confident enough to return to their forced labour jobs. Whilst underground Felix and Hella married; Hella told Ellen Compart that they wanted to make a commitment to one another, just in case their lives were cut short. After hearing about their wedding, Ellen bought Hella a small gift, presenting it to her at Aceta-Werke at IG Farben, where they both worked as forced labourers.[57] Elsewhere, another couple's luck had finally run out. Heinz and Marianne Joachim were living in the summer cottage in Petershagen 'illegally' rented by Gerhard and Hanni Meyer. They were arrested there on 9 June.[58]

18

INTERROGATIONS, EXECUTIONS AND SURVIVAL (1942–1944)

It has been said that shortly after his arrest, Herbert Baum was taken to the Siemens Elmo-Werke where he had been a forced labourer, and held in front of the door by Gestapo men who hoped his comrades would give themselves away. Not a soul did.[1] He was then sent to Alt Moabit prison. It is not difficult to imagine the treatment that Baum received at the hands of the Gestapo. No interrogation minutes or pre-trial documents were kept so there are few specific details of Baum's time as a prisoner, but usual practice was a cold cell and only bread and water for sustenance.

The Gestapo employed sleep deprivation and exhaustion exercises as well as other more 'creative' methods of torture. They knew that Baum was the leader of Goebbels' purported 'club of saboteurs and assassins' and treated him accordingly. He may very well have taken full responsibility for his group's actions, if he told them anything at all. Baum probably did little to hide his utter contempt for the Gestapo and everything they represented. Herbert Baum, born 10 February 1910 – German, Jew, communist and anti-fascist – died on 11 June 1942 at the age of 30, beaten and tortured to death. The Gestapo reported to the Court that Baum had 'committed suicide'.[2]

The Gestapo interrogation officers were getting frustrated. After three weeks in custody Heinz Birnbaum and Heinz Rotholz were still not cooperating, denying any knowledge of 'illegal organisations', even after rough handling. The Nazis therefore asked permission from their superior officer to beat the prisoners with sticks.

With the permission of Gestapo control station SS Colonel Bovensiepen they were twice subjected to severe means of interrogation by being beaten with sticks. Birnbaum was 'severely' interrogated on the 30th of June 1942 and the 7th of July 1942. Rotholz was 'severely' interrogated on the 1st of July 1942 and the 7th of July 1942.[3]

After six long weeks of stewing in the detention hall at Alexanderplatz, on 3 July Martin Kochmann finally had a hearing in front of a judge. Martin ('Alfons Buys') told the judge that he was Belgian; that he knew German because it was his mother's tongue; and that he was homesick and wanted to go home. The judge informed the factory administration and a young Dutchman was sent for to identify him.

The Dutchman looked Martin up and down and, much to Martin's surprise, declared that he recognised him as a homesick fellow worker who had run away. Because of the man's testimony, 'Alfons Buys' was free to return to the labour camp in Spandau under the Dutchman's supervision. Martin went to get his bicycle and returned to his liberator. He told the Dutchman, 'Well, listen, that'd be a shame if you spend your money on the fair for me! So I'll go back with the bike.' The young man smiled a knowing grin and said, 'Good!'[4] As the S-Bahn pulled away towards Spandau, Martin rode his bike in a different direction to Gartenfelde. He abandoned his bike at the train station and began walking to Charlotte Paech's flat. By chance he met Richard Holzer on Soldiner Strasse.[5]

Felix Heymann and Hella Hirsch – now Hella Heymann – seemed to have beaten the odds. They had returned to work after two weeks underground, and no Gestapo men had knocked on their door. Sadly, however, their luck ran out on 8 July. That day Felix's landlady told him that the police were looking for him, Hella and her sister Alice, who lived in the flat with them. Felix could not locate Hella and Alice to tell them the news; he had to disappear fast.[6]

Ellen Compart went to work on 8 July at the Aceta-Werke division of IG Farben, where Hella Hirsch worked the shift before her. Walking down a corridor, Ellen went to the locker room where she always changed into her work clothing. Upon arriving in the locker room, she saw Hella; 'The gentle girl with big, sad eyes was handcuffed and being led away by two big police officers.' Ellen hugged her friend, saying very loudly, 'I will go see your mother. Don't worry. It must all be a mistake.' As Hella was taken away, Ellen stood stunned. She had expected to be arrested along with her friend.[7] Hella's sister, Alice, was also arrested that day at her forced labour job and taken to Alt Moabit prison.[8]

Meanwhile Felix Heymann went to the Gesundbrunner train station in Wedding and met Wolfgang Knabe. Felix told him that he had no place to live because the police had been to his apartment, and asked him for help to find a place to stay. Saying that he would talk to his wife about putting him up for a while, Knabe invited Heymann to come over to his apartment the following day, which he did. The Knabes offered Felix a small room, fed him, and Wolfgang gave him 4800g worth of bread ration tickets, for which Felix paid 27 Reichmarks. Felix gave Wolfgang an additional 50 Reichmarks to get him more stamps. Admitting that he was going to attempt to flee Germany, he left the Knabes' home a week later. Wolfgang was worried that the Gestapo would discover that he had helped Felix.[9]

On the same day as Hella and Alice were arrested, Harry Cühn was enjoying a boat ride on Lake Havel in the outer western environs of Berlin. In the middle of his excursion he suddenly had a feeling of dread; he knew he had to get to Balsam-Eis, the ice cream parlour where he had first met his fiancée, Edith Fraenkel. Arriving at the establishment on Olivaer Platz, one of the owners, Jupp, greeted Harry with a serious look on his face. He had received a telephone call from Siemens Elmo-Werke; Edith has been arrested.

Edith and her mother lived on Pfalzburger Strasse in Wilmersdorf. Other Jews were quartered in their flat until their deportation, amongst them a Jewish lawyer, Dr Maas, and his Christian wife. Harry was desperately looking for someone who would be able to locate exactly where Edith was being held, and Maas referred him to a Dr Jacobsohn. Harry met with Jacobsohn, who had been an officer in the First World War. He could not do anything to help, but recommended a gentile colleague, Masius, who, said Jacobsohn, 'has great integrity.'

Masius was 'a very wonderful person,' wrote Cühn, who was quite impressed with the lawyer who had been either a captain or major in the First World War. Masius became public defender for Edith and one or two of the other Baum group members. Harry knew that Masius would do everything in his power to defend Edith in court. Considering the circumstances, that was all he could hope for.[10]

At 10.00am on 15 July, Hildegard Loewy's mother heard sharp knocking at the door of their flat. Opening the door she saw two men in suits; one of the men greeted her with 'Gestapo!' 'We are here for Hildegard Loewy,' said the other. Hilde was standing in the living room and overheard the exchange.

She quickly hid a photograph of her boyfriend, Georg Israel, under a copy of Franz Oppenheimer's book, *Die sozialer Forderung der Stunde* (The Social Demands of the Moment). The men entered the living room and Hilde identified herself. Her mother was in shock as the Gestapo men escorted Hilde downstairs. Peering out the window, she saw them put her daughter in a black sedan and drive away. Hilde was taken to Alt Moabit prison.[11]

On the same day Lothar Salinger, Helmuth Neumann and Siegbert and Lotte Rotholz were also arrested. The Rotholzes were dragged from their beds, both being ill with scarlet fever. Herbert Budzislawski managed to escape capture; while at work he overheard that someone was 'interested in him', and sped out via a rear exit.[12]

That same day Ursula Ehrlich arrived at the flat of Gerda and Willi May at Wat Strasse 3 in Wedding in an agitated state, having just heard that her fiancé, Lothar Salinger, had been arrested. She was accompanied by Ellen Compart. The young women decided to go underground together to avoid arrest. Ellen told her parents of her plans, stuffed 90 Reichmarks in her pocket and headed for Wat Strasse with her friend. Ursula said that there must have been a traitor; otherwise the Gestapo would not have been able to act so quickly and arrest so many people.[13]

The next day – 16 July 1942 – the first Baum group trial was held in Special Court V in Berlin.[14] Nazi 'justice' was swift and held no surprises. The trial of the ten accused lasted one day and all were found guilty of 'Preparation of High Treason' and given the death sentence. They were Marianne Baum, Joachim Franke, Hilde Jadamowitz, Heinz Joachim, Sala Kochmann, Hans Mannaberg, Gerhard Meyer, Werner Steinbrink, Irene Walther and Suzanne Wesse. Sala, due to her fractured skull and spine, was wheeled into court in her hospital bed. Execution by guillotine was scheduled for 18 August 1942.[15]

Meanwhile Felix Heymann was still on the run. He stayed with a friend called Kleczewski in his flat on Königsberger Strasse for a few days, then spent a fortnight with a forestry worker called Doll, who let him sleep in a hayloft. Felix paid 20 pfennig a day for his morning coffee and another 20 pfennig a day for his rustic accommodations.

Martin Kochmann spent the three weeks following his unusual liberation by the Dutchman at the farm of Otto Sielisch in Kummersdorf, 25km south of Berlin. Martin knew the farmer from the days when the Baum group took trips in the countryside. Martin did farm work from sunrise to sundown, falling fast asleep in the barn after dinner, completely unaware of the trial that had taken place on 16 July. On 18 and 19 July, however, he returned to Berlin to visit Charlotte Paech and purchase food stamps in Spandau. He spent two nights at the flat of Gustav Paech, Charlotte's former husband. Martin then returned to the farm in Kummersdorf with Charlotte for one week, where they both worked, then they both returned to Berlin.[16]

During the spring of 1942, Charlotte had been convicted of aiding and abetting in an abortion and received a deferred one-month prison sentence (see Chapter 15). On 27 July, upon returning to Berlin with Martin from the farm in Kummersdorf, she was summoned to serve her sentence. However, afraid that as a Jew she would end up in a concentration camp or even Auschwitz, she wanted to avoid reporting to the prison. Her lover, Richard Holzer, had recently escaped to Hungary with his Hungarian passport, and she decided to follow him. She and her ex-husband, Gustav, came up with a plan. Gustav offered to take over Charlotte's flat and care for their young daughter, Eva. He also said that he would advise the Barnimstrasse women's prison that she would be arriving shortly to begin her sentence. Charlotte felt that this plan left Gustav vulnerable, be he reassured her that everything would be alright and that she shouldn't worry about him.[17]

Now living underground, on 27 July Charlotte Paech and Martin Kochmann were taken in by Rita and Herbert Meyer and their young daughter Barbara, who lived at Neanderstrasse 7 in Mitte. After leaving the Meyers' flat a week later, Paech spent the next four weeks with a farmer called Grasse in Kummersdorf. She travelled back and forth between the farm and Berlin in order to visit a couple in Neukölln called Roth, whose address she had given Richard Holzer if he needed to contact her. She would also visit Martin, Rita and Felix Heymann. Felix's father, Max Heymann, answered a knock at his apartment door late one night and was shocked to see his son, gaunt and unshaven, standing before him. Max and his wife Grete were happy to see Felix, but terrified that the Gestapo would find him at their house. Felix fell asleep on their sofa and his mother draped a blanket over him; she knew that he would be gone again shortly.[18]

Arriving in Berlin for a visit on 18 August, Charlotte discovered that Gustav Paech had been taken into custody on 31 July. He was arrested because she had not reported to the Barnimstrasse women's prison on 27 July as he had said she would. Their eight-year-old daughter, Eva, was given to Gustav's mother for safekeeping. While his ex-wife was hiding out at Rita Meyer's flat, Paech underwent brutal Gestapo interrogation.

The knowledge that they beat out of him – including the names of the Baum group members he had helped – was used to build a case of 'aiding and abetting the commission of high treason' against him. After the interrogations Paech was placed in 'protective custody' in Sachsenhausen concentration camp, where he also stayed during his later trial.[19] Charlotte had no idea where her daughter was, and since she was underground, there was no way for her to find out. She thought it was too dangerous to go to Gustav's apartment as she was sure that it had been under surveillance by the Gestapo and that her conversations with her former husband had been overheard by the secret police.

While in Berlin on 18 August, a red poster caught Charlotte's eye. She was shocked to discover that it announced the executions of Marianne Baum, Joachim Franke, Hilde Jadamowitz, Heinz Joachim, Sala Kochmann, Hans Mannaberg, Gerhard Meyer, Warner Steinbrink, Irene Walther and Suzanne Wesse that very day at Plötzensee prison.[20] Beatrice Jadamowitz was being held in the cell next to her sister Hildegarde at the Alexanderplatz police presidium jail. When the SS came to transfer her to Plötzensee to be executed, Hilde went to her sister's cell, which was opened, to kiss her and hold her one last time. 'We could kiss each other goodbye,' writes Beatrice. 'She seemed cheerful and confident. Anyway, I had this impression. Perhaps she wanted to spare me.'[21] All ten condemned prisoners were let out of their cells and allowed to smoke cigarettes together. Someone even gave Joachim Franke a cigarette. Quite surprised, he said, 'You do this for me, now?'[22]

A Prussian institution, Plötzensee prison was constructed between 1869 and 1879 on over 60 acres abutting the Plötzensee, a lake. Surrounded by a 20-foot wall, the prison is located in the Charlottenburg district of Berlin, on Hüttigpfad off Saatwinkler Damm. During the Nazi period, Plötzensee was primarily the site of execution of resistance fighters and others deemed 'enemies of the state' by the notorious People's Court. Its execution chamber had a guillotine and gallows (built in 1942) set behind it.

The guillotine had been taken to Plötzensee under strict secrecy from Bruchsal prison on 14 February 1937, under orders from Hitler himself. Bruchsal itself had received the *Fallbeil* ('falling axe', German for guillotine), in 1856 from the city of Baden. It was built that year by the Johann Mannhardt company in Munich for 1000 guilders. Before the arrival of the guillotine at Plötzensee, executions were carried out on the block with an axe. A red-brick building used for storing cleaning utensils was converted into an execution chamber. The concrete floor was tiled, which made it easier to mop up the blood, and a drain and water line were also installed before the guillotine was fully operational.

Condemned prisoners at Plötzensee were kept in a large cell block building (House III), a short walk from the execution chamber. They spent their final hours – or sometimes days – shackled and guarded in special cells on the ground floor, which was called the 'house of the dead'. The only visitors allowed were prison officials and the condemned's attorney. Brigitte Oleschinski writes, 'A production-line death by beheading or hanging was the ghastly culmination of an inexorably merciless procedure. Administrative ordinances regulated every last detail, the process becoming increasingly streamlined as the number of executions rose.'

Plötzensee's executioner in August 1942 was Ernst Reindel, who received an annual salary of 3000 Reichmarks and a special bonus of 60–65 Marks for each execution. This bonus was also paid to his three helpers. He was a stocky man who wore an absurd black costume for his work: top hat, tails, no shirt, dark trousers and a mask.[23]

When it was Sala Kochmann's turn on the guillotine, she was wheeled in her hospital bed from the 'house of the dead' to the execution chamber. Because of her spinal injuries she could not move; she also had plaster casts on her neck and other areas of her body. After wheeling the bed as close to the machine as possible, the executioner and his three assistants lifted Sala from her bed and carried her to the board of the guillotine. Since moving even slightly caused Sala much pain, the process of being lifted and carried must have been excruciating. She was a heavy-set woman, which made it even more difficult to carry her. While being carried, Sala would have been able to see the guillotine and the gallows behind it. Given her injuries she likely cried out in pain as the executioner and his assistants dropped her onto the board – probably face up – and then adjusted the top of the lunette firmly against her neck. One can only imagine the effect her screams had on her comrades waiting their own turn on the *Fallbeil*. The emotional impact of the sound of the heavy blade landing with a thud, followed by absolute silence, and then a second, much lighter thud, is unimaginable.

The efficiency of the 'production line' is documented in the execution book of Plötzensee. It took a mere 37 minutes – from 5.00am to 5.37am – to snuff out the lives of Herbert Baum's ten comrades on 18 August 1942.[24]

As their friends died, other members of the Baum group were still in hiding. On the final Sunday before Charlotte Paech left the farmer Grasse in Kummersdorf, she was sitting in a field when a young soldier approached her and sat down nearby. There was an airport in Kummersdorf so it was not unusual for soldiers or Luftwaffe pilots to visit the farm to buy food. They had a pleasant chat about unimportant things and he asked to see her again. She explained that she was from Berlin and that she was returning the next day. The soldier then thanked her for an enjoyable afternoon and left. Charlotte did not know that they would soon meet again.[25]

Martin Kochmann remained with Rita and Herbert Meyer a week longer than Charlotte. Then he arranged a stay with another farmer, Paul 'Papa' Siebert, in Klein-Köris, 69km south of Berlin, one of the farms the Baum group had visited in happier times. After being there a short time, however, he became ill and returned to Rita and Herbert Meyer's flat in Mitte. Charlotte returned to the Meyers to care for her sick friend; she writes that Martin

> had a terrible sore throat with a very high fever. We did not know what we should do and all stayed with Rita ... All around us people were being picked up by the Gestapo. One day there was a knock at the door – there was no bell – Rita answered and it was the Gestapo. But they only asked about the Jews next door whom they wanted to get. And when they were at the door the apartment was filled with illegal Jews![26]

Felix Heymann was also still on the run, paying short visits to friends and relatives. One day he went to the apartment of his cousin Wolfgang Heymann on Paulsborner Strasse 91. Wolfgang was shocked to see him, but did not send him away. Some days later his comrade Bernhard Heymann, who was not a relative, had a similar reaction when he opened his door at Wullenweberstrasse 3 late one night to find Felix standing there.[27]

On 7 October the Gestapo finally came for the Meyers and Charlotte. Upon being arrested, Charlotte asked for her purse so she could use the toilet; she had poison hidden there to take in case she was caught by the Gestapo. The officer escorted her to the bathroom but changed his mind. He tore the purse out of her hands and rifled through it. Finding the poison, he angrily beat Charlotte and dragged her off the Alexanderplatz police presidium jail. Later that same day, Martin Kochmann knocked on the door of the Meyers' flat. Waiting behind the door were the Gestapo, who were only too happy to let Martin inside.[28]

Upon arrival at the Alexanderplatz police presidium jail, Charlotte was put in a wire metal cage in the middle of an empty room, along with another woman she did not know. She told the woman to be quiet, tied a noose with her belt, and attempted to commit suicide. When Charlotte climbed up the wall of the cage in order to jump, however, her cellmate began screaming and the officers came and took her belongings away from her.[29]

The officer in charge of Charlotte's case turned out to be none other than the 'soldier' with whom she had a pleasant chat over a month before. She asked him why he did not arrest her then, and he bellowed that he wasn't ready to take her in, that she had to return to Berlin and lead them to her comrades. Her first interrogation session lasted from 10.00pm until 4.00am. That night her jaw was split and 'otherwise they weren't soft on me either.' She was told by her interrogation officer that she was the last one arrested from her group (which was not true).[30] Everything that she had wanted to hide by committing suicide was already known! She decided that she would just have to wait and see what fate had in store for her. She was placed in a dark cell with no window, her only comfort a hard bed without a pillow or blanket. She was interrogated every day, day and night, fed only bread and water, deprived of sleep and subjected to exhaustion exercises. She was repeatedly asked for the location of Richard Holzer and for the names of other group members. Eventually she decided to stop talking completely, and after three weeks she was left alone. Compared to the daily brutality it was heavenly.[31]

Meanwhile Rita Meyer was taken to Gestapo headquarters on Burgstrasse, where she was kept in a cell in the basement. Then she was taken to the police jail at Alexanderplatz, where Charlotte Paech was also being held at the time. She was then transported again, this time to Lehrterstrasse prison, where she had a chance to see her husband, Herbert, but was unable to speak with him.[32] 'I want to say once more that the fascist methods were incredibly brutal,' writes Rita, 'both physically as well as psychologically.' After her capture she was expected to confess, but when that was not forthcoming, her husband was tortured in her presence. 'They would wring him like a piece of laundry until he could not breath and turned blue. It was easier to endure pain yourself than watch a person one loved being tormented. It was very hard but I did not break.'[33]

While Charlotte Paech and the Meyers were in custody, Ellen Compart was being helped to stay underground by Gerda May, who, being a Jew married to the Christian Willi May, was allowed to have certain 'Aryan' documents. Amongst these was a postal identity card, which very few Jews were allowed to possess, used to pick up packages and mail from a local post office. In order to get a postal ID one had to fill out a form (name, address, height, weight, hair and eye colour) and submit a photograph. Even though Gerda had a *Kennkarte* marked with a large 'J' for 'Jew,' if a police officer looked at her postal card he would assume that she was an 'Aryan'.

Gerda went to her local post office to get a postal ID for herself. A short time later, she returned with a photo of Ellen – the resemblance between them was striking – and submitted it as a photograph of herself. She explained by saying that she had lost her original postal card, when in reality she was getting Ellen a vital identification document. She had the chutzpah to go a third time in order to get a postal ID for a Jewish dentist. However, each time someone applied for a postal ID, his or her name, address and other information was put on a list, and now Gerda May's name was on three different lists. These lists were given to the Gestapo.[34]

Gerda was eventually called down to Gestapo headquarters for questioning about her postal ID applications. At the time she was pregnant with her third child. It was not the fact that she had applied for postal cards three separate times that caught the eye of the Gestapo, but the photograph that she had submitted with her second application.[35] 'This is not your photograph!' a Gestapo officer snarled at Gerda. He held it up in the air and looked at it while looking at Gerda. She argued that the photograph – which was actually of Ellen Compart – was indeed her. She asserted herself and even felt confident enough to yell at the Gestapo man, and he let her go home. But she had to return twice more and reiterate her assertion that it was a photograph of her. Eventually a postal ID card arrived in the mail with Ellen Compart's photograph on it. Thus Ellen Compart 'became' Gerda May and lived in her apartment with her husband Willi.[36]

Felix Heymann was being passed around from safe house to safe house; Eva Jerochim transferred him to Käthe Simon, who sent him to Hedwig and Heinrich von Kordisch.[37] Less than a week after the arrests of Charlotte Paech, the Meyers and Martin Kochmann, Felix Heymann was finally arrested by the Gestapo on 12 October. The next day he attempted to take his life but was not successful. Time ran out for Herbert Budzislawski one month later, on 13 November, when he too was apprehended.[38] Budzislawski, who was the first to declare his allegiance to Baum in 1933, was the last Baum group member to be caught in the aftermath of the 'Soviet Paradise' action.

After Felix's suicide attempt, he was taken to the Jewish Hospital where there was a special 'police ward'; patients were sent there by either the Gestapo or the prisons, because Jews could not be admitted to public hospitals. Bruno Blau was a Jewish cancer patient married to an 'Aryan', and was in the same ward as Felix Heymann in October 1942:

> Among the patients I met there was a young man – his name was Heymann – who had been arrested for taking part in communist activities, and who had tried to take his own life by slitting his carotid artery. As soon as he was able to leave his bed, he was picked up early one morning by two Gestapo officials, who stood at his bed until he had finished dressing … Heymann was a trained metalworker [lathe operator] and was especially intelligent and well-read.[39]

The second trial of Baum group members took place on 10 December 1942. The accused were Heinz Birnbaum, Edith Fraenkel, Alice Hirsch, Hella Hirsch (Heymann), Marianne Joachim, Hildegard Loewy, Hanni Meyer, Helmuth Neumann, Heinz Rotholz, Lotte Rotholz, Siegbert Rotholz and Lothar Salinger.[40]

Harry Cühn, who knew Heinz Birnbaum well and was Edith Fraenkel's lover, attended the trial and reported on Birnbaum's statement to the People's Court: 'We are here not as political fighters; we have been condemned as Jews.'[41] At the conclusion of the trial, Cühn saw the twelve defendants rise and face the judge as he read the verdict:

> The penalty against the defendants Heinz Rotholz, Birnbaum, Hella Hirsch, Hanni Meyer, Marianne Joachim, Salinger, Neumann, Hildegard Loewy and Siegbert Rotholz in accordance with existing legal regulations … is either life imprisonment or the death penalty. An inconsequential case this is not. It is the death penalty, however, that seems correct for these defendants. In the current struggle for existence of the German people, the defendants serve the enemy, which is also the vilest enemy of the civilised world, Bolshevism. They prepare its way and thereby undermine the resiliency of the German people, and seek to bring it to its death. Such actions demand the protection of the people and Reich. This punishment is all the more imperative, because the defendants are all Jews and as such had every reason to keep quiet and not, as in 1918, stab Germany in the back. Therefore the said defendants shall be given the death penalty.

Three of the defendants, however, had their sentences commuted to prison terms: eight years for Lotte Rotholz; five years for Edith Fraenkel; and three years for Alice Hirsch.[42] Upon completion of the trial, the three young women were taken to the district court prison on Kantstrasse and then transferred to Cottbus prison, southeast of Berlin, to complete their sentences.[43]

Three attorneys, all Nazi party members, were assigned to work on behalf of the accused; it was through their hard work that Lotte Rotholz, Edith Fraenkel and Alice Hirsch received prison terms instead of the death penalty. Amongst these lawyers was Masius, to whom Harry Cühn had been recommended after the arrest of Edith Fraenkel. They also attempted to get pardons or lesser sentences for the other defendants after sentencing on 10 December 1942. They called attention to the fact that their fathers had fought for Germany during the First World War and were honest, patriotic German Jews. Heinz Rotholz and the others set to work writing appeals on their own behalf to submit to the court. The officials at the People's Court were not pleased by this move by the defence council, but were required to process the appeals which were not signed with the de rigueur 'Heil Hitler' salutation.

Reports about the prisoners' behaviour in jail were requested, of which that concerning Siegbert Rotholz survives. In it he is complemented on his attitude and work performance while at Alt Moabit prison, but his strong belief in communism is stressed.

> He is apparently unable to recognise that his deed was a criminal one and therefore is due to be punished. His death sentence did not shake him, and he was even able to smile about it. Special circumstances that might warrant a pardon have not emerged.[44]

Harry Cühn was able to speak to Heinz Birnbaum and Edith Fraenkel after the verdict; Heinz asked him for a last cigarette, but Harry knew the People's Court was a non-smoking building and had left his cigarettes at home.

> The incident with the one cigarette will never leave my mind, because I still blame myself about the fact that I did not even have a single cigarette to give him. This burdens me even now [1993]. Yes. Because I never saw my friend 'Buber' ever again.[45]

On 10 December, Rita Meyer was taken to Alt Moabit prison where she was put into a Jew cell with Marianne Joachim, who had just received her death sentence in the People's Court earlier that day. She writes, 'The fascists had Jew cells in their prisons, which gave us a chance to be together and exchange information.'[46]

One day early in January 1943, Ellen Lewinsky received a note which had been smuggled out of Plötzensee prison by a friend visiting a prisoner. It was from Heinz Birnbaum: 'Dear Ellen, I am freezing cold all the time. Please send me some warm clothing. Heinz.' She flushed the note down the toilet and got to work knitting a woollen sweater and gloves for her friend. Ellen gave the clothing to her contact, who took it to Plötzensee.[47]

Heinz Birnbaum awoke in Plötzensee prison in cell 46 on the morning of 4 March 1943. He knew that his life would end that evening. He had applied for a pardon, but there was little chance. At 1.00pm footsteps approached his cell, and the door was opened to reveal the prison administration inspector Rohde, who was impeccably dressed in red, and Plötzensee's prison doctor, Dr Schmidt, who wore a crisp, white gown. Inspector Rohde told him that his appeal for a pardon, according to the decree of the Reich Minister of Justice, had been rejected. He also told Heinz that the sentence would be 'enforced' at 6.30pm. According to the two men, Birnbaum was 'calm and collected' when told of his imminent death.[48]

A few hours before his scheduled execution, Heinz was taken to a cell in House III. Once inside the cell, he was shackled and placed under armed guard. From there it was a short walk to the execution chamber. At precisely 6.30pm Judge Dr Beselin, the prison's enforcement director, dressed in red, and Karpe, the Court Clerk, dressed in green, were standing in front of his cell. The guard then removed the shackles from Birnbaum's wrists and ankles and Heinz rubbed the back of his neck; the night before an old shoemaker had carefully shaved his hair short to expose the skin. Firmly pulling Heinz's hands behind his back, the guard tied them together with a length of rope. The condemned did not resist. A police sergeant escorted Heinz from the cell to the guillotine; each time he ushered a prisoner from the 'house of the dead' to the execution chamber he received a payment of eight cigarettes.

At 6.32pm Birnbaum stood facing the execution chamber. Heinz looked straight ahead as his identity was 'demonstrated' by Beselin. Karpe started a stopwatch and stared as the seconds ticked away. The executioner Röttger, bare-chested and wearing a top hat, tails, dark trousers and a mask, was accompanied by his three assistants, the brothers Thomas and Richard

Arnold and a man named Hehnen, all dressed in black. A pastor wearing a black robe was standing nearby; there was no rabbi.

Röttger received his command from Dr Beselin: 'Executioner. Exercise your office!' The pastor muttered a short prayer as the executioner slithered up to Heinz, leading him by the arm to the *Fallbeil*. Heinz allowed himself to be placed on the guillotine without any struggle. Standing on the left side of the machine, the executioner pulled the lever. The heavy blade fell and Röttger declared, 'Mr Prosecutor, the ruling is enforced'. The clerk then clicked the stopwatch and wrote a number on a small notepad. A document signed by Beselin and Karpe reads, 'The execution from the demonstration until its completion took 18 seconds.'[49] That day also saw the deaths of Hella Hirsch (Heymann), Marianne Joachim, Hildegard Loewy, Hanni Meyer, Helmuth Neumann, Heinz Rotholz, Siegbert Rotholz and Lothar Salinger.

After her brutal three-week interrogation in October 1942, Charlotte Paech was left in her cell for five months, until shortly after the executions of 4 March 1943. Then she was taken to Fehrbellin, a women's 'work education camp' northwest of Berlin. According to Nazi security chief Ernst Kaltenbrunner, 'the working and living conditions for the inmates [in a work education camp] are in general harder than in a concentration camp. This is necessary to achieve the desired results.'[50] Paech spent only a fortnight in Fehrbellin, but it was devastating. She was treated so sadistically that she was barely able to move. Taken back to Berlin, she underwent further Gestapo interrogations. Then she was put in Lehrterstrasse prison where, for the first time since her arrest, she shared a cell with other Jews. 'When we were close to death,' Paech explains, 'we weren't fed and the insects had a feast.'

Charlotte was indicted for high treason along with Martin Kochmann, Felix Heymann and Herbert Budzislawski and was scheduled to go to court to face charges on 29 June. However, before she could face those charges, she was scheduled to be tried for war economy offences, having given food to three comrades with bogus food coupons, which were discovered on her. Found guilty of this crime, she was sentenced to one and a half years in prison in Leipzig! She was then told that she couldn't be taken to Leipzig because she was scheduled to go to court in Berlin for the treason case. But there was a administrative error: the transportation orders for her to go to Leipzig had already been written and processed, and a private policeman had been hired to personally deliver her to Leipzig-Kleinmeusdorf prison. Thus Charlotte was handcuffed and escorted on the train by the policeman. Upon arriving in Leipzig, they took a horse-drawn wagon from the train station to the prison, but she was refused entry. She was a Jew and Leipzig-Kleinmeusdorf was an Aryan prison. She was then taken to three other prisons in Leipzig with the same result. She ended up in Leipzig Detention Prison and was scheduled to be returned to Berlin the next day. However, she did not leave as scheduled, as she fell ill with scarlet fever and was quarantined.[51]

On 11 May 1943 three former comrades of Joachim Franke were sitting in the 'house of the dead' at Plötzensee prison: Werner Schaumann, George Vötter and Artur Illgen. It now appeared that Franke had betrayed his associates in a frantic attempt to save his wife Erika, giving up anyone he could think of. Besides the people documented in the pages of this book, there were dozens more who fell foul of their association with Franke, people who donated money to the cause, bought an anti-fascist newspaper or uttered an anti-fascist sentiment. Franke even offered to be a Gestapo spy; according to the report of his last interrogation, Franke said, 'As a motive for the start of my illegal activities I can only indicate that I hoped to get the central leadership of the KPD and hand them over to the Secret State Police.' It seems that Franke did achieve his goal, as Erika was acquitted for lack of evidence. Why was she set free? A document written by Criminal Secretary Otto Neumann states, in part, that 'Joachim F. in his last police interrogation provided information about the accused that has been considered credible.'[52]

Walter Bernecker, who took part in the 'Soviet Paradise' action with Franke, didn't even survive his Gestapo interrogations. Karl Kunger was executed on 18 June, just a few weeks after Schaumann, Vötter and Illgen. Rita Meyer went on trial before the *Strafsenat* (trial court) on 25 June 1943 with eight other defendants, individuals who had been caught buying or selling the goods that Birnbaum, Steinbrink, Baum and Holzer had 'confiscated' from the Fruendliches in May 1942. Her husband Herbert had died in custody. After sentencing, Rita was sent to Auschwitz. Her five-year-old daughter Barbara was murdered, but there is no record of where or when. Rita vividly remembers her introduction to Auschwitz: 'When I opened my eyes a Soviet woman doctor named Klawa was standing next to me. She bent over me and said that I was still alive. If it had not been for Klawa and the other friends, German, Soviet, Polish communists, I would not have survived.'[53]

Another Baum group trial took place less than a week later, on 29 June 1943. The defendants were Martin Kochmann, Felix Heymann and Herbert Budzislawski.[54] Facing the judge, the three defendants listened to the verdict:

The conditions for a reduced sentence under paragraph 2 of the provision are not being considered, because, although no serious consequences of crimes committed by the accused benefiting the enemy are demonstrable, those such results were intended by the defendants. The attempt to change Germany by way of an internal decomposition to Bolshevism demonstrates, not only an extremely anti-state viewpoint of the perpetrators, but in this case represents such a dangerous threat to the security of the Reich that it must be opposed with all its might.

Accordingly, the Court's decision for all three defendants is the death penalty. This punishment is considered necessary even for the defendant Budzislawski, since he ultimately supports the enemy's desire to deliver Germany to Bolshevism.

The deprivation of civil and political rights has not been recognised because the defendants do not have such rights as Jews.[55]

Charlotte Paech had been charged along with her three comrades, but was not present at the trial. To the great surprise of the Senior State Attorney, she was still in the Leipzig Detention Prison. Having been quarantined for scarlet fever, she was visited once by a doctor in the first week of her illness, who had diagnosed her then never returned.[56] She had thus been left in administrative limbo, and a week before the trial, on 23 September, the senior prosecutor at the People's Court returned the charges against her. This was because Nazi law – specifically Section 1 of the 13th Ordinance of the Reich Citizenship Law – stated clearly that criminal acts by Jews that were punished by the police were no longer judicial matters.[57]

On 16 July Charlotte's quarantine was lifted and she was taken back to Berlin in handcuffs by a private policeman. Arriving around midnight at a detention prison, she was told that she had been sentenced to death. She was also told, however, that it wasn't clear if this decision was official or not, and that she had to wait for an execution date from the court. No surviving documents show that she was formally sentenced to death. She was then put in a cell with five women who were awaiting execution; three of them were taken away while Charlotte was there. 'Never,' writes Paech, 'never in my life will I ever forget my last nights with them.'[58]

During an air raid on the night of 3/4 September 1943, the guillotine at Plötzensee prison was damaged and rendered inoperable. At that time there were over 300 condemned prisoners in House III, which was also damaged in the attack. Three prisoners escaped but were caught shortly thereafter.

This activated the circular issued by the Reich Ministry of Justice on 27 August which allowed for the speeding up the execution of death sentences due to the risk of air raids.

A few days after the air raid, on 6 September, a Ministry of Justice report stated, 'The roof of the execution chamber was stripped; the tile floor was partially destroyed; and the guillotine was damaged by fire, torn out of its underpinnings, and lay on the floor. The extent to which it remains serviceable must be determined by closer inspection, which has already been delegated to Tegel prison.' The Ministry considered having death sentences carried out at the Wehrmacht target ranges by either police or military firing squads. However, on 7 September, the Ministry of Justice – in response to Hitler's personal request – decided to shorten the clemency proceedings and execute all condemned prisoners in Plötzensee by hanging on the gallows that stood behind the damaged guillotine.

In order to streamline the process of forwarding the death warrants to Plötzensee, the names of the condemned were conveyed via telephone from the Reich Ministry of Justice to the prison, where a clerk sat at the ready with a prepared list. A Ministry representative would tell the clerk a name, the clerk checked his list and then told a prison official to put that person in a line, and the condemned was hung from a meat hook on the gallows. This procedure left something to be desired; that night four prisoners whose clemency proceedings had not yet been completed were executed, including a 17-year-old whose family had been assured that he was likely to be spared.

Amongst the 300 condemned prisoners in the 'house of the dead' on 7 September were Martin Kochmann, Felix Heymann and Herbert Budzislawski. Shackled and unable to leave their cells, they and the other prisoners were terrorised by the air raid going on overhead. A fire broke out and many of the cell doors were torn open by the shockwaves of exploding bombs. It was general knowledge that the guillotine had been damaged, and some of the prisoners believed that they would live a few extra days. They did not know about the plan to put the gallows into operation.

Amongst the eyewitnesses that documented the horror of 7 September 1943 were two prison chaplains, the Protestant cleric Harald Poelchau and his Catholic colleague, Peter Buchholz. Poelchau writes:

As darkness fell on 7 September the mass murders began. The night was cold. Every now and then the darkness was lit up by exploding bombs. The beams of the searchlights danced across the sky. The men were assembled in several columns one behind the other. They stood there, at first uncertain about what was going to happen to them. Then they realised. Eight men at a time were called by name and led away. Those remaining hardly moved at all.

Kochmann, Heymann, and Budzislawski had their shackles removed and were directed to stand in one of the columns. Names were called out: 'Hermann Vogt! Afred Krueger! Alfred Noack! Hans Heinrich Festersen! Ernst Hirning! Fritz Lemme! Friedrich Riemann! Willem Ekhart!' As each group of eight was led away, the remainder moved up the line.

A green-clad clerk sat with a list in front of him. As each man was hung by his neck on the gallows, the clerk drew a small cross next to his name. The clerk ran his finger down the page, drawing his little crosses as the executioner, a cigarette dangling from his lips, and his three assistants did their murderous work. More names were called out. More tiny crosses were drawn. More men apathetically shuffled up the columns. Then suddenly Martin, Felix and Herbert were the front three men of their column.

'Martin Israel Kochmann! Felix Israel Heymann! Herbert Israel Budzislawski!' This was the last time they were ever to hear their names spoken. They were led away with five other men. The clerk ran his finger down the list to number 32 and drew a cross next to 'Kochmann', then to number 33 and drew a cross next to 'Heymann', and finally to number 34 and drew a cross next to 'Budzislawski'. They were the last of the Baum group to be executed.

Protestant cleric Harald Poelchau continues:

Once the executioners interrupted their work because bombs thundered down nearby. The five rows of eight men already lined up had to be confined to their cells again for a while. Then the murdering continued. All these men were hanged ... The executions had to be carried out by candlelight because the electric light had failed. It was only at about 8.00am that the exhausted executioners paused in their work...[59]

That night the executioner Röttger was instructed by the prison authorities to 'reduce the number of prisoners quickly.' For the 186 people he killed that night he earned 5580 Reichmarks. He later described the process: 'The condemned had the noose placed around his neck. Then he was lifted. Then I take the loop and hang it on the hook as one would hang a dress.'[60]

Harry Cühn was allowed to visit his lover Edith Fraenkel in Cottbus prison. Edith kept asking Harry about her mother, and he repeatedly told her that she was doing well, even though in fact she had been arrested and was in the Kantstrasse prison. He did not want to upset or worry her further. One day in early October 1943 Harry went to Cottbus to see Edith but she was not there. He was told that she had been taken to Grosse Hamburger Strasse by the Gestapo. Harry knew that it was a transit camp to Auschwitz, and he rushed back to Berlin, taking a taxi from the Freidrichstrasse train station to Grosse Hamburger Strasse.[61]

Located in the Scheunenviertel sub-district of Mitte, the transit camp was on the site of two former Jewish institutions, the Jewish Community School for Boys and the Jewish Home for the Aged. They appeared unchanged except for the bars on all the windows and the blinding floodlights at night. Next to the transit camp were a series of air-raid shelters on the former grounds of the oldest Jewish cemetery in Berlin, which was in use from 1672 to 1827. In 1943 it was desecrated, the broken gravestones used to reinforce the walls of the shelters.[62]

Arriving at the transit camp, Harry made it his business to meet and get to know the Nazi in charge: Master Sergeant Walter Dobberke. The SS Master Sergeant could be mean and stubborn, and any breach of regulations sent him into a rage. He does not appear to have been an anti-Semite however, as he could be found enjoying an evening game of Skat with a Jew whom he had given 25 lashes a few hours before. Additionally, Dobberke did not see any reason whatsoever to hide the fact that he had a Jewish girlfriend who worked at the Jewish Hospital, where Charlotte Paech had been a nurse.[63]

Bruno Blau left an account of Walter Dobberke, written in 1952:

According to the unanimous judgment of former centre internees, no objections could be made to the treatment of Jewish inmates by the camp director Dobberke. He mistreated the inmates only if he thought that he had been lied to, or if he suspected some other resistance; otherwise, however, to the extent that it was within his power, he eased their lot in many ways, although he had the power to turn life into hell for them. One could get a great deal from him with a bottle of spirits made in the pharmacy or the hospital, and the hospital's director did his best to keep Dobberke in a good mood. At any rate, the inmates of the transit centre had it much better than the inmates of the police prisons.

It was the Jewish 'order keepers' who brutalised the prisoners at the transit camp, rather than Dobberke. Blau wrote that 'Some of them treated the Jews in their charge badly, beating them, too, especially the assistant leader Blond, who disappeared immediately after the Russians marched in.'[64]

Harry Cühn was not allowed to speak to Edith, but he spoke with Dobberke every day in order to build a rapport. He also spoke with Dr Jacobsohn, the Jewish lawyer whom he first contacted when Edith was arrested. No longer a lawyer, Jacobsohn had been given the job of steward at the transit camp by the Gestapo. He helped the Gestapo in the hope that he, his wife and young son would not be deported. Jacobsohn told Cühn that he could not offer much help because of his situation, but that it was believed that those who were sent to Thereisienstadt were more likely to survive. By 1943 everyone knew what Auschwitz meant. Harry went to Dobberke and tried to convince him to help. He told the SS man that Edith was not Jewish, that there was a pending investigation to prove it, and that she was not involved in the attack on 'Soviet Paradise'. Dobberke said there was nothing he could do and that he should talk to Jacobsohn, who could only offer to put Edith on a transport to Thereisienstadt. Harry could not free his lover, but better Theresientstadt than Auschwitz.

Alice Hirsch and Lotte Rotholz were also released from Cottbus prison at the same time as Edith Fraenkel and taken to the transit camp on Grosse Hamburger Strasse.[65] They had no Harry Cühn to fight their corner. On 14 October, the Gestapo put together a list of 75 people from the transit camp who were destined for Auschwitz. The following day, 15 October, Dobberke handed Jacobsohn a list of people to be rounded up. The former lawyer saw the name at the top: '44 Osttransport'. Lotte Rotholz was number 63 on the list and Alice Hirsch was number 64. The two young women, along with 73 other Berlin Jews, were put on the transport that day and taken to Auschwitz, where they arrived a few days later and were gassed.[66]

In 1944 Charlotte Paech was still being held in a Berlin detention prison, fearing a death sentence that did not exist. One day she was escorted down several hallways and corridors until she arrived at a small room, where a Gestapo officer was waiting. Believing her death was perhaps a few hours away, she was shocked to find herself being held in his arms. He pulled her towards him, kissing her neck and pressing himself firmly against her. His advances were violently rejected; he did not attempt to force himself upon her.

The Gestapo officer took her outside to a truck and put her in the back where two old Jewish men were sitting. Completely confused, Charlotte did not know what to think. The Jews handed her sandwiches and apples as the truck sped away. These two men were stewards at the transit camp on Grosse Hamburger Strasse run by Dobberke. During their conversation, she discovered that Jewish Hungarian women had been picked up and brought to the transit camp en route to deportation to Ravensbrück, and that Richard Holzer's mother was amongst them. Through the Jewish stewards she arranged to speak with her lover's mother for half an hour after arriving at the transit camp. A short time later the older woman was deported.[67]

On 16 October 1944 a transport list was compiled in Theresienstadt. Called transport 'Er' ('he'), there were 1500 names on the register; Edith Fraenkel was number 653. She and the others were put in box cars and transported to Auschwitz. Two days later, on 18 October, Edith perished in the gas chambers of the death camp.[68] All Harry Cühn's efforts had been for naught.

Meanwhile a fire had broken out at Gestapo headquarters, destroying, damaging or misplacing a vast number of documents. Charlotte Paech's confinement became more bearable because her dossier could not be located and therefore her status was in flux. Transferred to the camp on Schulstrasse, she was allowed to work as a nurse once again. For the first time, Lotti thought that she just might survive after all.

One day, however, she was told that her case was being reopened and that new hearings were scheduled. The warden's secretary told Paech that the documents in her case had been located and sent to the Gestapo security office on Kurfürstenstrasse. Charlotte was sure that if she were taken to court the only result would be transport to Auschwitz. Desperate, she became friendly with prisoners who worked outside the camp during the day, and through them she made contacts. She was found a place to stay by a circle of the Confessional, if she could escape the camp.

It was all up to Lotti to find a way out. To her, the choice was an easy one. If she was going to be killed anyway, then what was the difference whether she died escaping from the prison or after arriving at Auschwitz? The prison camp was located in the morgue of the Jewish Hospital where she had worked for fourteen years, and her knowledge of the place helped her plan her escape. She was also aided by the fact that the outer wall had been partially destroyed by seventeen Allied bombs.

Each day her imprisonment became more difficult. Three times she attempted to escape through an open door, but each time she was caught by guards and had to make up plausible excuses for being so close to it.

Then one day she heard that a second wire fence was to be erected around the circumference of the prison. She knew that she would never be able to escape through two wire fences. She had to make her move. An inmate who was putting up the fence told her that it would be finished on Monday. It was Saturday. She only had one day.

Charlotte had a reputation for being shy and modest, which helped her in her plan. Early on Sunday morning she approached the Gestapo officer on duty, who was one of the nicer ones, and calmly asked if he would allow her to take a walk along the fence.

'When did you become crazy?' he responded. 'How dare you ask such a stupid request!'

She mentioned her death sentence, saying that the only thing she wanted after two and a half years of imprisonment was to walk along the fence to feel free one last time. The Gestapo man looked her up and down, thought for a minute.

'Today between 1 and 2.00pm will be good. We will take a walk together.'

She thanked him and he sent her away. But she felt desperate because she knew she could not escape with him beside her, and that afternoon she told him that she was feeling ill and was not up to taking the walk.

She knew that there was no Gestapo patrol on Sundays from 3.00–7.00pm. During that time, Jews were responsible for patrol duty. On that particular Sunday, it was the turn of Mose Blond, who was known as being unpleasant and a Gestapo informant. Paech later wrote that 'He was a dog.' One time she saw him beat a young girl with a whip until she bled. Charlotte wanted her escape to get him in trouble.

At 4.30pm the Jews from the camp had their daily walk. Paech began making a lot of noise. She demanded that Blond allow her to walk outside of the fence, telling him that the Gestapo officer had given her permission. She begged Blond for several minutes until he gave in. She walked up to the fence and strolled back and forth, back and forth. She intuitively felt that the other prisoners knew her intent, because they tried to distract Blond.

Blond was speaking with an inmate when Paech vanished into the hospital grounds outside the fence. She hid for one and a half hours and heard the search party coming towards her. After years as a helpless prisoner she had to take the initiative. Finding a small opening in the wall, she pushed her way through it and found herself on the street outside the camp. She walked ten kilometres to reach her first hideout; it was only the first stop on the long road to liberation.[69]

AFTERWORD

LEGACY OF THE BAUM GROUP

The 'Soviet Paradise' action was an example of flawed heroics by a desperate group of anti-fascist Jews and their non-Jewish comrades. His followers never asked Herbert Baum how he expected to carry out an arson attack when he had no experience of such things, and how he planned to get away with it. But it was nevertheless an act of heroism, a rare act of resistance against a brutal regime.

The consequences were terrible, for the Baum group, those who helped them on the run, and the wider Berlin Jewry. Many were imprisoned, executed or died in concentration camps. But there were some survivors. Richard Holzer lived in Hungary during the remainder of the war and came back to Berlin to marry Charlotte Paech, who was never recaptured after her escape from prison. Ellen Compart and Ursula Ehrlich survived underground in Berlin, and both later moved to America. Rita Meyer survived Auschwitz and Ravensbrück; liberated by the Red Army, Rita spent two years in hospital before she was well enough to live on her own and move to the Soviet sector of Berlin. Gerda May survived in Germany, as did her gentile husband Willi. Gerda returned to the Soviet sector of Berlin, while Willi moved to America to be with Ellen Compart, with whom he had lived while she was pretending to be Gerda. Ari Steinbach survived the camps and also moved to America. Harry Cühn survived on luck and moxie in Berlin and stayed in what became West Berlin.

Several of those who had escaped Berlin during the early years of the war returned after 1945, including Walter Sack, Gerhard and Alice Zadek,

Günther Prager, Herbert Ansbach, Franz Krahl, Paul Friendlaender and Ismar Zoellner. For the most part, they settled in East Berlin. But that is another book.

NOTES

Chapter 1

1 Barta, Rudi, letter to the author, 6 March 1988.
2 Ibid, 16 April 1988.
3 Pikarski, *Jugend im Berliner Widerstand. Herbert Baum und Kampfgefährten* pp.48–49; Brothers, 'On the Anti-Fascist Resistance of German Jews' pp.377–79.
4 Rosenstock, 'The Jewish Youth Movement' p.97.
5 Ibid.
6 Ibid, pp.97–98.
7 Barta, Rudi, letter to the author, 16 April 1988.
8 Ibid, 6 March 1988.
9 Abraham, Max, letter to the author, 11 November 1985.
10 Rita Zocher deposition.
11 Barta, Rudi, letter to the author, 6 March 1988; comments to the author by Walter Sack, 6 July 1988.
12 Pikarski, p.132, 140; Kreutzer, '*Die Suche nach einem Ausweg, der es ermoglicht, in Deutschland als Mensch zu leben Zur Geschichte der Widerstandsgruppen um Herbert Baum*' p.150.
13 Norbert Wollheim interview.
14 Margot Deutsch-Verlardo interview.
15 Barta, Rudi, letters to the author.
16 Gerhard Zadek interview.
17 Pikarski, pp.48–50.
18 Pikarski, p.50.
19 Rita Zocher deposition.
20 Ballhorn, Herbert, letter to the author, 11 December 1984.
21 Ibid, 23 November 1984.
22 Ibid, letter to the author, 22 January 1985.
23 Ibid, letters to the author, March 1985 and 22 June 1985.

Chapter 2

1 Gross, 'The Zionist Students' Movement' p.144.
2 Ibid, p.145.
3 Gross, p.146.
4 Traverso, *The Jews & Germany: From the 'Judeo-German Symbiosis' to the Memory of Auschwitz* pp.23–24.
5 Gross, p.147.
6 Ibid, p.148.
7 Ibid, p.149.
8 Poppel, *Zionism in Germany 1897–1933: The Shaping of a Jewish Identity* p.71.
9 Ibid, pp.70–71.
10 Ibid, p.75.
11 Ibid, p.76.
12 Ibid, p.133.
13 Rinott, 'Major Trends in Jewish Youth Movements in Germany' p.88.
14 Gross, p.151.
15 Poppel, p.133.
16 Gross, pp.155–156.
17 Poppel, p.134.
18 Rinott, p.89.
19 Poppel, Table 7.
20 Ibid, p.134.
21 Gross, pp.158–159.
22 Ibid, p.159.
23 Moaz, 'The Werkleute' p.167.
24 Ibid, pp.167–168.
25 Rheins, 'The Schwarzes Fahnlein, Jungenschaft 1932–1934' p.176.
26 Ibid, pp.176–177.
27 Moaz, p.174.
28 Rheins, p.174.
29 Ibid, p.179.
30 Ibid, p.180.
31 Ibid, p.181.
32 Ibid, p.182.
33 Ibid, p.183.
34 Rosenstock, p.102.
35 Rheins, p.185.
36 Ibid, p.188.
37 Ibid, p.193.
38 Ibid, p.194.
39 Rosenstock, p.102.

Chapter 3

1 Rosenstock, p.101.
2 Ansbach, Herbert, letter to the author, 7 July 1987.
3 Richarz, (ed.) *Jewish Life in Germany: Memoirs from Three Centuries* pp.317–318.
4 Rinott, p.79.
5 Paucker, *Jewish Resistance in Germany: The Facts and the Problems* p.9.

6 Rinott, p.80.
7 Ibid, p.82.
8 Richarz, p.316.
9 Weitz, pp.160–161.
10 Crossman, Richard, (ed.) *The God That Failed* p.29.
11 For a more in-depth look at the issues surrounding the 'Red Assimilation,' see the following essays from the *Leo Baeck Institute Year Book* listed in the bibliography: Mosse, George L., 'German Socialists and the Jewish Question in the Weimar Republic'; Erpel, Simone, 'Struggle and Survival: Jewish Women in the Anti-Fascist Resistance in Germany'; Brothers, Eric, 'On the Anti-Fascist Resistance of German Jews'; Rinott, Chanoch, 'Major Trends in Jewish Youth Movements in Germany'; Maoz, Eliyahu, 'The Werkleute'; Rosenstock, Werner, 'The Jewish Youth Movement'; and Eckstein, George Gunther, 'The Freie Deutsch-Judische Jugend (FDJJ) 1932–1933.' Also see the written testimony of Gerhard Bry in: Richarz, Monika, (ed.) *Jewish Life in Germany: Memoirs from Three Centuries* (pp.369–378).

Chapter 4
1 Avidenko, A.O., 'Hymn to Stalin'.
2 Weitz, *Creating German Communism, 1890–1990: From Popular Protests to Socialist State* p.234.
3 Ibid, pp.234–35.
4 Bankier, 'The German Communist Party and Nazi Antisemitism, 1933–1938' p.326.
5 Lippmann, *Honecker and the New Politics of Europe* p.18.
6 Ibid.
7 Ibid, p.19.
8 Ibid, p.20.
9 Weitz, p.235.
10 Trotsky, 'Bureaucratic Ultimatism,' pp.4–5.
11 Weitz, pp.235–36.
12 Weitz, p.236.
13 Crossman, p.27.
14 Ibid, p.242.
15 Crossman, p.43.
16 Ibid, p.50.
17 Ibid.
18 Crossman, pp.29–30.

Chapter 5
1 Heiden, *Der Fuehrer: Hitler's Rise to Power* p.545.
2 Dawidowicz, *The War Against the Jews 1933–1945* p.63.
3 Heiden, p.266.
4 Ibid, p.544.
5 Shirer, *The Rise and Fall of the Third Reich* p.266.
6 Ibid.
7 Heiden, p.548.
8 Ibid, p.550.
9 Ibid.
10 Ibid, p.522.

11 Ibid.
12 Ibid.
13 Shirer, p.268.
14 Guerin, *The Brown Plague: Travels in Late Weimar and Early Nazi Germany* p.25.
15 Shirer, p.271.
16 Heiden, p.548.
17 Shirer, p.276.
18 Weitz, p.285.
19 Crossman, pp.44–45.
20 Weitz, p.285.
21 Crossman, p.35.
22 Ibid, p.51.
23 Ibid, p.52.
24 Weitz, p.285.
25 Trotsky, 'Against National Communism! (Lessons of the 'Red Referendum)'
26 Ibid.
27 Shirer, p.276.
28 Dawidowicz, *The War...* p.68.
29 Shirer, p.278.
30 Weitz, pp.285–286.
31 Ibid, p.286.

Chapter 6
1 Pikarski, passim.
2 Weitz, p.280.
3 Ibid, p.286.
4 George Manasse interview.
5 Benz and Pehle (eds.) *Encyclopedia of German Resistance to the Nazi Movement* p.68.
6 George Manasse interview.
7 Pikarski, p.45.
8 Ballhorn, Herbert, letter to the author, 22 January 1985.
9 Kreutzer, pp.97–98.
10 Barta, Rudi, letter to the author, 16 April 1988.
11 Ellen Compart depositions.
12 Dawidowicz, *The War...* pp.77–78.
13 Ibid, pp.232–233.
14 Ellen Compart depositions.
15 Schoeberner, *Artists Against Hitler: Persecution, Exile, Resistance* pp.50–51.
16 Ellen Compart depositions.
17 Shirer, p.333.
18 Ansbach, Herbert, letter to the author, 18 September 1985; Pikarski, p.132.

Chapter 7
1 Pikarski, pp.29–30.
2 Kurt Siering interview.
3 Ansbach, Herbert, letters to the author, 29 September 1986 and 5 December 1986.
4 Pikarski, p.154.
5 Ansbach, Herbert, letters to the author, 23 November 1985 and 20 May 1986.

6 George Manasse interview.
7 Kurt Siering interview.
8 Berlin Criminal Court document O.J. 529/34, 11 September 1934.
9 Pikarski, pp.30–31; Ansbach, Herbert, letters to the author, 29 September 1986 and 5 December 1986.
10 Otto Wendt interview.
11 Ellen Compart depositions.

Chapter 8

1 Ansbach, Herbert, letter to the author, 18 September 1985.
2 Pikarski, pp.32–33.
3 George Manasse interview.
4 Ibid.
5 Ibid.
6 Ellen Compart depositions.
7 Günther Prager interview.
8 Barta, Rudi, letter to the author, 6 March 1988.
9 Kreutzer, pp.111–112.
10 Ellen Compart depositions.
11 Pikarski, pp.33–34.
12 Ibid, p.132.
13 Ellen Compart depositions.
14 Dietrich, 'Kampfer und Augenzeugen unserer Ersten Reihe: Leitungsrunde bei 'Erich''
15 Alfred Eisenstädter interviews.
16 Pikarski, p.165.
17 Alfred Eisenstädter interviews.

Chapter 9

1 Pikarski, pp.37–38.
2 Weitz, p.294.
3 Crossman, p.62.
4 Pikarski, pp.37–41.
5 Weitz, pp.294–295.
6 Alfred Eisenstädter interviews.
7 McDonough, *Opposition and Resistance in Nazi Germany* pp.6–7.
8 Pikarski, p.42.
9 Weitz, p.297.
10 Otto Wendt interview.
11 Kreutzer, p.101.

Chapter 10

1 Cox, *Circles of Resistance: Jewish, Leftist, and Youth Dissidence in Nazi Germany* pp.67–69.
2 Ansbach, Herbert, letter to the author, 23 November 1985; Alfred Eisenstädter interviews.
3 'Ring, Bund Deutsch-jüdischer Jugend.'
4 Ilse Kessler (née Prager) interview; on Inge Gerson, see Brothers, Eric, 'Profile of a German-Jewish Resistance Fighter,' passim.

5 Ellen Arndt interview; Pikarski, p.134.
6 Ellen Compart depositions; Dr Arnold Paucker remembers seeing one of the flyers
('Hitler, Germany's gravedigger') shortly before emigrating from Berlin in 1936. Letter
to the author, 8 September 1986, London.
7 Ellen Compart depositions; see also: Brothers, Eric, 'On the Anti-Fascist Resistance...'
pp.375–376.

Chapter 11
1 Pikarski, pp.55–57.
2 Rita Zocker deposition.
3 Schatzker, 'The Jewish Youth Movement in Germany in the Holocaust Period (I):
Youth in Confrontation with a New Reality' p.165.
4 Ilse Heller telephone interview.
5 Kellerman, 'From Imperial to National-Socialist Germany. Recollections of a
German-Jewish Youth Leader' p.322.
6 Ibid, p.324.
7 Ilse Heller interview; Inge Aptekmann interview.
8 Ellen Compart depositions.
9 Rita Zocher deposition.
10 Sarin and Dvoretsky, *Alien Wars: The Soviet Union's Aggressions Against the World, 1919 to
1989* p.2.
11 Ibid, p.3.
12 Ibid, pp.4–5.
13 Lustiger, 'German and Austrian Jews in the International Brigade' p.298.
14 Ibid, p.301.
15 Ibid, p.303.
16 Ibid, p.312.
17 Alfred Eisenstädter interviews.
18 Gerhard Zadek interview.
19 Ansbach, Herbert, letter to the author, 23 November 1985; see also: Sachs, Henry, letter
to the author, 25 January 1986.

Chapter 12
1 Rita Zocker deposition.
2 Ellen Compart depositions.
3 Erpel, pp.404–405.
4 Ellen Compart depositions.
5 Alfred Eisenstädter interviews.
6 Dawidowicz, *The War...* pp.133–137.
7 Kreutzer, p.112.
8 Lustiger, p.301.
9 Alfred Eisenstädter interviews.
10 Ilse Kessler interview.

Chapter 13
1 Alfred Eisenstädter interviews.
2 Ilse Kessler interview; diary frontispiece inscription from Marianne Prager to Ilse

Prager 21 May 1939.

3 Gerhard Zadek interview.

4 Pikarski, pp.60–62.

5 Günther Prager interview; Pikarski, pp.60–62.

6 Weitz, p.302.

7 Sarin and Dvoretsky, pp.40–41.

8 Ibid, pp.43–44.

9 Weitz, pp.302–303.

10 Crossman, p.70.

11 Alfred Eisenstädter interviews.

Chapter 14

1 Weitz, p.303.

2 Sarin and Dvoretsky, p.51.

3 Pikarski, pp.87–88.

4 Alfred Eisenstädter interviews.

5 Ibid.

6 Kwiet, 'Forced Labour of German Jews in Nazi Germany' p.390.

7 Ibid, p.392.

8 Ibid, p.395.

9 Ibid, p.396.

10 Kwiet, 'Forced Labour…' pp.396–397.

11 Pikarski, p.91.

12 Ibid, pp.92–94.

13 Ellen Compart depositions.

14 Alfred Eisenstädter interviews.

15 Ibid.

16 Ibid.

17 Ibid.

18 Ibid.

19 Kreutzer, p.107.

20 Ibid, p.111.

21 Ibid, pp.114–115.

22 Charlotte Paech-Holzer deposition; Scheer, *Im Schatten der Sterne: Eine jüdische Widerstandsgruppe* pp.405–407.

23 Kreutzer, p.107; Scheer, p.407.

24 Eschwege, p.164; Cox, p.20, 89, 127; Scheer, p.408.

25 Scheer, pp.407–408.

26 Alfred Eisenstädter interviews.

27 Pikarski, pp.94–96; Moaz, 'A Jewish Underground in Germany,' pp.7–8. The following make an unsubstantiated claim that 50 people attended Rudi Arndt's memorial: Mark, 'The Herbert Baum Group: Jewish Resistance in Germany in the Years 1937–1942' p.61; Eschwege, 'Resistance of German Jews against the Nazi Regime' p.171; Steinberg, 'The Herbert Baum Campaign' p.31. I agree with Pikarski, who had the testimony of witness Ilse Haak who attended the memorial. This view is shared with Scheffler, 'Der Brandanschlag im Berliner Lustgarten im Mai 1942 und seine Folgen' p.114.

28 Ellen Arndt interview. That Heinz Birnbaum and others performed sabotage at Schubert-Werke was confirmed in statements to the author by Fred Cassel, who was a

Jewish sub-foreman there. Fred Cassel interview.

29 Engelmann, *In Hitler's Germany: Everyday Life in the Third Reich* pp.235–238; information on Erich Elkan is found in Engelmann, passim.

30 Alfred Eisenstädter interviews.

Chapter 15

1 Kwiet, 'Forced Labour…' p.393.

2 Pikarski, p.94.

3 Ellen Compart depositions; Kreutzer, p.113.

4 Gerda Lüth interview.

5 Kreutzer, p.121.

6 Pikarski, pp.144–145.

7 Kreutzer, p.121.

8 Pikarski, p.155.

9 Kreutzer, p.121.

10 Pikarski, p.152.

11 Ibid, pp.142–143.

12 Kreutzer, p.121.

13 Letters to the author of 22 July 1985 and 16 January 1986 from Inge Berner; *Tafellied* set to the tune of '*Stimmt an mit hellen hohen Klang*' written by Alfons Joachim 22/24 August 1941, from Ilse Kessler.

14 Kreutzer, p.129; Cox, pp.88–89; Pikarski, p.118, 156; Steinberg, pp.31–32; Eschwege, pp.173–174; Mark, pp.62–63.

15 Ellen Compart depositions.

16 Gerda Lüth interview.

17 'Operation *Barbarossa*,' in Wikipedia

18 Cox, p.110.

19 Krutzer, pp.118–119.

20 Ellen Arndt interview.

21 Ellen Compart depositions.

22 Kreutzer, pp.122–124.

23 Ellen Arndt interview.

24 Cox, p.111; excerpt from *Der Weg zum Sieg* in Pikarski, pp.166–187; Wolfgang Diewerge, *Deutsche Soldaten sehen die Sowjet-Union. Feldpostbriefe aus dem Osten* (Berlin: Wilhelm Limpert-Verlag, 1941) Excerpts of this brochure are found in English at the online German Propaganda Archive. The cover art from this brochure was adapted for the poster for *Das Sowjet-Paradies*, the propaganda exhibition that opened in Berlin in May 1942. http://www.calvin.edu/academic/cas/gpa/feldpost.htm)

25 Cox, p.112.

26 Kreutzer, p.119.

27 Ibid, p.128.

28 Ibid.

29 Ibid, p.127.

30 Benz and Pehle, p.247.

31 Kreutzer, p.127.

32 Ibid, p.128.

33 Cox, p.112; excerpts from *Der Ausweg* in Pikarski, pp.191–201.

34 Pikarski, pp.103–105.

35 Scheer, p.409.

36 Kreutzer, p.128.

Chapter 16

1 People's Court judgment against Rotholz and others 10 J 207/42g 2 H 314/42 dated 10 December 1942; Kreutzer, p.124.

2 Kreutzer, p.124; Alfred Eisenstädter interviews; Rita Zocher deposition; Norbert Wollheim interview; George Manasse interviews; People's Court judgment against Rotholz and others 10 J 207/42g 2 H 314/42 dated 10 December 1942.

3 Ellen Compart depositions.

4 Pikarski, p.117.

5 Ibid, pp.118–119.

6 Kreutzer, pp.125–128

7 Steinberg, p.33; Scheffler, p.99.

8 Ellen Compart depositions.

10 Kreutzer, p.129.

11 Ibid, p.130.

12 Ibid, pp.130–131.

13 Ibid, p.132.

14 Ibid, p.132.

15 Brothers, 'Profile…' pp.31–32.

16 Pikarski, pp.120–121; Steinberg, pp.34–35; Mark, pp.63–64; Brothers, 'Profile…' pp.31–32, pp.35–36; Charlotte Paech-Holzer deposition.

17 Original photos of 'Soviet Paradise' exhibition sent to the author by Michael Kreutzer; *Das Sowjet-Paradies. Ausstellung der Reichspropagandaleitung der NSDAP. Ein Bericht in Wort und Bild.* Berlin: Zentralverlag der NSDAP., 1942. http://www.calvin.edu/academic/cas/gpa/paradise.htm; Rita Zocher deposition.

18 Kreutzer, pp.134–135.

19 Ibid, p.135; Martin Kochmann's personal qualities in Eisenstädter interviews and Paech deposition.

20 Kreutzer, p.135.

21 Ellen Arndt interview.

Chapter 17

1 Richard Holzer written testimony c.1948, cited in Kreutzer, p.135.

2 Kreutzer, p.135.

3 Ellen Arndt interview.

4 Kreutzer, p.136.

5 Ibid, p.135.

6 Historical Weather: Berlin-Tegel, Germany. 18 May 1942. http://www.tutiempo.net/en/Climate/Berlin-Tegel/18-05-1942/103820.htm

7 Kreutzer, pp.136–137.

8 Pikarski, p.123.

9 Lindenberger, 'Heroic Or Foolish? The 1942 Bombing of a Nazi Anti-Soviet Exhibit' p.127.

10 Benz and Pehle, p.180.

11 Pikarski, pp.123–125.

12 Kreutzer, p.139.

13 Ibid, p.137.

14 Ibid, p.139.

15 Ibid, p.153.

16 Special Court document 7.0. Js. 219/43g dated 25 June 1943.

17 Charlotte Paech-Holzer deposition.

18 Kreutzer, p.139.

19 Special Court document 7.0. Js. 219/43g dated 25 June 1943.

20 Kreutzer, p.139.

21 Ibid, p.140.

22 Lindenberger, p.129. Goebbels refers to 'An engineer at Siemens...' In Germany, an 'engineer' is a skilled tradesman who has completed an apprenticeship.

23 Kreutzer, p.141; Pikarski, p.126.

24 Bundesarchiv Bild 183-J03164. Photo: Hoffmann – August 1942.

25 Pikarski, p.126.

26 Kreutzer, p.141; Alfred Eisenstädter interviews.

27 Kreutzer, p.141.

28 Pikarski, p.126.

29 Kreutzer, p.141.

30 Special Court document 7.0. Js. 219/43g dated 25 June 1943.

31 Kreutzer, p.142.

32 Ibid.

33 Ibid, p.141.

34 Rita Zocher deposition.

35 Ellen Arndt interview.

36 Charlotte Paech-Holzer deposition.

37 Kreutzer, p.138.

38 Cox, pp.135–136.

39 Ibid, p.136.

40 Hildesheimer, *The Central Organisation of the German Jews in the Years 1933–1945* page unknown.

41 Scheffler, pp.93–94.

42 'Reinhard Heydrich,' Wikipedia.

43 Kreutzer, p.95.

44 Ibid, pp.142–143.

45 Baker, *Days of Sorrow and Pain: Leo Baeck and the Berlin Jews* pp.272–276.

46 Kwiet and Eschwege, 'Die Herbert-Baum-Gruppe' p.129.

47 Charlotte Paech-Holzer deposition.

48 Lindenberger, p.130.

49 Kreutzer, p.142.

50 'Reinhard Heydrich,' Wikipedia.

51 Hildesheimer, page unknown.

52 Kreutzer, p.143.

53 Ibid.

54 People's Court statement of charges against Kochmann, Heymann, Budzislawski and Paech 7.0. Js. 235/42g dated 9 March 1943.

55 Rita Zocher deposition.

56 People's Court statement of charges against Rotholz and others 10 J 207/42g dated 21 October 1942.

57 Ellen Compart depositions.

58 Kreutzer, p.140.

Chapter 18

1 Pikarski, p.132.

2 'The Gestapo's Methods of Examination'. The 'fact' that Herbert Baum had 'committed suicide' in People's Court judgment in the case of Rotholz and others 10 J 207/42/g/2 H 314/42 dated 10 December 1942, p.3. ('...Baum hat Selbstmord begangen.')

3 Gestapo document: Stapo IV A 1–1333/42 g. Rs. dated 5 December 1942; also 'The Gestapo's Methods of Examination.'

4 Kreutzer, p.142; Paech-Holzer deposition.

5 Kreutzer, p.141.

6 Ibid, p.144.

7 Ellen Compart depositions.

8 Kreutzer, p.144; People's Court charges against Rotholz and others 10 J 207/42g dated 21 October 1942.

9 Special Court document 7.0. Js. 219/43g dated 25 June 1943.

10 Kreutzer, p.148.

11 Kreutzer, p.114; People's Court charges against Rotholz and others 10J 207/42g dated 21 October 1942.

12 Kreutzer, p.140.

13 Ellen Compart depositions.

14 Kwiet/Eschwege, p.130.

15 Pikarski, pp.131–162; Paech-Holzer deposition.

16 Kreutzer, p.144.

17 Charlotte Paech-Holzer deposition.

18 Kreutzer, p.144.

19 Statement of charges against Jacob Israel Berger and Gustav Paech: 7. 0 Js. 235/42 g dated 9 March 1943.

20 Charlotte Paech-Holzer deposition.

21 Elling, p.113.

22 Rita Zocher deposition.

23 Oleschinski, *Plötzensee Memorial Center* pp.6, 8; 'List of Executioners,' Wikipedia.

24 Pikarski, p.128.

25 Charlotte Paech-Holzer deposition.

26 Kreutzer, p.145.

27 Ibid, p.144.

28 Ibid, p.140.

29 Charlotte Paech-Holzer deposition.

30 In fact Felix Heymann and Herbert Budzislawski were both arrested after Charlotte Paech.

31 Charlotte Paech-Holzer deposition.

32 Rita Zocher deposition.

33 Ibid.

34 Ellen Compart depositions.

35 Ibid.

36 Ibid.

37 Kreutzer, p.144.

38 Ibid, p.140.

39 Richarz, pp.461–462.

40 People's Court charges against Rotholz and others 10 J 207/42 g dated 21 October 1942.

41 Kreutzer, p.148.

42 Judgment and sentencing in the criminal case against Heinz Rotholz and others, 10 J 207/42 g, 2 H 314/42 dated 10 December 1942.

43 Kreutzer, p.148.

44 Steinberg, p.36; Kwiet/Eschwege, pp.133–134; Report on Siegbert Rotholz at Alt Moabit: 10 J 207/42g/10 Gas. 152/42 dated 23 December 1942.

45 Kreutzer, p.148.

46 Rita Zocher deposition.

47 Ellen Arndt interview.

48 Announcement of imminent execution of death sentence against Heinz Israel Birnbaum, 10J 207/42 dated 4 March 1943; Letter written by Heinz Israel Birnbaum in cell #46 of Plötzensee prison asking permission to send 50 Reichmarks to his aunt dated 9 November 1942; colour of Rohde and Schmidt's outfits in 'An der Richtstaate kein Hitler-Gruss.'

49 Enforcement of the death sentence against Heinz Israel Birnbaum 10J 207/42 Berlin-Plötzensee on 4 March 1943; names of Röttger's assistants in 'Wilhelm Rottger,' Wikipedia; 'An der Richtstaate kein Hitler-Gruss;' Oleschinski, p.17.

50 Moorhouse, *Berlin at War* p.129.

51 Charlotte Paech-Holzer deposition.

52 Kreutzer, pp.138, 147; Pikarski, pp.136, 142, 152, 155.

53 Erpel, pp.408–410.

54 Kreutzer, p.147.

55 Sentencing in the criminal case against Kochmann, Heymann and Budzislawski: 10 J 328/43 g 2 H 99/43 of 29 June 1943.

56 Charlotte Paech-Holzer deposition.

57 Kreutzer, p.147.

58 Charlotte Paech-Holzer deposition.

59 Oleschinski, pp.18–19; 'The Bloody Nights of Plötzensee,' p.1; Execution order from the Reich Ministry of Justice dated 7 September 1943; Kreutzer , p.147.

60 'Wilhelm Röttger,' Wikipedia.

61 Kreutzer, pp.148–149.

62 'Grosse Hamburger Strasse Cemetery.'

63 Von Wyden, Sonnst kommst du nach Auschwitz. Stella – ein Jüdin auf Judenjagd für die Gestapo im Berliner Untergrund (II)'

64 Richarz, pp.463–464.

65 Kreutzer, pp.148–149.

66 Letter I-8523/77/2597/84 from Kazimierz Smolen, 4 January 1985.

67 Charlotte Paech-Holzer deposition.

68 Letter I-8523/77/2597/84 from Kazimierz Smolen, 4 January 1985.

69 Charlotte Paech-Holzer deposition.

BIBLIOGRAPHY

Arnould, Roger, 'Une Francaise Dans La Resistance Allemande' in *Le Patriote Resistant* 410

Avidenko, A.O., 'Hymn to Stalin', Internet Modern History Sourcebook (6 December 1997) available at FTP: fordham.edu/hallsall/mod

Axelsson, George, 'Opposition Seen Within Germany' in *The New York Times*, 10 June 1942

Baker, Leonard, *Days of Sorrow and Pain: Leo Baeck and the Berlin Jews* (New York-London, 1978)

Bankier, David, 'The German Communist Party and Nazi Antisemitism, 1933–1938' in *Leo Baeck Institute Year Book* 32 (1987)

Benz, Wolfgang, and Walter H. Pehle (eds.) *Encyclopedia of German Resistance to the Nazi Movement* (New York: Continuum, 1997)

Brenner, Michael, *The Renaissance of Jewish Culture in Weimar Germany* (New Haven & London: Yale UP, 1996)

Brothers, Eric, 'Profile of a German-Jewish Resistance Fighter: Marianne Prager-Joachim' in *Jewish Quarterly* 34.1 (1987)

_____ 'On the Anti-Fascist Resistance of German Jews' in *Leo Baeck Institute Year Book* 32 (1987)

_____ 'Wer war Herbert Baum? Eine Annäherung auf der Grundlage von 'oral histories' und schriftlichen Zeugnissen' in Löhken, Wilfried and Werner Vathke (eds.) *Juden im Widerstand: Drei Gruppen Zwischen Ueberlebenskampf und Politischer Aktion, Berlin 1939–1945* (Berlin: Hentrich, 1993)

Brothers, Eric and Michael Kreutzer, 'Die Widerstandsgruppen um Herbert Baum' in *'Im Kampf Gegen Besatzung und 'Endloesung': Widerstand der Juden in Europa, 1939–1945* (Frankfurt: Judisches Museum der Stadt Frankfurt am Main, 1995)

Cox, John M., *Circles of Resistance: Jewish, Leftist, and Youth Dissidence in Nazi Germany* (New York: Peter Lang, 2009)

Crossman, Richard (ed.) *The God That Failed* (New York: Harper & Row, 1965)

Dawidowicz, Lucy S. (ed.) *A Holocaust Reader* (West Orange: Behrman House, 1976)

Dawidowicz, Lucy S. *The War Against the Jews 1933–1945* (New York: Bantam, 1981)

Dietrich, Leonore, 'Kampfer und Augenzeugen unserer Ersten Reihe: Leitungsrunde bei 'Erich'' in *Junge Welt* (10 February 1987)

Diewerge, Wolfgang, *Deutsche Soldaten sehen die Sowjet-Union. Feldpostbriefe aus dem Osten* (Berlin: Wilhelm Limpert-Verlag, 1941)

Dippel, John V.H., *Bound Upon a Wheel of Fire: Why So Many German Jews Made the Tragic Decision to Remain in Nazi Germany* (New York: Basic Books, 1996)

Dorpalen, Andreas, *German History in Marxist Perspective: The East German Approach* (Detroit: Wayne State UP, 1985)

Eckstein, George Gunther, 'The Freie Deutsch-Judische Jugend (FDJJ), 1932–1933' in *Leo Baeck Institute Year Book* 26 (1981)

Elling, Hanna, *Frauen im deutschen Widerstand 1933–45* (Frankfurt/Main: Roederberg Verlag, 1986)

Engelmann, Bernt, *In Hitler's Germany: Everyday Life in the Third Reich* (New York: Pantheon, 1986)

Erpel, Simone, 'Struggle and Survival: Jewish Women in the Anti-Fascist Resistance in Germany' in *Leo Baeck Institute Year Book* 37 (1992)

Eschwege, Helmut, 'Resistance of German Jews against the Nazi Regime' in *Leo Baeck Institute Year Book* 15 (1970)

Friedlander, Saul, *Nazi Germany and the Jews. Vol. 1. The Years of Persecution, 1933–1939* (New York: HarperCollins, 1997)

Glass, James M., *Life Unworthy of Life: Racial Phobia and Mass Murder in Hitler's Germany* (New York: Basic Books, 1997)

Gross, Walter, 'The Zionist Students' Movement' in *Leo Baeck Institute Year Book* 4 (1959)

Guerin, Daniel, *The Brown Plague: Travels in Late Weimar and Early Nazi Germany* (Durham and London: Duke UP, 1996)

Halter, Hans, 'An der Richtstatt kein Hitler-Gruss' in *Der Spiegel Online*. 19 February 1977 (http://www.spiegel.de/spiegel/print/d-40351220.html)

Heiden, Konrad, *Der Fuehrer: Hitler's Rise to Power* (Boston: Houghton Mifflin, 1944)

Hildesheimer, Esriel, *The Central Organisation of the German Jews in the Years 1933–1945* (Jerusalem, 1982 (in Hebrew))

Hitler, Adolf, *Mein Kampf*, 1925, trans. Ralph Manheim (Boston: Houghton Mifflin, 1976)

Kellermann, Henry J., 'From Imperial to National-Socialist Germany. Recollections of a German-Jewish Youth Leader' in *Leo Baeck Institute Year Book* 39 (1994)

Kreutzer, Michael, '*Die Suche nach einem Ausweg, der es ermoglicht, in Deutschland als Mensch zu leben Zur Geschichte der Widerstandsgruppen um Herbert Baum*' in Loehken, Wilfried and Werner Vathke (eds.) *Juden im Widerstand: Drei Gruppen Zwischen Ueberlebenskampf und Politischer Aktion, Berlin 1939–1945* (Berlin: Hentrich, 1993)

_____ "Walter Sack und der 'Dritte Zug.' Erinnerungen an die fruhe Geschichte der Widerstandsgruppen um Herbert Baum' in *Juden in Kreuzberg: Fundstucke, Fragmente, Erinnerungen* (Berlin: Hentrich, 1991)

Kwiet, Konrad, 'Historians of the German Democratic Republic on Anti-semitism and Persecution' in *Leo Baeck Institute Year Book* 21 (1976)

_____ 'Problems of Jewish Resistance Historiography' in *Leo Baeck Institute Year Book* 24 (1979)

_____ 'Forced Labour of German Jews in Nazi Germany' in *Leo Baeck Institute Year Book* 36 (1991)

_____ 'Resistance and Opposition. The Example of the German Jews' in Large, David Clay (ed.) *Contending with Hitler: Varieties of German Resistance in the Third Reich* (Washington and Cambridge, 1992)

Kwiet, Konrad, and Helmut Eschwege, 'Die Herbert-Baum-Gruppe' in *Selbstbehauptung und Widerstand. Deutsche Juden im Kampf um Existenz und Menschenwurde 1933–1945* (Hamburg, 1984)

Large, David Clay (ed.) *Contending with Hitler: Varieties of German Resistance in the Third Reich.* (Washington and Cambridge, 1992)

Laqueur, Walter, 'The German Youth Movement and the 'Jewish Question': A Preliminary Survey' in *Leo Baeck Institute Year Book* 6 (1961)

_____ *Young Germany: A History of the German Youth Movement* (New York: Basic Books, 1962)

Lelina, Miriam, 'Rita Zocher' in *Soujetisch Heimland* (Moscow, December 1978)

Lindenberger, Herbert, 'Heroic Or Foolish? The 1942 Bombing of a Nazi Anti-Soviet Exhibit' in *TELOS* 135, Summer 2006

Lippmann, Heinz, (trans. Helen Sebba) *Honecker and the New Politics of Europe* (New York: Macmillian, 1972)

Lustiger, Arno, 'German and Austrian Jews in the International Brigades' in *Leo Baeck Institute Year Book* 35 (1990)

Mark, Bernard, 'The Herbert Baum Group: Jewish Resistance in Germany in the Years 1937–1942' in Suhl, Yuri (ed. and trans.), *They Fought Back. The Story of the Jewish Resistance in Nazi Europe* (New York: Schocken, 1976).

Mason, Tim, *Nazism, Fascism and the Working Class. Essays* (Cambridge and New York: Cambridge UP, 1995)

McDonough, Frank, *Opposition and Resistance in Nazi Germany* (Cambridge University Press, 2001)

Moaz (Mosbacher), Eliyahu, 'The Werkleute' in *Leo Baeck Institute Year Book* 4 (1959)

_____ 'A Jewish Underground in Germany.' (Translated from the Hebrew into an English-language typescript, this article was released by the Organisation Department of the World Zionist Organisation in March 1965)

Moorehouse, Roger, *Berlin at War* (New York: Basic Books, 2010)

Mosse, George L., *The Crisis of German Ideology: Intellectual Origins of the Third Reich* (New York: Grosset & Dunlap, 1971)

_____ (ed.) *Nazi Culture: A Documentary History* (New York: Schocken, 1988)

_____ 'German Socialists and the Jewish Question in the Weimar Republic' in *Leo Baeck Institute Year Book* 16 (1971)

Paucker, Arnold, and Lucien Steinberg, 'Some Notes on Resistance' in *Leo Baeck Institute Year Book* 16 (1971)

Paucker, Arnold, and Konrad Kwiet, 'Jewish Leadership and Jewish Resistance' in Bankier, David (ed.) *German Society's Responses to Nazi Anti-Jewish Policy* (Jerusalem, 1997)

Paucker, Arnold, 'Jewish Self-Defense' in *Die Juden im Nationalsozialistischen Deutschland / The Jews in Nazi Germany 1933–1943* (1988)

_____ *Jüdischer Widerstand in Deutschland. Tatsachen und Problematik* (Berlin: Gedenkstatte Deutscher Widerstand, 1989)

_____ *Jewish Resistance in Germany: The Facts and the Problems* (Berlin: German Resistance Memorial Center, 1991)

_____ *Standhalten und Widerstand. Der Widerstand deutscher und ostereichischer Juden gegen die Nationalsozialistische Diktatur* (Essen: Klartext-Verlag, 1995)

_____ *German Jews in the Resistance 1933–1945: The Facts and the Problems* (Berlin: German Resistance Memorial Center, 1995)

_____ 'Resistance of German and Austrian Jews to the Nazi Regime 1933–1945' in *Leo Baeck Institute Year Book* 40 (1995)

_____ 'Responses of German Jews to Nazi Persecution 1933–1945' in Timms, Edward, Margarete Kohlenbach and Ritchie Robertson (eds.) *The German-Jewish Dilemma: From the Enlightenment to the Holocaust* (Lampeter, Wales, 1998)

Pikarski, Margot, '*Ueber die fuhrende Rolle der Parteiorganisation der KPD in der antifaschistischen Widerstandsgruppe Herbert Baum, Berlin 1939–1942*' in *Beitrage zur Geschichte der deutschen Arbeiterbewegung. 5* (East Berlin, 1966)

____ *Sie Bleiben Unvergessen: Widerstandsgruppe Herbert Baum* (East Berlin, 1968)

____ *Jugend im Berliner Widerstand. Herbert Baum und Kampfgefährten* (East Berlin, 1984)

Poppel, Stephen M., *Zionism in Germany 1897–1933: The Shaping of a Jewish Identity* (Philadelphia: Jewish Publication Society, 1977)

Reinharz, Jehuda, and Walter Schatzberg (eds.) *The Jewish Response to German Culture: From the Enlightenment to the Second World War* (Hanover and London: UP of New England, 1985)

Reinharz, Jehuda, 'Hashomer Hazair in Germany (II): Under the Shadow of the Swastika, 1933–1938' in *Leo Baeck Institute Year Book* 32 (1987)

Rheins, Carl J., 'The Schwarzes Fahnlein, Jungenschaft 1932–1934' in *Leo Baeck Institute Year Book* 23 (1978)

Richarz, Monika (ed.) *Jewish Life in Germany: Memoirs from Three Centuries* (Bloomington and Indianapolis: Indiana UP, 1991)

Rinott, Chanoch, 'Major Trends in Jewish Youth Movements in Germany' in *Leo Baeck Institute Year Book* 19 (1974)

Rosenstock, Werner, 'The Jewish Youth Movement' in *Leo Baeck Institute Year Book* 19 (1974)

Sarin, General Oleg and Colonel Lev Dvoretsky, *Alien Wars: The Soviet Union's Aggressions Against the World, 1919 to 1989* (Novato, CA: Presidio, 1996)

Schatzker, Chaim, 'Martin Buber's Influence on the Jewish Youth Movement in Germany' in *Leo Baeck Institute Year Book* 23 (1978)

____ 'The Jewish Youth Movement in Germany in the Holocaust Period (I): Youth in Confrontation with a New Reality' in *Leo Baeck Institute Year Book* 32 (1987)

____ 'The Jewish Youth Movement in Germany in the Holocaust Period (II): The Relations between the Youth Movement and Hechaluz' in *Leo Baeck Institute Year Book* 33 (1988)

Scheer, Regina, *Im Schatten der Sterne: Eine jüdische Widerstandsgruppe* (Berlin: Aufbau-Verlag, 2004)

Schleffler, Wolfgang, 'Der Brandanschlag im Berliner Lustgarten im Mai 1942 und seine Folgen' in *Jahrbuch des Landesarchivs Berlin* (Berlin, 1984)

Schmidt, Walter, *Damit Deutschland lebe* (East Berlin, 1959)

Schilde, Kurt, *Jugendorganisationen und Jugendopposition in Berlin-Kreuzberg 1933–45. Eine Dokumentation* (Berlin, 1983)

Schoeberner, Gerhard (ed.), *Artists Against Hitler: Persecution, Exile, Resistance* (Bonn, 1984)

Seligmann, Avraham, 'An Illegal Way of Life in Nazi Germany' in *Leo Baeck Institute Year Book* 37 (1992)

Shirer, William, *The Rise and Fall of the Third Reich* (New York, 1962 (1983))

Steinberg, Lucien, 'Der Anteil der Juden am Widerstand in Deutschland' in *Studien und Berichte aus dem Forschungsinstitut der Friedrich-Ebert-Stiftung: Stand und Problematik des Widerstandes gegen den Nationalsozialismus* (Bad Godesberg, 1965)

____ 'The Herbert Baum Campaign' in *Not as a Lamb. Jews Against Hitler* (London, 1974)

Strauss, Herbert, 'The Jugendverband: A Social and Intellectual History' in *Leo Baeck Institute Year Book* 6 (1961)

Strauss, Herbert, 'The Jugendverband: A Social and Intellectual History' in *Leo Baeck Institute Year Book* 6 (1961)

Taleikis, Horst, *Aktion Funkausstellung: Erinnerungen in der Neufassung von Wolfgang Teichmann* (East Berlin: Dietz Verlag, 1988)

Traverso, Enzo, *The Jews & Germany: From the 'Judeo-German Symbiosis' to the Memory of Auschwitz* (Lincoln and London: Nebraska UP, 1995)

Trotsky, Leon, 'Against National Communism! (Lessons of the 'Red Referendum)' in *The Militant* (19/26 September and 10 October 1931) available at FTP: marx.org/ TrotskyArchive/1930-Ger/

_____ 'Bureaucratic Ultimatism' in *Germany, What Next?* (Trotsky, January 1932) available at FTP: werple.net.au/~deller/bs/1931/tihtm)

Verbeeck, Georgi, 'Marxism, antisemitism and the Holocaust' in *Leo Baeck Institute Year Book* 35 (1990)

Von Wyden, Peter, 'Sonst kommst du nach Auschwitz. Stella – ein Jüdin auf Judenjagd für die Gestapo im Berliner Untergrund (II)' in *Der Spiegel Online*. 26 October 1992 (http://www.spiegel.de/spiegel/print/d-13680169.html)

Weisenborn, Gunther, *Der lautlose Aufstand. Bericht uber die Wiederstandsbewegung des deutschen Volkes 1933–1945* (Hamburg, 1953)

Weitz, Eric D., *Creating German Communism, 1890–1990: From Popular Protests to Socialist State* (Princeton: Princeton UP, 1997)

Wippermann, Wolfgang, *Die Berliner Gruppe Baum und der judische Widerstand* (Berlin: Gedenkstatte Deutscher Widerstand, 1991)

Zadek, Alice and Gerhard Zadek, *Mit dem letzten Zug nach England* (Berlin: Dietz Verlag, 1992)

Primary Sources

Criminal Court statement of charges and judgment against Hans Dunst, Herbert Paessler, Georg Puls, Arno Hilber, Heinz Mittmann, Paul Nowy and Martin Kochmann; 11 September 1934; O.J. 529/34. Institute for Marxism-Leninism; Central Party Archive; East Berlin, GDR: NJ 648/7.

Excerpt of a report of the Berlin leadership of the KJVD from November 1935 on the KJVD sub-district southeast. Institute for Marxism-Leninism; Central Party Archive; East Berlin, GDR: I 4/1/49.

Letter in frontispiece of diary from Marianne Prager to Ilse Prager dated 21 May 1939.

Tafellied written by Alfons Joachim for Marianne Prager and Heinz Joachim, 22/24 August 1941.

Telegram to SS Führer Heinrich Himmler from Berlin Chief of Police Security describing 'Soviet Paradise' arson attack dated 19 May 1942. Bundesarchiv, Koblenz, Germany: Ns 19 neu/1771.

Führerinformation 1942 Nr. 81 dated 23 July 1942. Bundesarchiv Koblenz: R43 11/1559a.

People's Court of Berlin statement of charges and judgment against Heinz Israel Rotholz and others; 21 October 1942 and 10 December 1942; 10 J 207/42g. Berlin Document Center, West Berlin.

Letter written by Heinz Israel Birnbaum in cell #46 of Plötzensee prison asking permission to send 50 Reichmarks to his aunt dated 9 November 1942; 10 J 207/42 2 W 314/42. Institute for Marxism-Leninism; Central Party Archive; East Berlin, GDR: NJ 1642/3.

Gestapo document to People's Court concerning the case against Heinz Israel Rotholz and Heinz Israel Birnbaum dated 5 December 1942; Stapo IV A1–1333/42g. Rs. Berlin Document Center.

Findings of the managing committee of the detention facility Alt Moabit concerning Siegbert Israel Rotholz dated 23 December 1942; 10 J 207/42g/10 Gas. 152/42. Berlin Document Center.

People's Court judgment against George Vötter, Charlotte Vötter, Werner Schaumann, Beatrice Jadamowitz, Artur Illgen and Adolf Bittner dated 8 December 1942; 10J 232/42g. Berlin Document Center.

People's Court of Berlin statement of charges against Karl Kunger and others dated 27 January 1943; 10J 256/43g. Berlin Document Center.

People's Court of Berlin judgment against Karl Kunger and others dated 19 March 1943; 10 J 256/42 g/2 H 19/43.

Announcement of the upcoming execution of the death sentence against Heinz Israel Birnbaum dated 4 March 1943; 10J 207/42. Institute for Marxism-Leninism; Central Party Archive; East Berlin, GDR: NJ 1642/15.

Death verdict carried out against Heinz Israel Birnbaum dated 4 March 1943; 10J 207/42g. Institute for Marxism-Leninism; Central Party Archive; East Berlin, GDR: NJ 1642/15.

Red poster announcing the executions of the following people on 4 March 1943: H. Rotholz, H. Birnbaum, L. Salinger, H. Neumann, S. Rotholz, H. Hirsch, H. Meyer, M. Joachim and H. Loewy. In: Margot Pikarski, *Jugend im Berlin Widerstand: Herbert Baum und Kampfgefährten.*

Statement of charges against Jacob Israel Berger and Gustav Paech dated 9 March 1943; 7. o Js. 235/42 g. Yad Vashem.

Statement of charges against Martin Israel Kochmann, Felix Israel Heymann, Herbert Budzislawski, and Charlotte Sara Paech dated 21 May 1943; 10 J 328/43 g. Berlin Document Center.

Criminal Court statement of charges against Wolfgang Knabe, Hildegard Knabe, Heinrich von Kordisch, Hedwig von Kordisch, Heinz Overbeck and Käte Sara Simon dated 25 June 1943; 7.o. Js. 219/43g. Institute for Marxism-Leninism; Central Party Archive; East Berlin, GDR: NJ 1407.

Summonses to appear in court (sent from People's Court to Alt Moabit prison) for Herbert Israel Budzislawski, Felix Israel Heymann, and Martin Israel Kochmann; all three documents call for the accused to appear at 9.00am on 29 June 1943. Institute for Marxism-Leninism; Central Party Archive; East Berlin, GDR: NJ 1400/1.

Judgment against Martin Israel Kochmann, Felix Israel Heymann, and Herbert Budzislawski dated 29 June 1943; 10 J 328/43 g/2 H 99/43. Berlin Document Center. Execution order from the Reich Ministry of Justice dated 7 September 1943. Plötzensee prison. http://www.gedenkstaette-Plötzensee.de/zoom/07_4_e.html

Internet Sources

'The Bloody Nights of Plötzensee', Plötzensee Memorial Center http://www.gedenk-staette-Plötzensee.de/07_e.html
Das Sowjet-Paradies. Ausstellung der Reichspropagandaleitung der NSDAP. Ein Bericht in Wort und Bild (Berlin: Zentralverlag der NSDAP, 1942) http://www.calvin.edu/academic/cas/gpa/paradise.htm
'The Gestapo's Methods of Examination.' From a directive from the *Gestapo* chief, Müller. http://www.americantorture.com/documents/torture_memos/TM0.pdf
'Grosse Hamburger Strasse Cemetery.' http://www.jg-berlin.org/en/judaism/cemeteries/grosse-hamburger-strasse.html
Historical Weather: Berlin-Tegel, Germany. 18 May 1942, http://www.tutiempo.net/en/Climate/Berlin-Tegel/18-05-1942/103820.htm
Juden im Widerstand. Drei Gruppen zwischen Ueberlebenskampf und politischer Aktion, 1939–1945 http://juden-im-widerstand.de/en/index.html
Oleschinski, Brigitte, Plötzensee Memorial Center, Gedenkstätte Deutscher Widerstand, 2002: 80 pp.http://www.gdw-berlin.de/pdf/englisch-screen.pdf
'Ring, Bund Deutsch-jüdischer Jugend' http://juden-im-widerstand.de/ring.html
http://en.wikipedia.org/wiki/List_of_executioners
http://de.wikipedia.org/wiki/Wilhelm_Rottger

Interviews

Norbert Wollheim on May 1985 in Queens, New York.
Ellen Arndt (née Lewinsky) on 18 April 1985 in New York City.
Ellen Compart on 2 January 1985 in Boca Raton, Florida.
Alfred Eisenstadter on 28 January, 7 June and 5 October, 1985 in New York City.
George Manasse on 10 October and 21 October, 1984 via telephone and 17 December 1985 in Baltimore, Maryland.
Ilse Kessler (née Prager) on 18 December 1985 in Baltimore, Maryland.
Margot Deutsch-Verlardo on 12 March 1987 conducted by Kerstin Wacholz in London.
Manfred Lindenberger in June 1987 conducted by Herbert Lindenberger.
Günther Prager on 4 July 1988 in East Berlin.
Gerhard Zadek on 6 July 1988 in East Berlin.
Otto Wendt on 6 July 1988 in East Berlin.
Walter Sack on 6 July 1988 in East Berlin.
Kurt Siering on 6 July 1988 in East Berlin.
Kurt Gossweiler on 6 July 1988 in East Berlin.
Gerda Lüth (née Fichtmann) on 10 July 1988 in East Berlin.
Fred Cassel in 1985 in Bronx, New York.

Letters to the Author

Max Abraham	11.11.85, 19.11.85, 19.05.86
Herbert Ansbach	03.06.85, 18.09.85, 23.11.85, 20.05.86, 29.09.86, 05.12.86, 02.04.87, 05.06.87, 07.07.87, 16.11.87, 05.12.87
Ellen Arndt (née Lewinsky)	14.11.84, 15.12.84, 04.08.85
Herbert Ballhorn	23.11.84, 11.12.84, 22.01.85, 05.02.85, 03.85, 22.06.85, 12.03.86
Rudi Barta	06.03.88, 16.04.88
Inge Berner (née Gerson)	11.05.85, 22.07.85, 06.08.85, 07.10.85, 16.01.86, 30.06.87
Margot Deutsch-Verlardo	18.11.85, 15.04.86
Ilse Kessler (née Prager)	28.03.85, 14.07.85, 12.11.85, 22.11.85, 06.01.87, 12.07.87
Herbert Lindenberger	12.06.87, 22.06.87
Hermann Lindenberger	20.09.87
George Manasse	24.09.84, 05.10.84, 28.11.84, 23.01.85, 08.02.85, 12.05.85, 20.06.85, 01.03.86, 27.12.86
Dr Arnold Paucker	08.09.86
Werner Rosenstock	19.09.85, 24.10.85, 06.01.86
Henry (Heinz) Sachs	25.01.86
Norbert Wollheim	23.11.84

Letter I-8523/77/2597/84 from Kazimierz Smolen, Director of Panstwowe Muzeum Oswiecim Brzezinka dated 4 January 1985

Written Depositions

Ellen Compart	1985–1986, Boen Raton, Florida, USA
Charlotte Paech-Holzer	(no date), East Berlin
Rita Zocher (née Resnik, formerly Meyer)	1979, Yad Vashem, Israel

INDEX